THE POLITICAL ECONOMY OF INTEGRATION IN THE EUROPEAN COMMUNITY

The Political Economy of Integration in the European Community

Jeffrey Harrop

Edward Elgar

Published by
Edward Elgar Publishing Limited
Gower House
Croft Road
Aldershot
Hants GU11 3HR
England

Gower Publishing Company
Old Post Road
Brookfield
Vermont 05036
USA

British Library Cataloguing in Publication Data
Harrop, Jeffrey
  The political economy of integration in
  the European community.
  1. European Community countries.
  Economic development. Grants and Loan
  from European Community
  I. Title
  337.1′42

Library of Congress Cataloging-in-Publication Data
Harrop, Jeffrey.
  The political economy of integration in the European
Community.
    Bibliography: p.
    Includes index.
    1. European Economic Community.   2. Europe—Economic
integration.   I. Title
HC241.2.H3935 1989   337.1′42   88–16590

  ISBN 1–85278–008–8
        1–85278–188–2 (pbk)

Reprinted 1989

Printed and bound in Great Britain at
The Camelot Press Ltd, Southampton

To Nancy and Graeme, the new Europeans

Contents

Preface

I have been fortunate over the years in visiting European institutions and have benefited from discussions at the European Community in Brussels with members of the Commission, the Council and the Economic and Social Committee; and also at the Parliament in Brussels, Luxembourg and Strasbourg. Other visits to the Council of Europe in Strasbourg and to NATO in Brussels have increased my awareness of the role of these other organizations.

I am grateful to many colleagues who have stimulated my interest in the European Community. These include Bill Robertson in my early days at the University of Liverpool; Professor Stuart Wilson at the University of Hull who was quick to recognize the need for a course on the European economy to complement – and eventually to replace – more established courses on the Commonwealth; Professor Stephen Holt, now at the University of Kent, who led me to specialize even more deeply in the field of European integration. His enthusiasm for the subject proved infectious, and his successor at the University of Bradford, Professor Kenneth Dyson, has been a fertile source of new ideas and encouragement.

Particular thanks are offered to those who have read sections of the book; for example, Professor Stephen Holt at the University of Kent; Tony Jones at Leeds University, who also took over some teaching when I was on study leave; Rosemary Fennell in the Agricultural Economics Unit at Oxford University; and Michael Shackleton of the European Parliament in Luxembourg. In addition, my own colleagues in Bradford, Kevin Featherstone and Peter Wilson, have provided constructive comments on several chapters.

Finally, my indebtedness extends to my family who have had to take second place during the writing of this book, and particularly to my wife for preparing the manuscript for publication.

JH

List of abbreviations

AASM	Associated African States and Malagasy (countries which participated under the Yaoundé Convention)
ACP	African, Caribbean and Pacific (countries which participate in the Lomé Convention)
BRITE	Basic Research in Industrial Technologies for Europe
CADDIA	Co-operation in Automation of Data and Documentation for Imports, Exports and Agriculture
CAP	Common Agricultural Policy
CET	common external tariff
CFP	Common Fisheries Policy
Comecon or CMEA	Council for Mutual Economic Assistance (grouping of East European Countries)
COMETT	Community Programme for Education and Training in Technologies
COPA	Committee of Agricultural Organisations (Comité des Organisations Professionelles Agricoles des Pays de la Communauté Economique Européenne)
COREPER	Committee of Permanent Representatives (Comité des Représentants Permanents de la CEE)
CUBE	Concertation Unit for Biotechnology
EAGGF	European Agricultural Guarantee and Guidance Fund (Fonds Européen d'Orientation et Garantie Agricole FEOGA)
EBN	European Business and Innovation Centre Network
EC	European Community
EC(6)	European Community: Belgium, France, West Germany, Italy, Luxembourg and the Netherlands
EC(9)	The EC(6) plus Denmark, Ireland and the UK
EC(10)	The EC(9) plus Greece
EC(12)	The EC(10) plus Spain and Portugal
ECE	United Nations Economic Commission for Europe
ECs	European Communities (EEC, Euratom and ECSC)
ECSC	European Coal and Steel Community
ECU	European Currency Unit (a basket of European currencies)
EDC	European Defence Community
EEC	European Economic Community
EFTA	European Free Trade Association
EIB	European Investment Bank
EMCF	European Monetary Co-operation Fund

EMF	European Monetary Fund
EMS	European Monetary System
EMU	Economic and Monetary Union
EP	European Parliament
EPU	European Payments Union
ERDF	European Regional Development Fund
ESC	Economic and Social Committee
ESF	European Social Fund
ESPRIT	European Strategic Programme for Research and Development in Information Technology
ETUC	European Trade Union Confederation
EUA	European Unit of Account
EURAM	European Research on Advanced Materials
Euratom	European Atomic Energy Community
EUREKA	European Research Co-ordination Agency
EUT	European Union Treaty
EVCA	European Venture Capital Association
FAST	Forecasting and Assessment in Science and Technology
FEOGA	Fonds Européen d'Orientation et Garantie Agricole
GATT	General Agreement on Tariffs and Trade
GDP	Gross Domestic Product
GNP	Gross National Product
GSP	generalized system of preferences
IEA	International Energy Agency
IMF	International Monetary Fund
JET	Joint European Torus
LDC	less developed country
MCA	Monetary Compensatory Amount
MFA	Multi-Fibre Arrangement
NATO	North Atlantic Treaty Organization
NIC	Newly Industrializing Country
NTB	non-tariff barrier
OCA	optimum currency area
OECD	Organization for Economic Co-operation and Development
OEEC	Organization for European Economic Co-operation
OPEC	Organization of Petroleum Exporting Countries
R & D	research and development
RACE	Research into Advanced Communication Technologies for Europe
SEA	Single European Act
SPRINT	Strategic Programme for Innovation and Technology Transfer in Europe
STAR	Special Telecommunications Action for Regions
STABEX	Export Revenue Stabilisation Scheme

STRIDE	Science and Technology for Regional Innovation and Development in Europe
SYSMIN	Scheme for Mineral Products (Système Minérais)
UA	Unit of Account
UNCTAD	United Nations Conference on Trade and Development
UNICE	Industrial Confederation of the European Community (Union des Industries de la Communauté Européenne)
UNRRA	United Nations Relief and Rehabilitation Administration
VAT	Value Added Tax (TVA, taxe sur la valeur ajoutée)
VER	voluntary export restraints
WEU	Western European Union

Introduction

This book on the European Community (EC) is aimed mainly at undergraduate students, in particular those studying within the context of an inter-disciplinary European Studies degree, and whose chief interest is in Economics. The increased provision of such courses at both undergraduate and post-graduate level partly reflects the more European orientation in the UK, signalled by UK entry to the EC in 1973. At that time there was also an awakening of general public consciousness about the EC and since then there has been a growing demand for information about it. Some universities responded by providing Adult Education courses, and some of the material and ideas for this book were first collected for a diploma course in European Studies at the University of Hull and later for a similar course run jointly by the Universities of Bradford and Leeds.

The book has a common format to each chapter. Initially there is an outline of some of the basic issues; this is followed by the heart of each chapter which examines the progress of economic integration in the EC. Finally, the consequences of integration are examined from the perspective of the UK. The view from this angle is not intended to reflect any undue national preoccupation, but to meet the needs of most readers for an understanding of the extent to which the UK has become integrated in the EC and some of the difficulties which it has experienced.

Each chapter is self-contained and readers interested in a particular aspect of the Community need only turn to that chapter. However, I hope they will go on to read the rest of the book since one of the purposes in writing it has been to show the links between the different economic sectors which have provided the momentum to the process of integration.

The EC provides a natural interdisciplinary area for analysis, crossing the boundaries of many individual subjects. The two main disciplines considered here are Economics and to a lesser extent Politics. The book adopts a political economy approach covering both economic policies and institutions. It was felt that a wholly theoretical positive economics book would fail to encapsulate fully the multi-dimensional elements of Community developments over the past 30 years or more. Interpretation of these developments is naturally influenced by value judgments and from a UK economic perspective the writer's views of its relationship with the EC may appear somewhat critical at times.

Actual knowledge about the Community is still generally low and while readers should become better informed, with as much up-to-date material as possible, it is not the main purpose to provide facts, dates and a mass of detailed descriptive and legislative material for students to memorize. The main aim is to go beyond the descriptive level to a real understanding of the issues and principles which underlie the various sectors of economic integration in the EC.

I became conscious when gathering material over the years that it was accumulating faster than it could be digested. It became urgent to produce something concise and concrete and the late 1980s mark a very appropriate time to analyse past developments. This is because with the Mediterranean enlargement full membership of the EC now appears to be complete – apart from the possibility of Turkish membership or a reapplication for Norwegian membership. The Community has also re-examined its long-term political destination on which it failed to make much progress in the past; the Single European Act in 1986 marked an important step forward in this field.

It was evident that the book could not be wholly exhaustive in coverage and I decided to focus on the main developed sectors of economic integration. Some sectors are excluded, such as transport. While a common transport policy was seen in the Treaties as a vehicle for opening up trade, progress has been slow – despite recent extensions from rail and road transport to shipping and air transport. Commission proposals to create more competition have often lacked political support. Other areas such as energy are only touched upon briefly as part of the ECSC in the chapter on regional policy. Environmental policy is likewise omitted, apart from a mention at the beginning of the chapter on industrial policy. These areas are excluded not because they are unimportant – and indeed the completion of the internal market presupposes the implementation of many common policies in some of these areas – but to enable a sharper focus to be given in depth in other sectors: the customs union, agriculture, industry, regions, monetary and fiscal integration, external trade and enlargement. Agriculture is still perhaps the most important problem on the EC's agenda, with a mistaken pursuit of a higher share of the international market, by a price support policy covering less efficient marginal producers. Agriculture is a problem because of its centrality and influence on other sectors; for example, regional policy, monetary integration and the use of Monetary Compensatory Amounts (MCAs), and because of its high budgetary costs. It is industrial policy which needs to be placed higher on the agenda so that the Community can raise its international market share in high technology products.

For readers who wish to pursue areas excluded here, or to work even more thoroughly through the areas covered in the book, there are many sources available. The EC itself produces many publications – indeed, the mountain of printed papers can be compared with the agricultural surpluses! Nevertheless, some of these are valuable and readers are encouraged to sift through some of the Community material which is housed in European Documentation Centres in many libraries. There is material emanating from the Commission – with reports from the various Directorates-General, from the Parliament, the Council and the Court of Justice. Material from the latter and from other bodies such as the Economic and Social Committee (ESC) and the European Investment Bank (EIB) is somewhat less profuse.

There is plentiful documentation covering both primary legislation (relating to the founding of the ECSC in 1951 and the EEC and Euratom in 1957), with secondary legislation promulgated daily and published in the Official Journal. Community legislation is of four types:

1 *Regulations* which must be imposed and are directly applicable in the law of all member states;
2 *Directives* which are binding as to ends to be achieved, but leave to the national authorities the means of introducing them;
3 *Decisions* which are addressed to specific groups, which are binding in their entirety;
4 *Recommendations* and *opinions* which have no binding legal force.

The term 'Community' is preferred to that of 'Common Market', even though the latter has tended to receive wide usage, particularly in the UK, and is being reinforced by the emphasis on the completion of the internal market by 1992. However, the EC's goal has been to move beyond the stage of a Common Market along a road leading not only to economic union but towards a real community. It is more appropriate to talk about a European Economic Community (EEC), or just to refer to the European Community (EC) which avoids neglecting the social and increasingly important political dimensions of the Community. The term EC is also favoured by its citizens; for example, Eurobarometer polls in 1984 and 1985 indicated that more than 70 per cent of the respondents favoured the EC, whereas less than 30 per cent chose the term Common Market. Strictly speaking, one should refer to the European Communities since there are three of them: the European Coal and Steel Community, Euratom, and the European Economic Community. However, a decision was taken formally to merge their separate institutions in 1965 and they are treated in the book under the singular abbreviated title EC.

The process of international integration is one of combining countries together, leading towards a union between them in a regional bloc. The term integration has been chosen since in many respects it conveys more precisely the development of the EC than other words which are sometimes used: consultation, collaboration, concertation, co-ordination or unification. Progress towards integration has developed considerably in the post-war years between countries which consider that the elements they share are more important than those which divide them. The book is concerned with a very limited model of integration in western Europe, specifically that of the EC. While focus on its key features exemplifies many aspects of integration, readers should recognize the distinctiveness of the EC experience, bearing in mind that other examples of integration exist in the rest of the world (Robson 1980).

Unlike the more centrally planned economies in eastern Europe where integration in Comecon has taken a different form, integration in the EC has been rooted firmly in market principles. Market signals determine the allocation of resources and the Treaty of Rome reflected a liberal approach, mainly that of West German industry. Over the years the EC has developed some more interventionist policies, alongside those of individual member states with their more mixed economies. Some would favour going even further in this direction, arguing that otherwise the EC will remain an 'Uncommon Market' (Holland 1980).

1 Organizational stepping stones

Part I Disintegration and integration in Europe

A Pre-1945

During the nineteenth century the European economy became much more highly integrated, based initially on overlapping regional industrial developments and freer trade. The formation of the *Zollverein* in 1833 created a large free trade area and it enabled tariff concessions to be extracted from other countries. Italy was unified in 1860, creating a free trade area. Other countries signed treaties to reduce tariffs, such as France with the UK. Numerous international organizations were established, relating to spheres such as communications (Pollard 1974). However, a setback was provided by depression in the late nineteenth century which encouraged greater protectionism; also, national power caused international rivalry which was to result in the two catastrophic world wars in the first half of the twentieth century.

The First World War resulted in devastating losses of labour and capital, and for the first time even the victors had to conclude that war did not pay. It has been estimated that the war resulted in a slowdown of industrial production by approximately eight years; that is, the 1929 level of production, assuming pre-1914 trends, would have been achieved in 1921 (Svennilson 1954). The European economy disintegrated and the reshaping of national boundaries at the end of the war increased the number of separate customs unions in Europe from 20 to 27. Territorial realignments caused massive problems, creating dislocation in industrial links; for example, coal in the Ruhr and iron in Lorraine. Both Germany and the Austro-Hungarian Empire suffered substantial territorial losses. Massive reparation payments were imposed on Germany and these exceeded its capacity to repay them, contributing to instability in the 1920s (Aldcroft 1978, pp. 60–4). Inflationary finance and massive borrowings were undertaken. Unfortunately much of the borrowing was not used for productive investment, nearly half of it was short-term and eventually countries were borrowing just to pay back interest on the earlier borrowings. A collapse of the financial system resulted, and in the late 1920s capital inflows into Germany were withdrawn, especially by the USA, resulting in enforced deflation.

Economic activity turned down after 1929 and the depression was aggravated by speculative activity. The Great Depression was international in scope and marked a deep collapse in industry, trade and finance. While there was some recovery after 1932, this was very weak in North America and also weak in some European countries such as France and Austria. The most successful economic recoveries took place in Sweden, the UK and Germany. In Sweden it was based on enlightened budgetary policies, unlike the UK where there was greater concern with balanced budgets. In the UK cheap finance for investment stimulated key sectors such as housing. Recovery was also helped by the growth of new industries, and sales to an expanding domestic market were assisted by protection. In Germany a great economic recovery occurred on a different basis with a massive growth of public spending, particularly on armaments. Germany's export trade was also well adjusted to the new trends in world demand, with a larger share being held by metal manufacture, machinery and chemicals. In its trade policy Germany sought to raise its level of self-sufficiency. The weaker European countries fell under German economic hegemony and its expansionist military ambitions plunged Europe and the rest of the world into yet another devastating war.

The adverse effects of the Second World War were similar to those of the First World War; there were massive losses of labour and capital and millions of people were killed and wounded while others found themselves as refugees. Homes were in ruins and the transport system disrupted supplies, with shortages of essentials such as food and fuel. There was massive financial indebtedness to the USA which finally established itself as the major power in the world.

B   *Post-1945*

Peace did not automatically result in an improved situation and in the late 1940s there was continuing political and economic chaos. The division of Europe into two parts resulted in the Soviet Union consolidating its hold over eastern European states. The Soviet Union was seen as posing a threat to the West, turning the screw at sensitive points, such as Berlin. In some west European countries, for instance France and Italy, the Communist parties scored major electoral gains.

Attempts to achieve integration in the past by military aggression had recently failed disastrously under Hitler, just as they had under Napoleon. Given the impermanence of European history there was a need to create an irreversible process of integration on a new basis. Most European countries were in such a dreadful condition that there was a greater receptiveness to integration.

It was not so much the ideas for integration that were new, but the conditions which were conducive for this to occur after 1945. Unlike the failure of Count Coudenhove-Kalergi's ideas to be applied after the First World War, the collapse of continental nations at the end of the Second World War left them with little choice but to integrate. A peaceful process of integration on a voluntary basis was the only way to full recovery and to provide Europeans with a better future. Wartime resistance movements had gradually recognized this fact. The immediate practical problem was how to turn the dreams and aspirations of integration into reality. The driving force in this was provided by leading national figures who, through the force of personality and persuasion, were able to enlist the support of the political élite. Jean Monnet's role was crucial and his ideas were favourably received by politicians such as Robert Schuman in France, Konrad Adenauer in Germany and Alcide de Gasperi in Italy. These politicians came from the frontier areas which had been disputed areas ravaged by war.

Other support was forthcoming from political parties, with Catholic political parties, for instance, being more prepared to consider supranational instead of national solutions (Spinelli in Hodges 1972). Spinelli himself perceived scope for tapping popular support of the general public for the process of integration (Pryce 1987, p. 24). There was a high level of public support for European unification in the 1950s, even including the UK at that time.

The external influences on integration, in particular from the two superpowers − the USA and the USSR, created a constellation of new international circumstances. The USA was generally supportive of European integration, providing its own federal model as one which Europe could imitate. In contrast the USSR constituted a very threatening element, with fear of further extension of Soviet imperialism pushing European countries closer together for their own protection and security. Cold war pressures were especially acute in the early post-war years, but even in the mid-1950s there were constant reminders of vulnerability to Soviet power; for example, intervention in Hungary in 1956. That, along with other international events such as the Suez crisis, provided the background for renewed economic integration in the EEC.

Part II   European organizations

Although there were different views about the process of integration and the best ways of achieving it, there was much goodwill and idealism; these ideals were well-reflected in the Council of Europe.

A   The Council of Europe

This was established in 1949 and its founding members comprised: the UK, France, Belgium, the Netherlands, Luxembourg, Denmark, Norway, Sweden, Ireland and Italy, with other countries joining later. Its aim is expressed in Article 1 of the Statute: 'To achieve a greater unity between its members for the purpose of safeguarding and realizing the ideals and principles which are their common heritage and facilitating their economic and social progress'. The phrase 'Council of Europe' was used by Winston Churchill in 1943 and its title reflected Britain's influence on the structure of the organization. It was an intergovernmental organization, based on unanimity in decision-taking and having a consultative assembly.

It was decided to locate the Council in Strasbourg on the ravaged Franco-German border. The Council has been concerned with all matters excluding defence, and its prime concern is to organize co-operation in social and human rights, public health, education, culture and sport, youth activities, the environment and planning, local and regional authorities and law. It has a large membership, though it is limited to European Parliamentary democracies which provide basic human rights. Its most tangible achievements are enshrined in the Council's Conventions and Agreements. A most important Convention is that for the Protection of Human Rights and Fundamental Freedoms to create a civilized society. After it came into force the European Commission of Human Rights was set up, and later the European Court of Human Rights. Although the Council failed to achieve political unity in western Europe, its initiatives in the field of human rights and meetings of its parliamentarians have represented useful achievements.

B Defence organizations

Other organizations have been established mainly to help states to tackle their many national problems more effectively in a co-operative framework; this is exemplified by the defence and security problems of western Europe. The division of Europe into two halves has resulted in western European defence initiatives, notably in co-operation with the USA.

Various organizations have been created, starting with the Dunkirk Treaty between Britain and France in 1947, followed by the Brussels Treaty in 1948. This agreement between Belgium, France, Luxembourg, the Netherlands and the UK provided for automatic mutual defence assistance in western Europe. It was concerned with the possibility of a revived German aggression, but the main preoccupation was with the Soviet Union. It established a military agency, the Western European Defence Organization. The French refused to agree to the rearmament of an independent Germany. France, along with other members of the ECSC, agreed to set up a European Defence Community (EDC). Although a treaty to establish this was set up in 1952 it was not ratified by the French. France would not participate in a European army which included Germany unless Britain also took part and the latter's support was lacking. The failure of the EDC and of Spaak's proposals to combine the institutions of the ECSC and the EDC into a European Political Community marked a failure for the federal approach to integration.

In 1954 the rejection of the EDC gave way to the extension of the Brussels Treaty Organization to include West Germany and Italy in the Western European Union (WEU). It enabled the rearmament of West Germany to occur in an acceptable form. WEU also facilitated political consultations between the EC and the UK (until the latter joined the Community). WEU was not a very effective organization, but difficulties in developing a security and defence profile for the EC, such as Ireland's neutrality, led in 1984 to attempts to reactivate the WEU. France decided that it wanted to contribute more fully to discussions on European security; hence 1984 marked the first ministerial meeting for eleven years. Both Spain and Portugal decided to apply to join the other seven members of the WEU in 1984. WEU is an intergovernmental body and though militarily it is part of the North Atlantic Treaty Organization (NATO) defence system, it has the advantage of including France, which lies outside the integrated military structure of NATO.

Although a strengthening of the European pillar of NATO is thought by some to be desirable, it is NATO, founded in 1949, which has constituted the main basis of Western defence. It linked ten European countries with the USA and Canada (Germany, Greece, Turkey and Spain joining later). Its treaty is brief and not set out in arcane language, the core of it being Article 5 which begins 'The Parties agree that an armed attack against one or more of them in Europe or North America shall be considered an attack against all of them'.

NATO strategy is based upon *détente* and deterrence and if the latter fails then its flexible response will be to defend itself. Nations face many competing demands on their limited resources and quantitatively NATO is inferior in conventional forces to the Warsaw Pact. However, an aggressor requires a large enough quantitative superiority to be certain of success. The qualitative technical superiority of NATO has also lessened with recent improvements to equipment in eastern Europe. NATO has a triad of forces: conventional, non-strategic nuclear forces, and strategic nuclear forces. NATO needs to hold any attack by the Warsaw Pact as far foward as possible with its conventional defence. The concern is that if this failed NATO would be forced to resort to the use of nuclear weapons at a very early stage. The historic arms agreement in 1987 to eliminate intermediate nuclear forces has been criticized strongly by NATO Commanders such as General Rogers, the predecessor of the current Commander General Galvin, on the grounds that it would significantly diminish the doctrine of flexible response.

The European members of NATO in 1975 created the Independent European Programme Group (IEPG) and in 1984 this was given the new stimulus to create a European defence industry. The aim is to go beyond collaboration, creating a common market in military products in the same way that the EC has done in civil products. Perhaps, looking a long way ahead, at some stage the IEPG may become part of the EC Commission.

C   Economic organizations

The United Nations Relief and Rehabilitation Administration (UNRRA) provided some relief and rehabilitation during the war and early post-war years. European governments created a few emergency organizations to complement UNRRA's activities and these were subsequently absorbed into an Economic Commission for Europe (ECE) to facilitate reconstruction throughout the whole of Europe. It was successful in bringing about all-European co-operation in research; in the exchange of technological and statistical information; and in the removal of many obstacles to East–West trade (Palmer and Lambert 1968).

The Organization for European Economic Co-operation (OEEC). The USA agreed to donate aid under the Marshall Plan, if European countries would come together to frame their own recovery programme. It has been regretted by federalists that the aid was not made conditional on the creation of supranational political unity. Although assistance was offered throughout Europe it was refused by the Soviets who distrusted American intentions. Hence, rather than channel US aid through the ECE, a new body was created, the OEEC, in 1948. Sixteen west European countries, plus the Commanders-in-Chief of the Western zones of Germany, signed the Convention establishing the organization. Canada and the USA became associate members of the OEEC in 1950; Spain and Yugoslavia also participated in it in the 1950s.

A major problem in all organizations has been whether to operate on an intergovernmental basis like the OEEC, or whether to operate at a more supranational level, as favoured by France at that time; though France has had to square this with its concerns relating to its own national independence. The decision-taking in the OEEC has been on the basis of unanimity to protect the interests of the smaller countries.

The basic international problem in the early post-war years was recognized as one of restoring freer trade and payments since if industry were to recover and expand it would need access to a large international market. Freer international payments were helped by the European Payments Union (EPU) which was set up in 1950 to assist countries which faced balance of payments deficits.

By the beginning of the 1960s over 90 per cent of trade was free from quotas. After this, attention focused mainly on the other impediments to both visible and invisible trade. Unfortunately, a lack of consensus on the approach to reducing tariffs was to lead to the fragmentation of the OEEC. This led it to concentrate more on other international issues, symbolized by its change in name to the Organization for Economic Co-operation and Development (OECD). Its membership was increased to include countries such as Australia and Japan and it has become more concerned with common international problems.

The European Coal and Steel Community (ECSC), the European Atomic Energy Community (Euratom), and the European Economic Community (EEC). The organizations discussed so far have been intergovernmental ones, in which decisions are the responsibility of a Council of Ministers and in which unanimity is the normal voting procedure. The Secretariat usually has little scope for initiative, whereas in the EC the Commission has far more weight than a Secretariat. Both the ECSC and the EEC were designed to be more supranational in character, in particular the former.

The Schuman Declaration in 1950 had proposed the pooling of French and German coal and steel in an organization open to all European countries. In 1951 Belgium, France, Germany, Italy, the Netherlands and Luxembourg (the Six) accepted the Schuman Plan and signed the ECSC Treaty. It allotted strong supranational powers to its High Authority and the Council did not appear in the original plans of Schuman and Monnet. In the EEC greater weight was given to the Council since countries were reluctant to relinquish sovereignty over many other sectors of their economy. The ECSC offered France some control of these key strategic and heavy industrial resources to prevent any potential renewed German aggression. For West Germany it offered better prospects than the system of Allied Control. Tariffs and quotas were removed to create a single market for coal, coke, iron ore, scrap iron, pig iron and steel among the Six, with some initial exemptions for Italian coke and steel products and Belgian coal. Generally, the creation of the ECSC worked out easier than expected, resulting in increased trade.

A limitation of the ECSC was its confinement to two main sectors and the recognition that to enjoy greater success, integration had to be widened to include other sectors. For example, although trade restrictions in the ECSC were removed by 1953, it was not until 1957 with the introduction of the international through rates for transport that competition took place on a fairer basis. In transport, countries tended to have lower freight charges for domestic products and subsidies for exports. Imports often had to face terminal charges for reloading at frontiers. Hence, there was a need to develop a common transport policy, and also to go further with energy policy beyond coal and to cover other energy sources.

The creation of the EEC in 1957 with the signing of the Treaty of Rome included oil, natural gas and electricity. Meanwhile, research on atomic energy came under Euratom which seemed to offer considerable potential for co-operation. Indeed, in some quarters there was greater optimism about Euratom than the EEC. For instance, France was very keen to form Euratom, whereas West Germany and the Benelux countries showed greater interest in achieving an EEC customs union. Unfortunately, the desire by national governments to control their own nuclear programmes has hampered the progress of Euratom. In addition, expectations of the role of nuclear power were too high, and only after 1973 did the need for such a supplementary energy source become vital.

The Benelux countries had already experimented with their own customs union. They agreed to form a customs union during the later stages of the war and from the beginning of 1948 they removed all intra-tariffs, establishing a common external tariff (CET) to outsiders, plus some attempt to harmonize economic policies. Benelux sought to go further and it was Paul-Henri Spaak, a Belgian closely involved with the process of post-war integration, who was chosen to chair an intergovernmental committee which produced the important report bearing his name in 1955/56; this laid the foundation stone for the Treaty of Rome.

The smaller European countries, not being major powers, have had less to lose through integration, though they recognized that there would have to be a satisfactory voting system to ensure that their views would not be overridden by larger European partners. The smaller members have been able to exercise international influence via the EEC, in particular when occupying the Presidency of the Council of Ministers. Both Belgium and Luxembourg house European institutions, with Brussels being acknowledged as the capital of the Community; these institutions are an important source of revenue and Luxembourg has fought hard to try to retain its position. These smaller countries are all highly dependent on trade, and access to an open trading system is crucial to them.

The EEC is the most important of the three Communities and economic spill-over has occurred with the interdependence of different sectors. The starting point was the customs union in which a precise and detailed timetable was laid down for removing intra-bloc trading barriers. Individual national tariffs were replaced by a common external tariff which was applied on imports from outside countries — this, the CET, was the visible symbol of the EC's presence to the rest of the world. In addition to creating a free flow of goods, a free flow of factors of production also took place. This first phase of integration created a Common Market in which the barriers which had been erected were steadily removed.

Another phase of integration has consisted of positive policies in new fields leading towards economic union, and this has proved difficult and contentious. Its economic justification has been to create conditions of fair competition and to avoid a situation of 'second best'. The latter arises if countries are importing from their partners not because of natural comparative advantage, but because of different national policies subsidizing particular sectors of the economy. For example, those countries with cheaper food, lower taxes, and lower charges for transport and energy, etc. would have an unfair trading advantage; hence the rationale for a high degree of economic integration. This has been carried out more highly in some sectors, such as agriculture, than in others.

Apart from natural economic spill-over, political pressures have also underscored the process of integration. The EC has shown a bureaucratic appetite for expansion into new areas, sometimes impinging upon the work of more specific organizations. Nevertheless, progress has not been as automatic as expected since countries have fought obdurately to defend particular national interests. The process of bargaining has often produced 'package deals', whereby countries have only been willing to make concessions in return for some quid pro quo in an ancillary area. Indeed, the actual formation of the EEC along with Euratom exemplified the linking of interests in its inception, but over the years the process has become more pronounced. In some respects it is paradoxical that at times inability to reach agreement on one issue has resulted in more widespread integration in other fields in which some countries perceive prospective gains. This process of integration may be a source of potential problems, and has on occasions invoked strong national interests which resulted in complete deadlock; for example, the Community seized up in the mid-1960s after the French boycott and its opposition to moving towards majority voting.

New goals were established for integration during the 1970s to move it towards a real Community. On the eve of EC enlargement in 1973, the widening of EC membership from six to nine was also to be accompanied by deeper integration in an attempt to create the ambitious goal of European union by 1980. In some respects Community enlargement actually seems to be incompatible with a deeper and faster process of integration. Nevertheless, the EC has sought to progress from microeconomic policies of integration in particular sectors towards macroeconomic integration. The progression towards monetary union became necessary since free trade and common pricing in a sector such as agriculture is undermined when national exchange rates are highly unstable. Monetary union in turn has reinforced the case for strengthening the Community's regional policy. Monetary integration itself can only be sustained by the adoption of convergent economic policies, in particular to avoid disparities in national rates of inflation. In the long-run, if macro-economic policy-making becomes more centrally controlled, with a larger budget, then, politically, institutions at a supranational level may develop more fully towards a political union − provided these are not frustrated by continuing national interests.

Unfortunately, a setback to macroeconomic integration was provided by the steep rise in oil prices after 1973. Since then the Community has resembled more closely a zero sum game in which gains made in one country are increasingly at the expense of another country. Progress is much easier where a variable sum game exists since all countries expect to gain real benefits from EC membership. The minimum condition that needs to be fulfilled is laid down by Paretian social welfare in stating that 'changes are desirable if it is possible to compensate losers so that no one is worse off and at least some people are better off' (Dosser *et al.* 1982, p. 5); hence some countries need to be better off and to compensate losers so that the latter are no worse off. The Community has now decided to reinforce its original basic theme of completing the Common Market, but to couple this with enhanced structural funding to help weaker member states, particularly those in southern Europe; otherwise the latter would lose out from the focus solely on the internal market which was the central feature of the Single European Act (SEA) which came into force on 1 July 1987.

European Free Trade Association (EFTA). The OEEC split created a Europe of 'Sixes and Sevens' in which seven countries opted for a looser free trade area instead of joining the Six in a customs union. Seven countries signed the Stockholm Convention in 1960: Austria, Denmark, Norway, Portugal, Sweden, Switzerland and the UK; they were joined later by Finland and Iceland.

The departure of the UK and Denmark from EFTA in 1973, along with the later withdrawal by Portugal, and their entry into the EC has led to the conclusion in some quarters that EFTA was a failure and that it has now disintegrated. That would be not only a premature but a mistaken conclusion. EFTA continues to exist, providing an interesting comparison, particularly for the three of its members mentioned which have belonged to both of its organizations. In 1973 the bridge-building between the enlarged EC and EFTA led to the establishment of much closer economic relations between the two organizations; this was decisively reinforced after the Ministerial Declaration of Luxembourg in 1984.

A primary and distinctive difference between EFTA and the EC is that the former has been concerned solely with economic integration. It never sought political integration as its goal, whereas the pursuit of political integration in the EC provided an obstacle to most EFTA countries to joining the EC. For example, Austria and Finland have been constrained by Soviet pressure, while Switzerland has been concerned with preserving its long-standing neutrality. Finland was only an associate member of EFTA, but decided to become a full EFTA member − after the departure of Portugal into the EC.

EFTA is an intergovernmental organization; its key institution is the Council which consists of occasional meetings attended by representatives of its member governments, while the Heads of the Permanent Delegations meet more frequently. EFTA has made little use of voting and has generally proceeded on the basis of unanimity. It lacks a body such as the Commission of the EC to provide initiatives for federal integration and it has only a very small Secretariat of under a hundred employees. The official language continues to be English, even though German might seem to be more appropriate given the membership of countries such as Austria and Switzerland. EFTA reflects pragmatic traditions, with its absence of supranational institutions. Unlike the growing workload of the Court of Justice in the EC, relationships in EFTA have been relatively harmonious with only a few disputes arising and those were referred to the Council. The operating costs of EFTA have been low, not only because of its limited economic scope and its falling membership, but also because of its low institutional overheads. For example, EFTA budgetary expenditure was only 7.0 million Swiss francs in 1967/68 and 9.4 million Swiss francs in 1978/79.

EFTA has been concerned with industrial free trade and each country retains its own tariff to outsiders. This necessitated rules of origin to prevent imports creeping in through the country with the lowest tariff. EFTA also failed to develop the range of common policies which characterize the EC. Nevertheless, EFTA has shown a high degree of success for its members in terms of macroeconomic performance. The growth of trade led to low rates of unemployment in all EFTA countries and the problem countries − the UK and Portugal − have transferred their problems into the EC.

EFTA now constitutes a more homogeneous group and some of its members would be better candidates to progress towards full economic integration than some of the new members which have enlarged the EC. Many EFTA countries have gained economic benefits from free trade access into the Community market, without paying the full price of membership. The EC's developments of the internal market by 1992 are now testing EFTA's ultimate intentions and if it wishes to maintain its preferential position with the EC then it may have to fall into line, perhaps ultimately applying the EC's CET and approximating taxes.

Part III   The United Kingdom
The UK's ambivalent post-war relationship with the EC has some-

thing of a tragic farce about it. Various phases can be distinguished and in the 1950s when the ECSC and the EEC were being formed and UK participation would have been welcomed, the UK aloofly remained outside. In the 1960s when the UK sought to join, the boot was on the other foot and British overtures were rejected. Finally, after eventually joining the EC in 1973, the UK has since agonized over whether it took the right decision, with the trauma of the referendum in 1975, followed by perpetual disputes over agricultural and budgetary issues.

The mistake of standing aside in the 1950s
The pressures underlying European integration were much greater on the continent than in the UK, which had held firm during the war. Although at that time Churchill had proposed a union between France and Britain, in the early post-war years the UK was reluctant to participate in any continental integration which went beyond intergovernmental organizations. The UK was unwilling to join the ECSC at its inception since the British coal and steel industries had been nationalized by the Labour government and there was opposition to placing these key industries under a higher supranational authority. At the time the UK produced about half the coal and about a third of the steel output of Europe so that its absence from the ECSC was significant, as was its later failure to join Euratom − in a field where the UK again had a strong position. The UK stood apart since it had very real doubts as to whether European integration could be successfully created in a durable way. With its glorious history, why should it choose to take the risky jump into the unknown instead of continuing with its more certain, reliable and traditional partners such as the USA and the Commonwealth? The UK had sufficient political power in the 1950s, and hoped that EFTA could provide a sufficient additional economic stop-gap. The UK was able to mould EFTA so that it could play a similar pivotal role in it to that which it exercised in the Commonwealth. EFTA was a complementary organization enabling the continuance of traditional Commonwealth trading links such as those for the import of cheap food. Unfortunately, the UK failed to maximize its opportunities in EFTA, partly because it was always seen as a temporary creation, and British business had to make special marketing arrangements for the different Scandinavian and Alpine markets.

The case for joining the Six was so much less compelling at the time than it was for its continental neighbours who appreciated the political and economic benefits from reconciliation. Whereas they opted for change, the UK chose continuity. It saw its past and its future as an outward-looking maritime power which did not wish to be drawn into an inward-looking continental bloc. In retrospect, the

UK made a crucial and major miscalculation in the 1950s. In took the safe decision, and the one that most people would probably have taken in the circumstances at that time. But with the benefit of hindsight it was a fundamental error — given that later the UK was to withdraw from EFTA and join the EC, which had been moulded and developed to suit different continental interests. The UK joined in an even weaker position with poorer terms.

Courtship of the Community from the 1960s
In the early 1960s the UK decided that it wanted to join the EC and its change in position can be attributed both to political and economic factors. The political arguments for joining increased because of the weakening links with the Commonwealth, whilst those with the USA also deteriorated, notably after the Suez crisis. Unfortunately, in 1963 entry negotiations were called off, after President de Gaulle stated that the time was not ripe for British membership of the Community. De Gaulle still harboured some resentment towards the UK and whereas Britain felt that it had treated France well during the war, de Gaulle was less than flattered by his war-time relationship with Churchill. In the 1960s de Gaulle was also very concerned about the dangers of increased American influence creeping into the Community via UK entry. In suggesting that Britain was not ready for membership one can detect a recognition of the greater competitive threat posed by British industry at that time than later. France would hardly accept such competition unless the UK accepted the key aspects of integration, particularly the Common Agricultural Policy (CAP). Negotiations became bogged down not only over agriculture and the Commonwealth, but over a multiplicity of other items.

The EC doubted whether the UK was prepared to play a constructive role in the Community. The United States, which had pursued an equal Atlantic partnership with Europe based upon the UK in the EC, found its strategy rebuffed. Instead of enlarging the Community, France and Germany reinforced their partnership, signing a Treaty of Co-operation which was ratified in 1963. West Germany added a preamble to the Treaty to reduce criticism from outside, such as that from the USA, though de Gaulle considered that it diminished the value of the Treaty (von der Groeben 1985).

The Labour government in 1966 decided to pursue British membership of the Community. This arose partly from some disillusionment with the Commonwealth and problems in particular countries such as the illegal UDI in Rhodesia. The Prime Minister and Foreign Secretary made a tour of capital cities in the Community, pointing out amongst other things the technological advantages which Britain could bring to the Community. In 1967 de Gaulle said '*non*' yet again.

De Gaulle may have been right in thinking that the British would not turn out to be '*communautaire*', though France itself has often been uncooperative when it suited national interests. For example, while de Gaulle was prepared to use the EC to pursue French economic interests, politically he believed that only national governments could deal with the high policy areas. In the EC, France withdrew from its institutions in the latter half of 1965 since it was concerned to perpetuate a national veto on decisions of major importance. Similarly, in 1966 France decided to withdraw from the integrated command structure of NATO. The French preferred their own '*force de frappe*', objecting to American dominance of NATO and being less certain of the US nuclear guarantee to Europe.

After the resignation of de Gaulle in 1969 the UK made better progress since France was prepared to recognize that the UK could provide some counterweight to the growing power of West Germany. France also saw that enlargement could be linked to the completion of the Community's budgetary system of own resources. The Hague Summit in 1969 cleared the way for a round of new and successful negotiations. The UK was worried about particular issues such as agriculture, fisheries, the Budget, and so on. In 1971 Heath and Pompidou compromised, with the UK accepting the own resources budgetary system, and France giving ground over its concern about the overhanging sterling balances.

The first enlargement, 1973
The UK agreed to accept the existing treaties, but negotiated a period of transitional adjustment for five years in which it aligned itself to the EC system. The UK would have preferred a shorter transitional period for its industry and a longer one for agriculture. The interests of the Commonwealth were accommodated for imports of dairy produce from New Zealand and sugar cane from important Commonwealth producers. The attempt to meet specific Commonwealth interests has aggravated subsequent agricultural problems in the Community, adding to its embarrassing surplus of farm products. The entry terms for the UK were approved by the House of Commons with a vote of 356 to 244 in favour of joining the Community. Ireland and Denmark also entered the EC.

It was inevitable that Ireland would be drawn towards the EC because of the UK's application. In some ways Irish membership was less contested than that of the UK since Ireland had not incurred the strength of French opposition. Ireland also stood to benefit strongly from the Community's agricultural policy and indeed the absence of agricultural concern in EFTA was one reason why Ireland was a non-member of that organization. A referendum produced overwhelming support in Ireland with an 83 per cent 'yes' vote for EC membership. Ireland has generally fared quite well, though the recent restraints on agricultural spending have proved unpopular. In addition, closer co-operation on issues such as European security, as part of the SEA, led to Irish delay in ratifying this. In May 1987 the Irish government arranged a referendum on the SEA, with a majority of 70 per cent in favour.

Denmark saw the UK as one of its major export markets agriculturally which had to be retained. In the EC efficient Danish farmers have been able to improve further on their already adequate incomes. The economic benefits have cemented Denmark in the Community, despite considerable opposition, and in 1986 a further referendum was necessary so that Denmark could sign the SEA.

A Nordic Council had been created in 1954 and Denmark co-operated closely with other Scandinavian countries. In joining the Community Denmark also expected Norwegian entry, but unfortunately whereas Denmark voted 63.5 per cent in favour of entry, the Norwegian referendum rejected membership with 53.5 per cent voting 'no'. The major sources of opposition in Norway were the primary and peripheral sectors comprising agriculture and fisheries, although it also included other fringe protest groups. These were confronted by industry, commerce, shipping and consumers, but in the end the more urban groups were defeated (Allen 1979). Norway negotiated a trade agreement with the Community, after hard bargaining over several sensitive industrial products and the level of fishing tariffs. At some stage Norway may still reapply for full membership of the EC in the future.

A referendum to resolve the issue of UK membership
The UK was relieved to have finally obtained its objective of membership of the Community, but it soon seemed to forget why it had joined and pressure resurfaced for a withdrawal. Although the UK had committed itself firmly to the EC for an unlimited time period, this was not necessarily considered to be binding since Westminster was in a position to revoke membership. The Labour government which was returned to office in 1974 was highly dissatisfied by the terms of entry achieved under the Conservative Prime Minister, Edward Heath. There is little doubt that the gradual weakening in the UK's bargaining position and its determination to join the EC almost at any cost had not resulted in the negotiation of the best terms. Community policies had moved on in areas such as agriculture, fishing and budgetary matters and these were to prove contentious for the UK. The Labour government sought a review of particular items and was determined to secure better terms. In June 1975 the UK underwent the innovation of a referendum (greater use is made of referenda in other European countries).

The old issues were reopened and the major political parties were divided. Consequently, the campaign was between two groups: Britain in Europe which was pro-market and the National Referendum Campaign, which was anti-market. The major political figures supporting Britain in Europe made important pleas. Edward Heath asked 'Are we going to stay on the centre of the stage where we belong, or are we going to shuffle off into the dusty wings of history?'. Roy Jenkins, who was President of the Britain in Europe organizing committee, argued that 'not to have gone into Europe would have been a misfortune, but to come out would be an altogether greater scale of self-inflicted injury'. In the pamphlet urging a 'yes' vote for Britain in Europe, some of the following points were made: traditions would be safe; jobs would be retained; food secured at fair prices; and ultimately no better alternatives were foreseen. The financial weight of this group was stronger than that of the National Referendum Campaign which urged a 'no' vote. The latter were concerned with the UK's right to rule itelf, and with the adverse effects on food prices, jobs and the trade deficit. They also recognized the favourable alternatives available to EFTA countries.

The decisive factor was the government's own position and its pamphlet entitled 'Britain's New Deal in Europe'. The Prime Minister, Harold Wilson, claimed that the renegotiation objectives had been substantially achieved. Therefore the government 'decided to recommend to the British people to vote for staying in the Community'. The voters were naturally inclined to trust the government's advice and certainly holding a referendum on whether to withdraw from the EC was a different matter from the decision not to hold a referendum on whether to join in the first place.

The referendum was a way of helping to heal the intra-party divisions which were most intense in the Labour Party. The turnout in the UK was 64.5 per cent and some 17 million people voted 'yes' to stay in the EC and about 8 million people voted 'no', although the result concealed wide regional and local variations. In the North less support was recorded, but only Shetland and the Western Isles voted against remaining in the Community.

The electorate has had considerable difficulty in understanding the complex subject of the EC and public opinion on the issue has been extremely volatile. Unfortunately, in the EC there tended to be an over-optimistic interpretation of the referendum result in deducing an apparently new-found enthusiasm by the UK for the Community. This was largely mistaken, but at least the main virtue of the referendum was that it settled the issue, confirming that the UK's future role and destiny lay in the EC. Withdrawal would have been a setback, although Greenland withdrew from the Community in February 1985. Obviously a UK decision to withdraw would have had far more devastating consequences.

2 The structure and operation of Community institutions

Part I   The decision-making process

It is important to understand the institutions which engage in decision-making and exercise power in the Community, and to consider the changes which have taken place in the interplay between them. It has been suggested that the EC's achievements have been constrained by failings in its decision-making and also that these need to become more democratic. The five institutions examined in this chapter are the Commission, the Council of Ministers, the European Parliament (EP), the Economic and Social Committee (ESC) and the Court of Justice. It should be borne in mind when discussing the European Communities that there have been differences between the ECSC, the EEC and Euratom, since each had separate Commissions and Councils, but with a common Parliament and Court. A Treaty to merge the three together was signed in April 1965 and entered into force in July 1967. Since that time there has been a single Commission and Council. The whole structure institutionally will be referred to as the EC, notwithstanding a few differences in the way in which the ECSC and Euratom operate on the basis of their original Treaties.

While the main concern of economists is with policy outputs, as shown in subsequent chapters of the book, it is important to understand the inputs which go into the decision-making process. This is crucial not only for political scientists, but for all those seeking to influence and participate in decision-making. It is true that there has still not been the decisive transfer of identity and power towards the Community which was hoped for and the key actors are still the nation states. Also, so far, the political spill-over brought about by European interest groups has not kept pace with the economic spill-over of integration. Nevertheless, over time more and more crucial decisions are being taken at the Community level, with far-reaching implications both for business and for citizens in the Community.

The decisions which are taken are not imposed secretively by the bureaucracy in Brussels, as perhaps the media might imply, but represent the articulation of many different views in a very open, participative and consensual system. This framework results in a very slow process of decision-making – on average a period of three years before proposals are turned into law, with difficult issues often taking very much longer. Thus there are considerable opportunities to influence policy-making, but to do this effectively it is necessary to identify the role of the institutions and to exercise timely and appropriate lobbying. It is preferable to do so at an early a stage as possible, starting when the Commission is formulating new legislative proposals, and these are being considered by experts and working parties. Further channels to reshape policies occur when the proposals are being considered by the ESC and by the EP, and since the latter now has enhanced powers to amend legislation it is likely to be lobbied far more in the future. Another opportunity to influence policy arises when the revised draft is being reworked by the Commission and discussed by the Committee of Permanent Representatives (COREPER), before being submitted to the Council of Ministers. Since policies evolve and are moulded to suit the different national interests of the twelve member states, there is considerable scope to modify legislation. While influence is best brought to bear at the European level, it should not be neglected at national level, both in the House of Commons and in the House of Lords, since the latter scrutinizes Community legislation closely.

It will be shown that power has shifted over time from the Commission — which is now just one among several other bodies — to the Council, and in particular the European Council. Furthermore, since direct elections in 1979 to the EP, the latter has increased its influence, tending to diminish that of the ESC. In addition, there has been a growing demand by the EP to enhance its powers further and some concessions have been made to it in the SEA; for example, the co-operation procedure between the three main institutions in certain areas, such as the internal market. Previously, the Council only had to approve the Commission's proposals or to amend them by unanimous vote. Now, in areas where the SEA provides for majority voting, the EP has been given strong powers to approve, reject or amend legislation.

Since the SEA only came into force in 1987 it is still early to predict and assess all the implications of this major and systematic revision of the Treaties. Nevertheless, there have been some early indications that the Council is not sticking to the basic rules of the co-operation procedure in some instances; for example, it has systematically rejected the EP's amendments on public procurements. In addition, a snag arose over the freedom of financial services in 1988 relating to insurance (excluding life assurance), since the Council's proposals do not bear much resemblance to the EC's opinions first expressed in the late 1970s, and the EP feels it should be reconsulted and the process started afresh. It is clear that the Council of Ministers and the European Council still remain the ultimate decision-makers, though the Community has once again set out on a new course continuing its 'journey to an unknown destination' (Shonfield 1973).

Part II   EC institutions

A   *The Commission*

Structure. The Commission is a small and open bureaucracy which employed about 11 000 staff in 1986, compared with under 6000 staff prior to the first enlargement of the EC in 1973. Around a quarter of its staff is engaged in linguistic work, made necessary by the use of nine working languages. The Commission is the Community's Civil Service and the distinction has to be drawn between the Commissioners and their staff.

The Commissioners are appointed for a period of four years, with the President being appointed for two years on the assumption that this will be renewable once. The experience of the first President, Walter Hallstein, of West Germany, in serving for longer, is unlikely to be repeated; it has also been difficult to match the excellent spirit of co-operation in the first Commission (Von der Groeben 1985, p. 47). The President has to mould the team together and has usually been an important national figure already. The Frenchman, Jacques Delors, succeeded Gaston Thorn from Luxembourg as President in 1985.

The President is assisted in his task by six Vice-Presidents. The Commission consists of two Commissioners from the larger countries and one Commissioner from the smaller countries. There has been some concern about it becoming unwieldy as a consequence of enlargement, but proposals to appoint only one Commissioner from each country have been turned down. In the allocation of portfolios between the Commissioners, some of these are thought to be more significant and rewarding than others; hence, some haggling occurs over the initial distribution of posts. Commissioners exercise influence according to their portfolios and their personal characteristics of charisma and drive. Some strong personalities, including those from smaller countries, such as Viscount Davignon, have often wielded considerable power (Butler 1986, p. 18).

Despite different political views, the national appointees have to work together effectively, transferring their new allegiance to the Community. While naturally they retain close links back home, they are definitely not delegates following national instructions. They have to act impartially in the Community interest and occasionally in doing this they have incurred national criticism. For example, in 1987 the two German Commissioners came under attack from a few national Ministers for failing to defend German agricultural interests and also its beer purity laws. However, Commissioners cannot be dismissed during their term of appointment either by their national governments or by the President of the Commission. Although the Commission as a whole is directly responsible to the

Parliament – which can dismiss it by a two-thirds majority – the Parliament cannot take formal action against individual Commissioners.

The Commission is organized into various Directorates-General and they are usually identified by number; for example, DG VI on agriculture is particularly important. There are no close horizontal links between the DGs, and the main organizational links are vertical ones.

The Commission takes several decisions routinely and other straightforward matters follow a written procedure; if no reservations are entered then the proposals are adopted. For more important issues, majority voting is used. Where a vote is taken the Commission operates like a college and the minority abide by the collective decision.

Each Commissioner is supported by the French form of private office or Cabinet, which helps to keep the Commissioner well informed and is usually filled with his own personal choice of staff. The Chef de Cabinet will step in as Deputy and represent an absent Commissioner. The power of the Chef de Cabinet may have reduced some of the authority of the Directors-General who run each of the 20 Directorates-General (covering broad policy areas). Beneath the Directors are the Heads of Division.

The allocation of posts in the Directorates-General are distributed to secure a balance between the twelve members of the Community. To enable this balance to be maintained after enlargement, some generous early retirement of existing staff occurred. The blending together of different nationalities has generally worked well, avoiding a splintering into rival national factions. The main dissatisfaction arises from career-minded staff who, although well paid, may feel that their promotion is restricted because of national quotas on staff in different grades and areas. However, in the lower-grade posts the quota is disregarded and a disproportionate number of staff are nationals of the countries in which the institutions are situated (Henig 1980, pp. 45–6).

Functions of the Commission. The Commission embodies the ideals of the Community and carries out a range of political and administrative functions which can be classified in five main ways. In the first instance, the Commission proposes new policies since the Treaty establishing the EC was more of an outline sketch than that of the ECSC or Euratom. Hence the Commission has filled in the detail of existing policies and initiated new policies. It is the master of both the form and the timing of new proposals, without which the Council cannot act. The Commission often has to modify these proposals, but tries to act as the powerhouse of closer integration.

Commission power is strongest where it can act on a clear Treaty provision supporting its action.

Secondly, the Commission carries out executive powers to implement the policies in the Treaties. It prepares decisions and regulations to implement the provisions of the Treaty, such as on trade, and enactments of the Council; for example, a mass of regulations is passed each year relating to the CAP. The Commission also administers Community Funds and Euratom research programmes. The Commission works closely with member countries to operate policies effectively, often by means of management committees, such as those for agriculture. While national administrators may lack the commitment to integration of the Commission, they have been helpful in monitoring proposals and in reducing the administrative burden.

Thirdly, the Commission acts as guardian of the Treaties; it fulfils a watchdog role and investigates any action which it considers to infringe the Treaties. It demands explanations for such actions which may arise from a misinterpretation of the Treaties. If the Commission is still dissatisfied with the explanations given, then it issues a reasoned opinion with which the state must comply. If the state does not do this the matter is referred to the Court of Justice, although in the case of competition and cartels the Commission has direct powers itself to fine offending companies.

Fourthly, the Commission has the formal right to attend Council meetings where it presents its views vigorously in order to pilot its legislation through. Likewise, the President of the Commission attends meetings of the European Council ('summit meetings'). The Commission seeks to steer through its own proposals, being the centre of bargaining and the thirteenth member of the Council, and even though the Commission has no vote it possesses the expertise. It mediates and strives to secure agreement between the differences of the member states – as does the President of the Council. The Commission is also the hinge between the Parliament and the Council at the second stage under Article 149. Often the overall policy outcome is simply one of establishing the lowest common denominator, far removed from the initial Commission proposal based on a strong, adventurous initiative for integration.

In addition to the functions outlined, a final responsibility of the Commission is to represent the EC in various international organizations and also in the Community's external relations with non-member countries. The Commission in conducting its activities has developed over time into a more bureaucratic organization. It has been suggested that such a highly-structured and mechanistic role is less consistent with its activities of initiating policies and engaging in mediation (Coombes 1970).

B   The Council of Ministers

Structure. The Council was given only a minor role in the ECSC but has had a very important position to play in the EC and its power has grown in significance. Ministerial representatives from the member states along with their officials make up the Council. Its meetings are usually in Brussels, but also in Luxembourg, and the latter having suffered from the decision of the Parliament not to hold meetings there, is keen to retain some Council meetings in Luxembourg.

Unlike the other EC institutions, the Ministers' mandate is to represent their own country. The most frequent visitors to Council meetings are the Ministers of Foreign Affairs and Agriculture. Ministers of Finance also meet on a regular basis, whereas other Ministers meet less frequently. Sometimes Ministers even from the same country may adopt contradictory positions; for example, Ministers of Agriculture have supported farming interests, whereas Ministers of Finance have been concerned to limit the financial expenditure on agriculture. The Foreign Ministers have the most important responsibility since they are also expected to provide the general role of supervision and co-ordination.

The Presidency of the Council is held by each member state on a rotating basis, and it is held for a period of six months. The President has an important job in exercising political weight of mediation to try to secure agreement − with the Commission's role being to produce the technical solutions to the problems.

The establishment of the Council's own Secretariat has altered the Commission's role in servicing the Council. The Council's Secretariat had nearly two thousand employees in 1986 and it is organized like the Commission into a small number of Directorates-General. The major administrative task of the Secretariat is to organize and administer the Council's decision-making; it makes EC legislation available in different languages and most of its staff tend to be translators and legal linguists.

The Council of Ministers has extended vertically over the years, spreading downwards to include COREPER. This has assisted the Council to cope with the growing volume of work. COREPER consists of both the Permanent Representatives themselves who deal with external questions and significant political questions, while beneath them their deputies focus more on internal issues. COREPER resolves many issues, providing the groundwork for the Ministers themselves, who can make greater progress on other important and difficult areas.

The vertical links of the Council have also extended upwards, reflected in the activities of the European Council; this consists of regular meetings of heads of governments. These summit meetings were not provided for in the Treaty of Rome, but it was agreed to establish them in 1974 and they are now written into the SEA under Article 2. Although they have limited the supranational character-istics of the Community in favour of inter-governmentalism, they have been vital in breaking the log-jam of business and in propelling the Community forward. The European Council has met three times a year and now meets twice a year; the meetings are held in the capital cities of the countries which hold the Presidency during the year. Although heads of government interact less frequently than Foreign Ministers, when they have enjoyed amicable personal relationships, these have been most helpful to the Community's progress. For example, Franco-German links are crucial and the meeting of minds between Schmidt and Giscard d'Estaing provided the Community with leadership in fields such as the European Monetary System. Sometimes relations have been strained and meetings unsuccessful since heads of government have become bogged down with too many details, which they have been incapable of comprehending, and an overlengthy agenda. Problems have been compounded by some indecisive national Ministers who might have settled some of the issues themselves in the Council instead of leaving these to be shifted upwards to the European Council. Perhaps with greater use of majority voting in the Council, then the European Council will be able to focus on fewer major problems; the European Council is the one body which can set a clear agenda of objectives (Tugendhat 1986).

Functions of the Council. Power resides in the Council of Ministers since it takes the decisions, but being the least supranational of the Community bodies it has provided a brake on developments. There has been some concern about the way in which decisions are taken; voting can be by unanimous vote, or by absolute or qualified majority vote (Commission Twentieth *General Report*, 1987, p. 29). The Treaty of Rome laid down a voting procedure in which in the earlier years most of the decisions required a unanimous vote, but in other areas such as agriculture a qualified majority vote was sufficient. France raised objections to Commission proposals in 1965 for a package deal to develop agricultural policies more completely and to move towards decision-making by majority voting. France not only opposed the substance of the latter, but objected to the way in which the Commission's proposals were first delivered to the EP before being forwarded officially to the Council of Ministers. The paralysis of the Community was resolved by an extraordinary meeting of the Council of Ministers, which was held in Luxembourg rather than Brussels, and the outcome was the so-called Luxembourg Compromise. De Gaulle was not prepared to see France outvoted where very important national issues were at stake. It was agreed, therefore, that countries would continue to negotiate with each other until unanimous agreement was reached. After the enlargement of the EC, most new members supported this national right of veto. However, in 1982, when the UK invoked the Luxembourg Compromise to veto a proposed increase in agricultural prices, for which the usual price fixing package had not been agreed satisfactorily, it was voted down. Nevertheless, the Luxembourg Compromise can still be invoked where important national interests are involved.

A general reluctance to make wide use of majority voting slowed down the decision-making in a search for compromise and consensus. It became obvious after the southern enlargement of the EC in the 1980s that changes were needed to bring about greater use of majority voting, otherwise the Community was likely to grind to a halt in many fields. The SEA has made an important breakthrough by introducing majority voting for most aspects in the creation of the internal market. It thus embodies a significant step forward in improving the Community's decision-making process.

Under the qualified majority voting system, the votes are distributed so that the 'big four': France, West Germany, Italy and the UK have ten votes each; Spain has been given eight votes; Belgium, Greece, the Netherlands and Portugal have five votes each; Denmark and Ireland have three votes each, and Luxembourg has two votes. From these total 76 votes a qualified majority consists of 54 votes, though when the Council is not acting on a proposal from the Commission, an additional condition is that the votes should be cast by eight members (Mathijsen 1985, p. 30). The 23 Mediterranean votes of Italy, Spain and Greece together put them in a position to block some decisions. With less scope for an individual national veto, countries need support for a blocking minority; hence Italy has a crucial role in southern Europe, since the other southern countries just fall short of a blocking minority. In northern Europe, the UK and Germany, along with one small country (Denmark or the Netherlands or Belgium) can likewise block measures in the areas which they feel strongly about — perhaps budgetary expenditure. In fact there is the dangerous prospect of an impasse over the cohesiveness of the Community between its northern and southern member states, with the former holding the purse strings over tackling issues such as Mediterranean regional imbalance.

C   The European Parliament

Structure. The European Parliament (EP) used to be called the Assembly. Its structure can be examined in two ways: the members of the European Parliament (MEPs) can be divided either by the national membership, or by their party political distribution. There were 410 MEPs after the first direct elections in 1979 and since the southern enlargement of the EC the total number of MEPs has now risen to 518. The 'big four' each have 81 MEPs; Germany, France, the UK and Italy. Spain has 60, the Netherlands 25, and there are 24 MEPs each from Belgium, Greece and Portugal, plus 16 from Denmark, 15 from Ireland and 6 from Luxembourg.

The MEPs, drawn from some 70 national political parties, have come together into a small number of political groups. These transnational groups seek a common approach to issues and ultimately they may grow into real political parties. The strength of the groups and their national membership in the EP in 1986 is shown in Table 2.1.

The largest transnational group is that of the Socialists, with MEPs belonging to it from every country except Ireland. Nevertheless, Socialist MEPs differ in their approach, with one cleavage, among others, being whether they represent urban or rural areas. There are also often differences in their links with the national party; for example, the Spanish Socialists have closer links with their national party at home than do others, such as their Danish colleagues.

The second largest group is the European People's Party, with MEPs from eleven states belonging to it − the exception being no representatives from the UK. The Christian Democrats in this group have mainly represented business interests, including agriculture, and have strongly supported the progress of European integration. British MEPs formed a more restrictive and largely national party group: the European Democrats. This third group is tightly knit and most coherent in its voting with very few dissidents. They have also been able to co-operate closely with other groups, especially the Christian Democrats, though the trade union wing of the latter has been a barrier to the Conservatives joining the European People's Party. The centre-right have an overall majority in the Parliament, though this has been less clearcut since Mediterranean enlargement.

The fourth largest group comprises the Communists and their allies. The group is dominated by the Italian and French Communists, but one can detect some differences between them; for example, the Italians have been more in favour of integration, developing a European strategy with some independence from Moscow, compared with French Communists. Conflicting views have made this grouping rather less effective than one would expect from its membership size, and this has been exacerbated since enlargement.

The group of Liberal and Democratic Reformists is perhaps least coherent ideologically since there are wide interpretations of the word 'liberal', but it has shown concern for a liberal economy based

Table 2.1 Group Membership by Nationality, 1986

	B	DK	D	E	F	UK	GR	IRL	I	L	NL	P	Total
Socialists	8	3	33	36	20	33	10	—	12	2	9	6	172
European People's Party	6	1	41	7	10	—	8	6	27	3	8	2	119
European Democrats	—	4	—	13	—	46	4	—	—	—	—	3	63
Communists and allies	—	2	—	—	10	—	4	—	27	—	—	9	46
Liberal and Democratic Reformists	5	2	—	2	11	—	—	1	5	1	5	4	41
European Alliance for Renewal and Democracy	—	—	—	—	20	1	1	8	—	—	—	4	34
Rainbow group	4	4	7	1	—	—	—	—	2	—	2	—	20
European Right	—	—	—	—	10	—	1	—	5	—	—	—	16
Independents	1	—	—	1	—	1	—	—	3	—	1	—	7
Total MEPs	24	16	81	60	81	81	24	15	81	6	25	24	518

Key: B – Belgium, DK – Denmark, D – Germany, E – Spain, F – France, UK – United Kingdom, GR – Greece, IRL – Ireland, I – Italy, L – Luxembourg, NL – Netherlands, P – Portugal.

Source: One Parliament for Twelve, 5th ed., September 1986.

upon private enterprise and democratic institutions to guarantee human and civil rights.

The European Alliance for Renewal and Democracy consists very much of French and Irish members who have strongly supported agricultural interests. Another smaller group in the Parliament, with 20 MEPs, is the Rainbow group. Its members reflect concern for environmental interests, especially in West Germany – this was confirmed further by the increase in the vote of the Greens in the national election in West Germany in January 1987. The Rainbow group has a broader base and also includes Regionalists from Spain and Italy seeking stronger regional independence. The final group, the European Right, consists of 16 neo-Fascists, with ten from France, five from Italy and one from Greece.

The parliamentary groups receive financial assistance and in 1979 Parliament laid down that if a group contained representatives from three countries or more, then ten MEPs constituted the minimum group size. Where MEPs were drawn from fewer member states, then 15 MEPs were needed from only two states, and if they all came from one member state, then 21 MEPs were necessary to constitute a political group. The speaking time in the Parliament is in relation to the strength of the groups. There are only a few MEPs who are independent of party groups – such are the perceived advantages of group assistance.

The political groups do much work, not just in Parliament itself, but in the 18 Permanent Committees; these are the engine room of the Parliament. Each group's membership of the Committees is proportional to its size, while the independent members have the right to membership of one Committee only. Some Committees have much more importance than others; for example, Agriculture, Budgets, Economic and Monetary Affairs, and the Political Committee. By increasing the number of its Committees, Parliament has shown that it is concerned to be a working Parliament (Bourguignon-Wittke *et al.* 1985, p. 42). The political groups have the right to fill the Chairmanships of the various Committees. The Committees appoint a rapporteur, following French tradition, who draws up a draft report for discussion, modification and redrafting and revision into a final draft resolution for adoption. The Committees' reports then go to a plenary session.

Parliament has been peripatetic; its Committee meetings and party group meetings are held regularly in Brussels and there is little doubt that it would have been more efficient and economic to site the Parliament itself in Brussels – alongside the Commission and the Council. Unfortunately, the location of the Parliament's activities has been very much a tug-of-war between Strasbourg and Luxembourg, with the Parliament's Secretariat based in Luxembourg alongside EC institutions such as the European Court of Justice and the EIB. The wish of France to consolidate Strasbourg's seat of the Parliament has been achieved by considerable financial expenditure to facilitate EP operations there.

Functions of the EP. The EP's role has been mainly consultative and advisory in non-budgetary matters, but since direct elections in 1979 it has tried to increase its powers based upon the strength of its democratic electoral support. With regard to the latter, about three in five voters in the Community turned out to vote in the 1979 and 1984 elections, with the range of turnout varying widely between the member states, there being a particularly high turnout in Belgium.

The normal functions of any parliament, apart from expressing views, are to legislate, to exercise financial responsibilities, and to control government. It has been argued that the EP does not properly fulfil the traditional powers of a national parliament (Herman and Lodge 1978). This is partly because some of the traditional parliamentary powers lie with the Commission and the Council. Parliament has sought to influence both these bodies, but in general has done so more effectively in the case of the Commission, since any accretion of the EP's powers is regarded as a direct challenge by the Council. The proposals from the Commission go to the EP for its opinion and often the Commission has made changes to incorporate its suggestions. The EP is also able to make its own initiatives, trying to encourage the Commission to legislate in particular fields.

Parliament has had considerable scope for questions, especially to the Commission. For example, in 1986 3023 written questions were tabled − 2671 to the Commission, 195 to the Council and 157 to the Conference of Ministers for Foreign Affairs (Political Co-operation). There were also in the same year 1277 oral questions − of which 800 were to the Commission, 290 to the Council, and 187 to the Conference of Ministers for Foreign Affairs (Commission 1987, p. 39).

The EP's budgetary powers have also been limited and confined mainly to the small non-compulsory expenditure, and it would like the last word on the vast amount of compulsory expenditure which takes place mainly in financing the CAP (these distinctions in the Community Budget are discussed more fully in Chapter 8). The conciliation procedure between the Parliament and the Council has been used extensively for the Budget.

It is the institutional weaknesses of the Parliament in relation to the Council which have most concerned the MEPs. It is true that national Ministers themselves have been appointed from elected MPs, but the operation of national officials in COREPER has been criticized, especially for not being accountable to the EP (Palmer

1981). The Ministers are held to account by attending the different Committee meetings. It has been suggested that Parliament should go further and use Congressional-type Committee hearings to interrogate Ministers (Tugendhat 1986).

The EP has been locked into a vicious circle in which it has·failed to command popular support since it has lacked the powers to match those of national parliaments. This has resulted in citizens focusing their main allegiance and expectations on the latter. One attempt to tackle the EP's remoteness from Community citizens has been to encourage those with grievances to appeal to its Committee on Petitions, and these public petitions rose in number from 57 in 1979 to 279 in 1986–7. Further institutional changes have been made to raise the EP's profile under the SEA (and some of these are discussed more fully later). They provide greater consultative powers for the EP, and a new system of co-operation. In addition, the Council has to obtain the approval and assent of the EP – by an absolute majority of its component members – for applications for membership of the Community, and for its association agreements. Early in 1988 the EP started to use the latter powers, for example to block three protocol agreements to the Community's trade agreement with Israel to show its condemnation of Israeli behaviour towards the Palestinians on the West Bank.

D   The Economic and Social Committee

The Economic and Social Committee (ESC) is marginal to the main decision-making process, though it has an influence on some policy details. The ESC consists of 189 representatives of interest groups in the twelve member states. It parallels the national systems for institutionalizing interest group participation – these have had a long history going back to the 1920s in Germany and France.

The ESC under the Treaties has to be consulted compulsorily on many issues: agriculture, freedom of movement of workers, right of establishment, transport, approximation of laws, social policy and funding, and vocational training; also, under the Euratom Treaty it has had to be consulted on various nuclear areas. The ESC has also had to be consulted on other areas where this has been appropriate; for example, regional, environmental and consumer policy, etc. Since 1974 the ESC has had the rights of initiative on questions affecting the EC; the high level of unemployment since that date has been one of the issues raised frequently.

The ESC consists of three groups: employers (group 1); workers (group 2); and various other interest groups (group 3) – representatives of agriculture, transport, trade, small enterprises, the professions and consumers. The trade unions in group 2 feel that on some issues the group 3 members tend to vote with the group 1 employers. The ESC's functions are consultative and its influence has tended to be eroded by the elected EP. It has been criticized further for being a 'quango' in its appointments, and in its procedures since it has been consulted only at a late stage (Taylor 1983). Its influence has also been diluted by the growth of independent interest groups themselves – even though not organized as powerfully transnationally as neo-functionalists expected. For farmers there is the Comité des Organisations Professionelles Agricoles (COPA); for employers the Union des Industries de la Communauté Européenne (UNICE) and for trade unions, the European Trade Union Confederation (ETUC).

If the ESC is to be of influence it has to have well-produced recommendations, but on some economic and social affairs each group has used the Committee as a platform for its own views, though on other issues like safety standards (for example, cars) the three sides have been much more in agreement. The Committee is an unelected body like the Commission and it has seen the latter as its ally, needing to prevent the overlap and duplication of the ESC with the stronger elected EP. The latter often waits for ESC deliberation, but also deals more directly with other pressure groups. The ESC sends its opinions to the Commission and Council, before the latter takes its decisions.

A consensus among the 189 members is difficult, so the ESC is divided up into nine sections representing key areas. If the Commission asks for an opinion it is sent to one of these sections. Each member of the ESC sits on two or three sections. A small study group is then set up, representative as far as possible of the three interest groups and member states. The study group elects a rapporteur and listens to the members, and where a very technical issue is concerned, such as that of nuclear power stations, then there is also a resort to outside expertise. In 1985 the ESC issued 98 opinions, including five on its own initiative. Issues involving coal and steel are referred to the ECSC Consultative Committee and in 1985 it had 21 proposals submitted to it; it issued two opinions and three resolutions.

E   The Court of Justice

The Court of Justice has no connection with the Council of Europe Court on Human Rights in Strasbourg. The Court of Justice sits in Luxembourg and its structure comprises 13 judges who are appointed for a period of six years, with provision for reappointment. While the judges come from member states, like members of the Commission, they are expected to be independent from the pressure of national governments. This is facilitated by judgments emanating from the Court instead of from individual Judges; hence governments do not know if any particular judge has supported its views or not (Henig 1980, p. 87).

The Judges are assisted by six Advocates-General, appointed from the member states. The office of Advocate-General is based on the French system and they prepare the ground for the Court by giving a reasoned opinion. There is an Advocate-General for each case.

The Court is supranational and its main function has been to ensure that in the member states Community law is applied with the Treaties being understood and implemented correctly. Where a citizen goes to the national court, if the latter is in doubt about matters it can refer to the European Court for clarification. Given the EC's prime concern is with economic integration then the Court has been occupied very much in ensuring that key economic objectives are carried out; for example, free trade, and the Court has ruled against different types of protectionist measures; the CAP has also resulted in numerous court cases. In addition, the Court has been active in tackling practices by businesses which are contrary to its competition policy.

The Court has resolved cases of infringement of the Treaty which have been referred to it. Member states have preferred not to bring proceedings against other member states, leaving it to the Commission to do so. The Court has also, among other things, ruled both on the actions and on the failures to act properly by Community institutions. Even the EP has gone to the Court claiming that the Council had breached its obligations under the Treaty to introduce a common transport policy.

The Court is sovereign, overruling national courts, but the latter apply the law. The European Court itself has no EC army or police force for this purpose! The Court of Justice is very active and has dealt with over 5000 cases since first taking up its duties in 1953. It has a growing workload and to relieve this the Single European Act has provided for the establishment of an additional European Court of First Instance.

F   The changing relationship between the institutions and the impact of the Single European Act

What was the initial relationship which was established between Community institutions and how has this changed over the years? In the first instance the Commission wielded great power with a strong Commission providing the driving force for integration. However, after the Luxembourg Compromise of 1966 to maintain a national veto, the Commission became somewhat subdued, lacking the leadership which was necessary to ensure the progress which neo-functionalists sought. The Commission has tried to create greater backing for its proposals, but it has had to be flexible and compromise, for example with the EP and particularly with the Council. Its main limitation which has to be emphasized is that it is no longer the dominant institution and is just one among several. Nevertheless, it remains the most central and permanent of the Community institutions, with some potential to restore part of its role since the SEA. For example, the SEA recognizes that implementation of EC legislation should be left more to the Commission. Furthermore, its powers in some fields, such as competition policy under Articles 85 and 86, have been highly developed already; more so than its potential power in other areas such as state aids in which the Commission has shown greater sensitivity to the wish of national governments to pursue their own industrial policies.

There have been many proposals for institutional change; for example, in 1979 the Spierenburg Report focused on the Commission's decline and made various proposals. These included recommendations to strengthen the role of the Commission President and to reduce both the number of Directorates and the number of Commissioners. Although some countries, such as the UK, are prepared to go along with proposals for one Commissioner, the enlargement of the EC has actually resulted in a further increase in the number of Commissioners.

Over the years the power of the Council increased, especially after the Luxembourg agreement in 1966. Countries have been able to block developments, and to alleviate this problem 'package deals' have been resorted to increasingly to offer compensatory gains to countries in some areas in an attempt to offset losses elsewhere and to secure agreement. But the pursuit by countries of their own national interests and their attempt to claim domestic victories has created slow, inefficient decision-making. With enlargement of the Community, complete paralysis would probably have occurred. Greater use of majority voting was recommended by the Committee of Three (Biesheuvel, Dell and Marjolin) in its Report in 1979. Certainly the wider application of majority voting under the SEA represents a valuable step forward in cutting through the vast growth of Community business to ensure that this is executed more effectively.

The elected EP has been concerned to increase its power in relation to the Commission and especially *vis-à-vis* the Council. Under the influence of Altiero Spinelli it took the lead in bringing about institutional reform by drafting a Treaty to establish European union. There was strong support for this, particularly from Italian and German MEPs, in keeping with the earlier Genscher–Colombo Plan. There was a Solemn Declaration on European Union in 1983 and the European Union Treaty (EUT) was adopted by the EP in February 1984 by 237 votes to 31, with 43 abstentions (Lodge 1986, pp. 35–6). It led the European Council at the Fontainebleau Summit in 1984 – having dealt with the UK budgetary issue – to establish two Committees on European union. These were the Dooge Committee on Institutional Affairs (along the lines of the earlier Spaak Committee which provided the basis for the Treaty of Rome) and the Adonnino Committee, which was concerned with improving the EC to create a so-called People's Europe. This included, among other things, aspects such as a Community flag, emblem and anthem; introduction of common postage stamps and minting of the ECU as European coinage. The European Council Meeting in 1985 proposed an inter-governmental conference in Luxembourg in autumn 1985 which led to agreement to amend the Treaty of Rome and to sign the SEA in 1986. Although this was a far-reaching development, especially for countries such as Ireland and Denmark which had difficulty in ratifying it, it fell short of the radical proposals by the EP for European union.

Some of the speeches and statements at the signing of the SEA reflected these disappointments. Andreotti, the Italian Minister for Foreign Affairs, felt that the SEA fell short of the joint decision-making which had been sought by both the Italian Parliament and by the European Parliament. The Vice President of the EP, Alber, also expressed the view that not enough had been done to give the EP more democratic control. However, various amendments have been made in the Treaties so that the EP is now recognized in the SEA by its preferred description of a Parliament and not as an Assembly.

The new system of co-operation, laid down in Articles 6 and 7 of the SEA, provides for very intensive consultation with the EP. Whereas under the existing Treaties the EP's opinion was only sought once, now it has another opportunity at the next to last stage. The EP first provides an opinion, and later the EP may, by an absolute majority of its component members (260 votes), propose precise amendments to the Council's position and may by the same majority reject the Council's position. If the EP has rejected the Council's common position, unanimity is then required for the Council to act on a second reading. Thus the EP's powers are much enhanced if it rejects the legislation, because the Council is likely to be mindful of the EP's vote and it seems possible that some of the member governments will go along with the EP's position preventing unanimity. With regard to amendments, the situation is more complicated and the EP's powers are weaker unless it can enlist the support of the Commission for its amendments. If the Commission's new version is acceptable, then the Council can enact a law by a qualified majority, whereas for the EP's position alone, unanimity in the Council is necessary. While the EP now has a say on two occasions – its opinion beforehand and amendment afterwards – this still falls short of allowing the EP to take over the legislative powers of the Council. Furthermore, the EP is constrained by the time provision at the final stage which provides that if the Council fails to act within three months, proposals shall be deemed not to have been adopted.

Both the Commission and the Council are having to pay greater attention to the Parliament. The co-operation procedure for key areas, such as the internal market, is leading the EP into the legislative area, more like a national Parliament. The EP is also monitoring what happens to its amendments and ultimately a failure to accept its views could lead to a threat to reject legislation outright or a vote of no confidence by the Parliament in the Commission and the latter's dismissal. Procedures in the SEA, while seeking to maximize close inter-institutional co-operation and dialogue, are still not without their problems. These could unfortunately lead to even more likelihood of deadlock – as seen in the past when the EP has exercised its budgetary powers.

Part III   UK adjustment to the institutions
The UK has had to adjust to different styles of legal and political systems. Its national voting system, based on the 'first past the post' system – rather than the system of proportional representation in other EC states – has distorted the representation from the UK political parties to the EP. For example, it has denied representation to the UK Liberals who might have strengthened Liberal forces in the EP. Both Labour and particularly Conservative MEPs have fitted uneasily into the EP's political parties. Although Labour MEPs are part of the Socialist group, the anti-market views of some Labour MEPs have reduced the cohesiveness of the Socialist group. Furthermore, the Conservative Party was unable to fit into existing party groups and hence form the European Democrats; this is virtually a national party group though it has included a sprinkling of Danish MEPs and now contains some Spanish MEPs. The European Democrats have tried to introduce a whipping system, though this has been much less effective than at Westminster (Daltrop 1982, p. 68).

The European Parliament has not had the impact which was hoped for, failing to receive anything like the degree of media coverage given to Westminster. Most of the major political personalities are still attracted to Westminster, with some MEPs from the UK using the European Parliament either at the beginning or the end of their political careers. National parliaments have been reluctant to see any overwhelming transfer in powers to the EP with a major difference in views, for example, between Mrs Thatcher in Westminster and Lord Henry Plumb in the EP. Nevertheless, national parliaments have lost some of their influence over the economic areas covered by the Community. Scrutiny of EC affairs is often limited and retrospective, with the scrutiny committees of the House of Commons, and the more effective one in the House of

Lords, sifting through material trying to highlight important issues.

The UK turnout in the European elections of 1979 and 1984 was low, with only about three in ten eligible voters actually voting. The only other countries to record a low turnout were Denmark, for example 47.8 per cent in 1979, and Ireland, 47.6 per cent in 1984. It has been suggested that between 1979 and 1984 there may have actually been some weakening of the mass commitment to European integration (Pridham 1986).

Lack of enthusiasm in the UK has also been shown by Eurobarometer national opinion polls in which most people consider that they have not benefited from EC membership. Various polls of public opinion conducted between spring 1983 and autumn 1985 showed that the percentage of people believing the UK to have benefited range from 34.8 to 39 per cent. In contrast, for the people of the EC as a whole, 58 to 64 per cent felt that their country had benefited. The lack of popular support for the EC has been brought about by the conflictual approach of the UK government over issues such as the costs of the CAP and the inequity of the Budget. Hence the UK has been less positive about the Community than other countries such as France or Italy (Hewstone 1986).

The UK has dispatched some distinguished political figures to the Commission, whose own self-image is one of a political bureaucracy. One of the most significant was Roy Jenkins who in his capacity as President of the Commission was successful in launching the EMS – unfortunately he failed to carry the UK into its crucial exchange rate mechanism. Other senior Commissioners appointed have included Christopher Soames, while the latest, Arthur Cockfield, was close to Mrs Thatcher – certainly until his proposals for harmonizing rates of VAT. The second Commissioner appointed has reflected a bipartisan political approach, being a member of the opposition party; for example, Stanley Clinton Davis was the other UK Commissioner, with a less powerful portfolio.

In the Council, governments have defended their own national interests tenaciously and the British have proved no exception with vigorous defence of crucial issues such as agriculture and the Budget. The pattern has tended to be one in which northern European countries have fought very strongly in the Council and created more difficulties than southern European countries. Nevertheless, the former have a good record in implementing the law, with relatively few cases against them, whereas the latter have raised problems of implementation. Certainly since the Fontainebleau Summit in 1984, which marked significant progress in tackling the outstanding budgetary problem, there has been a better phase in the UK's membership of the Community. Thus the UK's acceptance of the Community was reflected in the absence of the EC as an issue in the 1987 national election campaign. However, there is always a natural tendency both by the media and by politicians to use the Community as a scapegoat for the UK's own problems. The UK is keen on expanding into new co-operation in industry and technology, and also in defence co-operation.

Although the UK may not be wholly *communautaire*, it appears more committed to the Community, particularly at times when compared with other new entrants which have had to contend with some difficult problems of their own and contested Community competence; for example, Denmark, Greece and Ireland. The signing of the SEA shows how firmly embedded the UK has become in the EC. Its reservations were less than those of the other countries mentioned, though naturally there was some concern by anti-marketeers, which was shared initially by the British government (especially over the extension of powers by the EP and the extension of majority voting). But the outcome of the SEA was a pale shadow of the draft European Treaty, and the compromise disappointed the federalists since it omitted the word 'union' in its title. Yet the anti-marketeers consider that the SEA has gone too far in further eroding British sovereignty through the primacy of Community Law – even though this has arisen mainly from the Treaty of Rome rather than additional provisions in the SEA. In both the House of Commons and the House of Lords there was a large majority for the government. It was recognized quite sensibly that having joined the EC then the SEA offered an opportunity to exploit its potential further, in particular in the internal market in which majority voting suits the UK. Under the UK Presidency of the Council in the second half of 1986, many measures were pushed through to create an internal market since it was recognized that these would occur anyway once the SEA was in force.

The UK has also played an enthusiastic role in the development of foreign policy since it sees the Community as an important vehicle through which it can continue to exercise an influence in world affairs. Consultation on foreign policy has taken place since the Davignon Report in 1969; but this was kept at an informal intergovernmental level separate from the Community and France was prepared to accept this since it lacked any legal supranational element. There are regular meetings of Foreign Ministers, and the EC has reached common views on key international issues and its members tend to vote together at the United Nations. The SEA now carries foreign policy a stage further by recognizing that the Community 'shall endeavour to formulate and implement a European foreign policy'. The UK imprint in the SEA is shown clearly in foreign policy co-operation and the internal market. In other areas the UK has provided a brake on more rapid progress; for example, towards giving to the EP the even greater powers to which it ultimately aspires of full co-decision-making with the Council.

3 Free trade, the customs union and internal market

Part I GATT's efforts to maintain a free trade system

The signing of the General Agreement on Tariffs and Trade (GATT) in 1947, originally by 23 countries, was a crucial step forward in ensuring that a freer trade system would predominate in the post-war years. It has provided the best defence for the international economy, minimizing the re-emergence of a paralysing protectionism. It is founded on basic principles, such as that of non-discrimination. Advantages in trade conferred to one party have had to be extended to all, which then receive Most Favoured Nation (MFN) treatment. Since exceptions already existed for preferential agreements, such as those in the British Commonwealth, further advantage was taken of the exceptions which were made for customs unions.

Both the ECSC and the EEC took advantage of the concessions which were permissible, but have failed in some respects to comply fully with the conditions for creating customs unions: these were to cover virtually all the trade between member countries, whereas the ECSC only covered iron and steel. Yet when the ECSC required a waiver from GATT, the only opposition raised came from Czechoslovakia. The CET was not to be fixed at a higher or more restrictive level than that which the member countries themselves applied before the formation of the customs union. While the CET in the EEC was set below the tariff rates of some individual members, it initially involved the raising of tariffs in countries such as West Germany. The development of the EC since the 1970s has also manifested several restrictive tendencies; for example, the free trade area between the EC and EFTA excludes agricultural products. In addition, there has been concern over whether the extension of the customs union between the EC and certain Mediterranean countries can be completed within a reasonable time period (Hine 1985).

The EC has taken over from the individual member states which were the contracting parties to GATT, and has participated in many rounds of trade negotiations. These reduced the EC's CET from 12.5 per cent in 1958 down to about 6 per cent after the Tokyo round of negotiations. The main achievement of the Tokyo round, which ended in 1979 after six years, was to reduce nominal industrial tariffs in the developed world by nearly a third on average. Unfortunately, however, some countries, including those in the EC, have begun to infringe the general principles of GATT far more — partly as a consequence of recession. While agriculture, textiles and clothing were to a large degree exempt from GATT rules and discipline, trade in several other products has now become distorted by the use of quotas and by voluntary export restraints (VERs).

Community countries still retain national quotas on many imports which often pre-date the Treaty of Rome. These national quantitative restrictions are likely to be phased out with the removal of internal frontier controls in the single European market by 1992. Any controls will then have to be imposed on a Community-wide basis. While VERs have become more widespread, these are not really voluntary, but countries recognize that if they refuse to accept them they will be likely to experience a universal non-negotiable reduction in their exports. VERs have been accepted since they enable sellers to obtain higher prices in compensation for their goods than if other forms of trade restriction were used (Hine 1985). In the mid-1980s the EC had around 50 VERs, and over a third of Japanese exports to the EC were thought to be covered by these.

In an attempt to salvage GATT some 105 countries met for an eighth round of negotiations at Punte del Este in Uruguay in September 1986 and these are due to be completed by the end of 1990. Differences have arisen between developed countries and LDCs with the latter being sceptical about opening up trade in sectors such as services. In addition, the Code on Subsidies and Countervailing Duties negotiated during the Tokyo round has failed to tackle export subsidies effectively, particularly in agriculture; though there are even greater difficulties in doing much about agricultural production subsidies in which the EC is an obstacle to progress. Beforehand, suggestions had been made for a GATT-Plus (or Super-GATT) paralleling the kind of à la carte or variable geometry in EC integration, in which the leaders move on more quickly (Tsoukalis 1986).

Part II   The EC customs union and internal market

A   Key concepts of a customs union: trade creation and trade diversion

The most important characteristic of a customs union is a complete removal of tariffs between member countries. This constitutes a movement toward free trade, at least within the regional bloc. However, a customs union is also characterized by the imposition of a CET on imports from the rest of the world, and the higher its level the more adverse its impact on outsiders.

Whether a customs union is beneficial depends, amongst other things, upon the two concepts of trade creation and trade diversion.

Trade creation occurs when a country in the customs union finds it cheaper to import from a partner country. Instead of producing a good domestically, it switches its supply to the partner, which has a lower price since the intra-tariff is removed. Let us assume that there are three countries: 1, 2 and 3. Assume further that initially the price of a good, x, is £2 in country 1, £1.50 in country 2 and £1.40 in country 3. If country 1 imposed a 50 per cent tariff against imports, then it would produce the product domestically, since it would cost £2.25 to import it from country 2 (£1.50 plus 50 per cent tariff) and £2.10 (£1.40 plus 50 per cent tariff) to import it from country 3.

If countries 1 and 2 form a customs union (and country 3 remains outside, facing a 50 per cent CET), then country 1 imports the product from country 2 at the price of £1.50. Figure 3.1 helps to clarify these production gains, assuming for simplicity elastic supply schedules (quantity supplied at constant costs); also, for the present, any demand effects are ignored, with a completely inelastic demand schedule being shown in country 1.

The total cost to country 1 of producing the good domestically is the area under its supply schedule OABQ. The total cost of importing the same quantity OQ from country 2 is OCDQ. The difference between the two rectangles constitutes a resource saving of ABCD. It is apparent that there would be greater consumer gains

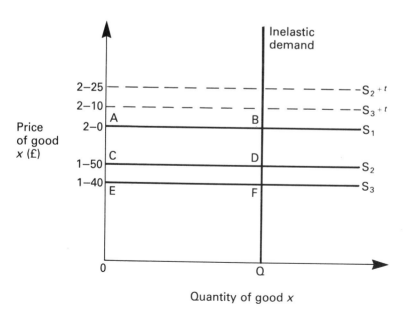

Figure 3.1   Trade creation

by enlarging the customs union to include country 3, since this would provide additional resource savings of rectangle CDEF.

A paradox exists as to why country 3 is excluded from the customs union. What are some of the implications for outside countries? The concept of trade diversion shows the consequences for outside country 3 which in the pre-customs union situation was the lowest cost supplier to country 1, but was excluded by 1's tariff; that is, the tariff of 50 per cent resulted in country 3 being priced out of the market. Let us assume, therefore, that a pre-customs union tariff of only 10 per cent was originally in force. Then country 1 imported from country 3, since the cost of importing from country 3 was £1.54 (£1.40 plus 10 per cent tariff), whilst the cost of importing from country 2 was £1.65 (£1.50 plus 10 per cent tariff). When a customs union is formed between countries 1 and 2, with country 3 excluded, trade is now diverted completely from a lower cost supplier outside the union to a higher cost member, since country 1 can save 4p by importing tariff-free from country 2 instead of from country 3 (which still faces the CET of 10 per cent).

Although in Figure 3.2 country 1 enjoys a consumer saving of rectangle ABCD by importing from country 2, it sacrifices welfare as shown by the rectangle CDEF, since country 3 has production costs of only OEFQ. The diversion of trade in this instance has clearly had adverse trading consequences for outside countries.

Jacob Viner, the pioneer of customs union theory, was mainly

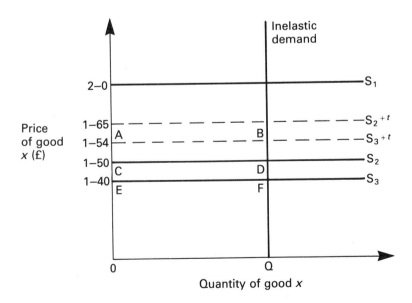

Figure 3.2 Trade diversion

influenced by classical economists in thinking about production changes — even though consumption changes had already been introduced into the international trade literature. It is necessary therefore to modify the earlier analysis by adding changes in consumption, since when prices are reduced (by removing tariffs), demand tends to increase. Figure 3.3 shows the normal downward sloping demand curve, plus a more normal upward sloping supply curve for the home producer.

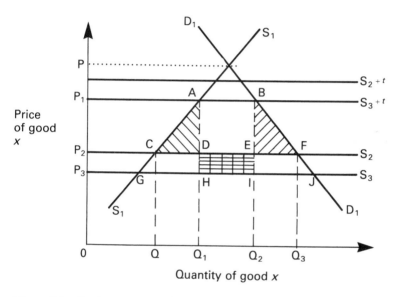

Figure 3.3   Trade creation and diversion

In Figure 3.3 the demand and supply curves in country 1 intersect at price OP. By importing good x consumers can enjoy a lower price than OP. With a tariff imposed by country 1 on imports from countries 2 and 3, country 1 produces domestically along its supply schedule up to OA and it imports quantity AB from country 3. What changes occur if a customs union is formed between countries 1 and 2 in which the lowest cost producer, country 3, is excluded? Since the EC is open to full membership by European countries, then many low-cost world producers are excluded.

In a customs union, country 1 reduces its own domestic supply to OQ and switches all of its imports to country 2 and imports CF. In the trade-creating effects of the customs union there is the supply-side effect discussed earlier; this is now shown by a triangular area ACD. The costs of producing quantity QQ_1 in country 1 is the area under its supply curve; that is, AQ_1QC, whereas the cost of importing the same quantity from country 2 is CQQ_1D. The triangle ACD is the production gain between these two areas.

The new element shown in Figure 3.3 is the increase in demand of $Q_2 - Q_3$ resulting from the lower price. Consumers are potentially better off, and using the concept of consumer surplus as a representation of consumer utility — notwithstanding its limitations — a consumption gain can be shown by the triangle BEF. Consumers are prepared to pay the prices shown along the demand curve. The utility from consuming $Q_2 - Q_3$ is shown by the area BFQ_3Q_2, whereas the expenditure incurred for $Q_2 - Q_3$ was EQ_2Q_3F. The difference between these two areas is the triangle BEF.

Since country 2 is not the lowest cost producer, trade is diverted from country 3. The trade diversion is rectangle DEIH and in conventional analysis is clearly harmful. However, it is possible that in the long-run country 2 could reduce its costs significantly; also, country 2 may on welfare grounds be a low income country. Furthermore, it has been argued that trade diversion empirically is not widespread and a general presumption in favour of customs unions should be retained (Bracewell-Milnes 1976). In addition, where customs unions have contributed to rising internal incomes and outside countries have been supplying complementary products, the latter have been able to derive benefits — this has been true particularly where the CET has been set at a low level. Customs unions which are bigger in membership are likely to be better since they reduce the likelihood of the lowest cost producer being excluded. Where the customs union partners have a high proportion of intra-trade and only a low CET to outsiders then the degree of trade diversion is likely to be small.

However, with completely free trade there would be no trade diversion at all and in Figure 3.3 there would only be gains: higher production gains AHG and higher consumption gains BIJ. Thus it has been argued (Cooper and Massell 1965) that a non-preferential trade policy which reduces protection will always be superior to the formation of a customs union. Yet if the traditional consumer gains for importing countries can be obtained by unilateral tariff reductions, why do countries rarely reduce tariffs unilaterally but instead favour the formation of customs unions?

B   *The rationale behind customs unions*

The initial reasons for forming customs unions were not wholly economic, including both strategic and political considerations. However, it is helpful where an economic explanation is given to focus not only on consumer gains, but in addition on the gains to producers in a customs union.

In Figure 3.4, a low cost supplier in one EC country — where D_i is

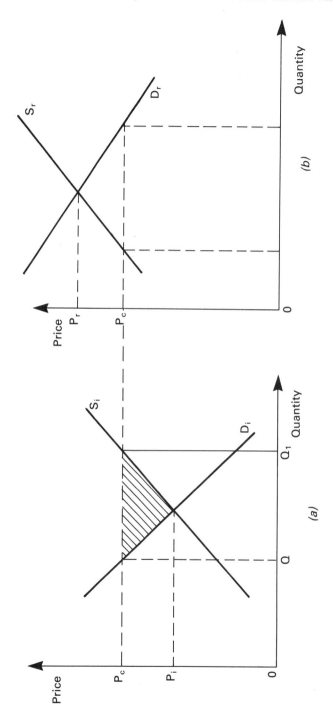

Figure 3.4 (a) *The market in an individual EC country*
(b) *The market in the rest of the EC*

domestic demand, S_i is domestic supply and a low equilibrium price OP_i prevails — is able to export quantity QQ_1 to the rest of the EC. A common price OP_c, which equals the EC price, then exists throughout the Community. Thus industry is able to expand along its domestic supply curve (S_i) supplying the rest of the EC — with subscript r in the diagram referring to the rest of the Community.

The concern with expanding production *per se* has led to perhaps the most cogent explanation for the formation of customs unions. Johnson (1965) argued that a country has some collective preference for domestic industrial and agricultural production which yields social benefits. In a predominantly trade diverting customs union, a country which has a strong preference for such production, but with only a weak comparative advantage internationally, can achieve its preferences. However, why do countries not achieve this by measures such as domestic subsidies and taxes? To achieve a sufficiently high level of production and exports countries would need to resort to export subsidies, and these have been used widely in agriculture. But industrially they infringe international trading agreements, whereas customs unions have been able to develop within the GATT framework. Therefore the constraints on the use of first-best domestic policies and constraints on trade policies help to explain the formation of customs unions (Jones in El-Agraa 1985).

Producer gains have been significant for another reason and this is that much of the trade expansion has been of an intra-industry type; that is, countries simultaneously export and import similar or even homogeneous products in the same industry. Freer trade has enabled countries to concentrate production in fewer, larger plants. While intra-industry trade has always existed, it has increased significantly within the EC (Grubel and Lloyd 1975, p. 134; Greenaway 1987, p. 108). In 1980 intra-industry trade ranged from 50 per cent for Italy to 65 per cent for both France and Belgium-Luxembourg. It exists particularly in differentiated products in which multinational companies are active, with a significant growth of intra-firm trade in, for example, passenger cars.

Countries in a customs union are able to derive other advantages. For example, by acting collectively rather than separately they are able to increase their bargaining power and their terms of trade may improve relative to outside countries. If the latter are producing competitive goods whose output is inelastic, then the price of their exports falls. EC countries have been able to get much better prices for their own exports relative to their import prices. Terms of trade gains of up to one per cent of GNP have been estimated (Petith 1977). However, later studies have been less optimistic about the size of these terms of trade gains, though they have confirmed that the larger the economic area, the more substantial is likely to be the improvement in the terms of trade (Marques Mends 1987, p. 106).

Finally, the customs union is important as the basic starting point along the road to more extensive integration in other sectors. A customs union, then, is part and parcel of the whole process of integration in a regional bloc.

C   Dynamic gains in a customs union

Modern industry is characterized by the growth of giant firms which are able to reap static and dynamic economies of scale within a large market such as that in the EC. These economies of scale enable firms to meet greater market demand by moving down their long-run average cost curves. Economies of scale are significant in the formation of all customs unions, not only the EC but also the customs unions which have been formed in other parts of the world between less developed countries (LDCs).

In the case of key industries such as the motor industry, a customs union between LDCs helps to make the actual production of cars viable, whereas in developed countries it enables cars which are already being produced to be produced at an even lower cost. Optimum economies of scale in the EC car industry would occur with a company output of up to 2 million cars annually, with every doubling of output up to this level reducing unit costs by about 10 per cent — no European manufacturer has yet reached this level of output. It indicates that the European market can accommodate only a few large firms. The more successful producers have been able to benefit from export opportunities and French car producers have significantly increased their net sales to other markets in the Community. West Germany has also been very successful in penetrating other EC markets, especially in a sector such as commercial vehicles. In the latter, economies of scale are lower, though the 100 000 unit producer had a cost advantage of about 16 per cent over the 20 000 unit producer (Owen 1983). In other sectors, for instance white goods, it is Italy which has shown the way forward. Economies of scale in products such as refrigerators and washing machines have enabled Italy to sell with great success in other markets within the Community. Some economists have placed particular emphasis on the role of economies of scale in lowering unit costs in such industries (Owen 1983).

The scope for exploiting economies of scale naturally varies from one industry to another. In some industries the level of concentration which has been reached may well be above that which is justified by the need for economies of scale alone. Furthermore, large firms operating in oligopolistic markets and lacking sufficient competition are often prone to some X-inefficiency. Nevertheless, the aim of the EC has been to provide a market size to try to match the economies of scale, standardization and productivity levels of the USA. There the market has been large enough to support a sufficient number of optimally-sized plants without resulting in the danger of monopoly exploitation which was a problem in national European markets.

While multinational companies can only develop on the basis of a large market, historically some of the world's major multinationals have actually grown up in small national markets such as Switzerland and Sweden. But they have been able to grow mainly by selling to the international market rather than to the domestic one alone. Membership of EFTA and the latter's free industrial trade agreement with the EC have further facilitated the growth of such multinationals, even if they did not cause it initially. The smaller EFTA countries have also been able to co-operate with the EC in some industrial sectors in which scale is crucial to success. Not being full members of the EC has not precluded co-operation by outside countries in sectors such as aerospace. Even before 1973 the UK, for example, was an active participant in European aerospace projects.

Apart from economies of scale, another mechanism of dynamic gain is provided by increased competition which can stimulate a higher level of efficiency. In a more competitive environment less efficient producers are undercut, being forced either to improve their production methods or to be driven out of business. Monopolies in domestic markets find their position undermined by exposure to highly competitive imports. But for gains to be actually realized, these firms have to compete effectively by altering their existing pricing policies (Hine 1985, p. 28).

A further benefit is that a large expanding market is conducive to a greater level of both indigenous and inward investment − a key factor in raising the rate of economic growth. In the heyday of EC expansion, businesses feared the consequences of not investing aggressively in new plant and equipment, but in the recession since 1974 investment has slackened. Although the EC has contributed to an increase in the aggregate rate of economic growth, some individual countries such as West Germany actually achieved a higher growth rate before joining the Community; also, the UK economic growth rate since joining the EC has not accelerated. While dynamic factors as a whole are important, they are unlikely to be sufficient to outweigh any losses which show up in a static analysis of customs unions (Lundgren 1969).

D   Empirical measurement

There have been many studies which have tried to measure the growth in trade which can be attributed to the formation of a customs union *per se*. The two basic approaches are either ex-ante or ex-post. The former is a system of simulating the effect of tariff changes on the pattern of trade, with results depending on demand

and supply elasticities. The ex-post method involves looking at the changes in trade patterns which have taken place as a result of a customs union. Balassa, for example, used ex-post income elasticities of demand (assuming that they would have been unchanged in the absence of the EC). He confirmed the predominance of trade creating effects and these were strongest in the early stages of the EC. However, to avoid overstating trade creation it is generally useful to try to normalize the expected trade shares more realistically by examining how income elasticities have changed in other countries outside the EC, such as the USA. Even with such downward adjustments they showed trade creation exceeding trade diversion by at least four times (Balassa 1975).

There are great variations in both the empirical results and also in the welfare analysis of the implications of trade creation and trade diversion (Jones in El-Agraa 1985). Nevertheless, some sensible orders of magnitude of static effects are possible and in several studies trade creation has been around $10 billion and trade diversion around $1 billion (Swann 1984, pp. 118–19). There are, though, one or two studies which show significantly lower aggregate trade creation and more trade diversion, such as those by Truman and by Kreinin (1974). Overall static customs union gains are limited, to one or two per cent of GNP, since not all goods and services are traded.

A particular dissatisfaction with traditional customs union analysis has been expressed by some economists. Marques Mendes (1987) goes further than the basic problems of trade creation and trade diversion and unreliability of their results, pointing out the neglect in measuring the important dynamic effects, let alone all the other features of the Community. He adopted a different approach, using the foreign trade multiplier to capture trade effects, relating those to output growth. His results showed the strong trade effects and concluded that in the EC, integration resulted by 1981 in a GDP that was 5.9 per cent higher than in the non-integration situation (1987, p. 104). This is a much higher result than earlier estimates by other economists, and the role of trade, the CAP, factor movements and so on, are all included in his analysis.

E   Intra-EC trade and the internal market
The removal of tariffs between countries in the EC was much easier than anticipated since the countries were in a fairly similar competitive position (apart from the South of Italy). Also, at a time of general economic growth in the 1960s, firms were able to expand and any factors of production which became redundant could be absorbed with relative ease into other sectors. Just over half of the EC's trade now consists of intra-trade (Eurostat 1986); this growth has been assisted not only by the removal of tariff barriers but also by other developments such as the emergence of greater similarity

in the pattern of consumer preferences. Once manufacturers have developed a competitive product, they look for exports in other markets which have similarity in both income per head and in the pattern of demand for those products. Thus more horizontal trade, at least in modern consumer durables, has developed between countries with similar factor proportions, and not as the Heckscher-Ohlin theory predicted between countries with different factor proportions. Many products are the result of innovation and the most developed EC countries with high R & D expenditure tend to dominate trade in new technological sectors. Export of such products enables both dynamic and static economies of scale to be reaped.

With the onset of economic recession since the early 1970s, member states in the Community have sought to exploit Article 36 of the Treaty of Rome far more — this allows justified exemptions to free trade. EC countries have started to make greater use of non-tariff barriers (NTBs) to defend their products. These NTBs, for example, can take the form of different technical standards to protect national health, safety and the welfare of citizens.

The lack of a complete common market still constitutes a significant obstacle to increasing the competitiveness of European industry. It is to rectify this that the Community is now pursuing vigorously the completion of the internal market for which plans were first published in a White Paper in June 1985. It will provide a catalyst for the Community's regeneration and agreement on this has proved possible since the lack of a single internal market is much more costly than the CAP, and tackling the former seems less intractable than the latter. The distinctive features are that it is a complete programme and set within the time period for completion by 1992, though there may be some slippage since it is not legally binding. The internal market, according to Article 13 of the SEA and the new Article 8a of the EEC Treaty, 'shall comprise an area without internal frontiers in which the free movement of goods, persons, services and capital is ensured'. Article 14 of the SEA and the new Article 8b of the EEC Treaty is concerned with a balanced implementation of measures, with the Commission to report to the Council on the progress made, with decisions taken on the basis of qualified majority voting. Article 15 of the SEA and Article 8c in the EEC Treaty recognize the heterogeneous nature of the Community since its enlargement, with provisions for temporary derogations.

The single internal market is one which is going to dominate all other issues over the next few years. The focus in this section is on the physical and technical barriers impeding the flow of goods and services in the customs union. Different aspects of the internal market are included in other chapters, such as taxation in Chapter

8, but it should be recognized that this is mainly the consequence of removing frontier controls, rather than any new macroeconomic preoccupation with fiscal (or monetary) integration. Indeed, the single European market indicates a re-commitment to microeconomics to reap the benefits accruing from the free play of market forces, running in parallel with more liberal policies in many member states.

The Kangaroo Group, a European Parliamentary pressure group, has drawn attention to the multiplicity of barriers which still exist (*The Kangaroo News* 1987). The two major sources of market fragmentation which are cited most frequently are different national production standards, followed by national purchasing policies. By contrast, delays at frontiers are a less significant factor; for example, the costs of national preferences have been estimated at a colossal £57 billion, compared with an annual cost of £17 billion for inspections at frontiers. One measure of market fragmentation is the continued practice by firms of charging different prices between national markets; for example, car prices have varied by up to 50 per cent, being cheapest in Belgium and dearest in Denmark. In an integrated market with resale arbitrage firms would be forced by competition to charge similar and low prices. European firms would then be better placed to compete with Japanese producers in many products, such as video-cassette recorders, where European producers have been at a 43 per cent disadvantage in cost relative to Japanese producers, partly because of high cost European parts from local sources (Booz Allen and Hamilton Inc. 1986, p. 2).

Firms are adversely affected by the existence of different national standards. In West Germany, the Standards Institute imposes very high standards, whereas most French and British standards have not been compulsory. In exporting products, firms complain that the Community is an 'uncommon market' and they have to make modifications to meet the separate national requirements for each European market. When every product has to be submitted for approval by each country, this leads to delays and often imported products may be subjected to a more thorough process of testing.

A test case of considerable significance was that of *Cassis de Dijon* 1979 in which a French liqueur made from blackcurrants was deemed to have too low an alcoholic content for the West German market. The European Court of Justice decided otherwise and it laid down that if a product had satisfied the standard requirements in one country then it should in principle be allowed to be imported into another member country. The ruling has since provided precedent for other cases, such as that concerning beer imports into West Germany and Greece. German law stated that beer could contain nothing more than malted barley, yeast, hops and water. Germany claimed that their law was not discriminatory since if national manufacturers made beer in this way they could sell to the German market. This claim was successfully contested by the European Court of Justice. However, Denmark, which has generally been progressive in opening up markets, has also banned imports of beer from other member states, unless it is in reusable beer bottles. While this may be a useful conservation measure, it again reduces imports of foreign beer because of the distance in comparison with the more convenient position of Denmark's own breweries.

The process of harmonizing standards has also been slow, often taking years to adopt, whereas technology may have moved on in the meantime. Since 1983 member states have had to notify the Commission in advance of any new standards they intend to introduce. A stand-still period has been imposed to allow time for the Commission to examine them, initially for three months, which can be extended up to twelve months. In addition, the procedure for complaints is being improved for those industries adversely affected by such barriers. Apart from trying to prevent the imposition of new national standards, the EC has achieved agreement by issuing European standards for many products. It has abandoned the idea of trying to harmonize every detail of a particular product, and it has tried instead to establish minimum standards for health and safety, exemplified by a mass of items ranging from pressure vessels to toys, with many further proposals of essential requirements for items such as construction products and machine safety. Likewise, to remove technical barriers for foodstuffs, instead of complicated specifications on their composition, the EC's food harmonization is based on 'framework' directives for food labelling, additives, food for certain nutritional uses, and materials and articles in contact with food. Common standards will be of great benefit to European producers, but they will have to operate on the basis that the whole Community market is in fact their home market. Unless this happens, the major beneficiaries may well be outside suppliers such as Japan and the USA since they much prefer to work to one standard rather than to twelve different national standards in the Community.

Although the customs union was completed in July 1968, checks at frontiers have continued. To simplify these, procedures were agreed on a package of customs changes from January 1988. The Single Administrative Document (SAD) has replaced about 100 export and import forms and Community transit documents (T-forms) used in the EC and for trade with EFTA. Some forms have had to be retained, though revised and aligned to the SAD, in order to provide proof that certain goods, such as those covered by the CAP, are used or disposed of in a particular way. Since 'Customs 88' there has also been a reclassification of tariff codes to a new harmonized commodity description and coding system. This consists of six digits recognized world-wide; seven and eight digits for EC sub-divisions and nine for the UK; for imports from outside the EC, and especially for agricultural products, an additional digit tariff is used. While the change in code has changed some duties, the overall effect is neutral. A new computer system for Customs Handling of Import and Export Freight (CHIEF) accommodates changes brought about by the SAD and the Community Integrated Tariff (TARIC), and these are expected to be implemented fully by 1990. Automation of customs data will speed up administration and cut costs for industry and commerce: the programme for Co-operation in Automation of Data and Documentation for Imports, Exports and Agriculture (CADDIA) is currently proving very successful.

There has been a new attempt to reduce national preferences for public contracts, since public procurement accounts for up to 15 per cent of the EC's GDP (though only a small proportion of contracts have gone to non-national suppliers). The reluctance to buy from outside suppliers has been aided by lack of proper advertising and by the complexity of tendering procedures. The bias in favour of national suppliers has continued, despite the adoption by the Council of Directives on Public Works contracting as long ago as 1971, and further Directives in 1977 on Public Supply contracts. Directives apply to contracts above particular threshold levels; for example, ECU 200,000 for supply contracts for regional and local authorities which are subject only to EC rules, and ECU 1 million for Public Works contracts. The exclusion of important sectors, such as transport, water, gas and electricity, and telecommunications, is being rectified to prevent the national industrial champion from preserving a monopoly of orders for power stations and telecommunications. This has resulted in excess capacity and higher costs in these sectors by European firms. For example, in telephone exchange switching equipment the Commission has estimated that open procurement will reduce the price per phone line to about £80 (compared with £53 a line in the US), resulting in only two Community suppliers. Open procurement will limit single tendering and lengthen the time period for bids. Also, better policing has been proposed to tackle non-compliance so that action can be instigated against offending purchasers. An attempt is being made to use European standards to define the technical specifications for contracts. For example, IT systems have been incompatible but Open Systems Interconnection (OSI) Standards are being developed and in 1987 the EC adopted a decision requiring public purchasers to specify these standards when buying IT systems.

Fragmentation of the market has prevented European firms from exploiting their competitiveness to the full. The lack of a single internal market has been estimated on average to have added some

15 per cent to total costs (Booz Allen and Hamilton Inc. 1986). The removal of unnecessary barriers will bring down some costs very quickly; for example, the wasteful costs of physical trading barriers which are especially onerous for smaller firms. Other benefits will emerge in the long-run as new business strategies are planned. Firms will re-appraise their activities to take advantage of cheaper sources of EC component supplies and lower costs of financial services and distribution. The greatest benefits will arise when business reorganization permits greater concentration on major product lines, reaping economies of scale and often rationalization of a firm's operations on one site.

The Community's timetable is to get rid of more than 300 physical, technical and fiscal barriers by 1992. Qualified majority voting will facilitate this — though there are some exceptions and it does not apply to tax measures, free movement of persons and the rights and interests of the employed person. In addition, countries will be even more reluctant to enforce measures with which they are not in agreement and there have already been too many instances of countries in the past failing to implement Community policy properly. Furthermore, greater powers given to the EP may delay progress, along with a reluctance of Southern European countries to concede to the entity of the internal market unless this is linked to their demands for compensation in other ways to create a more cohesive Community. Interest groups adversely affected by market forces can be expected to resist further liberalization, perhaps falling back upon other protectionist devices, such as state aids. Nevertheless, the SEA was clear in its goals, and by November 1987 the Commission had timetabled some 200 proposals, although less than 70 of these had actually become law (*The Times* 19 November 1987).

Part III   UK trade in the EC

The removal of tariffs on trade between the UK and the EC has led to a reorientation in the patterns of trade. In 1973 32.8 per cent of UK imports and 32.3 per cent of UK exports were conducted with the EC (Holmes 1983, p. 23). By 1986 51.7 per cent of UK imports and 47.9 per cent of UK exports were with the EC (HMSO 1987, p. 15). The main problem has been that imports from the EC have tended to rise faster than UK exports to the Community. This was to be expected to some extent, given the diversion in UK imports of agricultural products towards Community suppliers. Although North Sea oil has developed as a valuable export to the EC, in some respects, by pushing up the UK's exchange rate, this made it harder for the UK to export manufactured products.

A summary of UK transactions with the EC between 1973 and 1986 has shown the UK generally in balance of payments deficit and in only two of these years, 1980 and 1981, was the UK in small surplus in its current account transactions with the Community. In 1986 the deficit on all current account transactions had widened to £9165 million (HMSO 1987, p. 63). The general imbalance can be attributed mainly to the deficit on visible trade, but the UK has also been in small deficit on invisible trade with the EC, apart from a few years, such as 1981 to 1984. In 1986 the UK's deficit on invisibles was £783 million and this can be attributed mainly to government transfers associated largely with the Community budget which has offset the surplus on items such as private sector financial services.

Of major concern has been the growing imbalance on UK trade in manufactures. In 1973 the EC took 31 per cent of the UK's total export of manufactures and provided 39 per cent of its imports of manufactures. By 1984, although the EC received 39 per cent of UK exports of manufactures, it supplied 50 per cent of UK imports of manufactured products. The UK trade deficit with the EC in manufactured goods was £8.38 billion in 1984 and some 60 per cent of that deficit was accounted for by the UK's trade with West Germany (Dearden 1986). Unlike the UK, West Germany has enjoyed a massive trade surplus, especially in its trade with the Community. West Germany's export-import ratio on all trade in 1985 was 115.9, whereas for the UK it was 91.7 (Eurostat 1985). Key sectors such as the motor industry have accounted for a large part of the UK deficit; for example, by 1984 just over 60 per cent of UK motor vehicles originating in the EC came from West Germany. The total UK trade imbalance in motor industry products deteriorated from £2.3 billion in 1984 to £3.9 billion in 1986, and for the first time trade in parts and accessories also showed a deficit in 1986 of £346 million.

The export–import ratio of the UK in its trade has been in deficit in most manufactured sectors. Apart from road vehicles, there have been deficits in, for example, machinery, iron and steel, and textiles, though the UK did have a surplus in a few sectors such as clothing and chemical products (Holmes 1983). The UK performance has been disappointing, given the promising position from which many of its industries started in their trade with the EC (Han and Liesner 1971).

It would be wrong, however, to attribute all of the UK's trading problems solely to its membership of the EC. The UK's basic problem has been the low world income elasticity of demand for its exports and a high UK income elasticity of demand for world imports. Indeed, the UK's dilemma has been that it has not only been in deficit in its manufactured trade with the Community, but also with other developed countries. Furthermore, the export–import ratio for UK trade in manufactures with both Japan and North America has deteriorated far more than that with the EC.

The pattern for the UK has been one of tending to sustain trading deficits in manufactures with major developed competitors, and to offset these partially by running a trading surplus on manufactures with less developed countries. The UK trading imbalance in manufactures has resulted from ongoing microeconomic deficiencies, exacerbated by macroeconomic problems, such as a periodic overvalued exchange rate.

While UK industry has obtained export benefits in EC markets the UK trade balance has not benefited sufficiently because of rising imports – though precise estimates of the trade balance vary according to the sources used (Morgan 1980). In the light of the massive decline in the UK's domestic manufacturing output, one conservative estimate is that it reduced this by at least £3 billion, about 1.5 per cent of GNP, and the effect could easily be twice as high (Winters 1987, p. 328). Despite the adverse effects on domestic unemployment, Winters has taken the optimistic view that the welfare benefits to users and consumers of manufactured products could be high enough to outweigh the losses to home producers.

Apart from the lack of UK competitiveness in manufactured trade, it has also suffered from insufficient integration in sectors in which it is more competitively placed, such as financial services and air transport. Hence the extension of integration in these sectors is welcome and during the UK Presidency of the EC Council in 1986 it sought to consolidate integration in these sectors of the internal market where the UK can benefit from its comparative advantage. Financial services account for some seven per cent of the EC's GDP, and the aim of the internal market is to go beyond the rights of establishment in other member states to the direct provision of these services. For example, an EC non-life insurance services Directive will provide cover irrespective of where the insurer is established (though transitional arrangements in Greece, Ireland, Portugal and Spain will delay its application until after the end of 1992). Nevertheless, for the UK in opening up the market in financial services, it will be important to ensure that this does not have an adverse effect on those non-Community financial institutions which are already active in the 'City'. The UK will also have to compete with other countries which will begin to enjoy a more liberal and less regulated financial framework. But overall the UK clearly enjoys a comparative advantage in particular sectors, such as insurance and Stock Exchange dealings.

The single internal market is a source of new opportunities, but not without risks, and some manufacturing sectors may suffer from greater import penetration, without these being outweighed by extra export sales. Some industries, such as textiles, have already reorganized after long exposure to stiff international competition, and other industries now face similar rationalization. If British business fails to involve itself more actively in European Standards bodies, then problems will arise in working to new foreign technical standards. Once a harmonized standard has been agreed to by a majority vote in the Community, then conflicting national standards have to be removed. The UK recently has held the Secretariat of far fewer technical committees of the European Standardization Committee than either West Germany or France.

The view that the internal market is attractive since it is largely costless in budgetary terms neglects other costs, such as those imposed on depressed areas. Many local authorities have made use of public purchasing to stimulate development by favouring local suppliers. They have also exercised a social influence over the employment practices of their suppliers. The opening up of public procurement policies is likely to be a further source of imports and to dilute local economic development policies.

The UK has introduced a more active internal market publicity campaign than West Germany – the latter has done well already in industrial exports and is hesitant about opening up its protected service sector. Other countries, such as France, have been quick to publicize 'quatre-vingt-douze' (1992). In addition, Italian businessmen, in particular Carlo de Benedetti, the head of Olivetti, have begun to exploit the EC as a natural base for industrial growth. This was illustrated by his attempts to gain control of Belgium's Société Générale early in 1988. Parts of UK industry will similarly become even more vulnerable to foreign take-overs, whereas many continental countries are better protected against such incursions.

The single internal market will generate aggregate economic gains for the EC, and also for parts of the UK economy, such as high-tech industries and much of the service sector. (The importance of the service sector in terms of employment is shown in a 3-variable graph in Chapter 4.) Nevertheless, in the short-term some of the changes will be uncomfortable and result in further job displacement in weaker industrial sectors.

Dynamic effects on the UK economy. It was always hoped that there would be strong dynamic effects on British industry in the EC, arising primarily from the opportunities for greater economies of scale, a sharper competitive climate and faster growth; these will be further reinforced in the single internal market. There are some distinct examples of industries in which static and dynamic economies of scale have been reaped, but often the greatest gains have been made by continental producers in industries such as passenger cars, commercial vehicles and in white goods (Owen 1983). Given the UK's relative decline in manufacturing industry, then the truth about the dynamic effects may be closer to some of the early gloomy predictions (Kaldor 1971).

The benefits for consumers of lower prices from a process of 'Darwinian destruction' have to be set against some of the adverse effects on UK producers. Although some firms have been jolted into greater efficiency as a result of more competition, others have been unable to survive, resulting in a substantial loss of domestic capacity. Furthermore, excessive competition by lowering profits can inhibit some much needed long-term investment. Nevertheless, it does appear that the heightened competitiveness in the Community may have helped to tackle the 'British disease', whereas only a few years ago pessimists concluded that the main hope lay in spreading the disease to others! (Einzig 1971)

The assumption that membership of the Community would automatically shift the UK on to a higher plateau of economic growth was over-optimistic. Certainly the UK has become a more attractive location for inward investment and its growth rate was good in 1973 – the year of entry into the Community – but the subsequent economic recession reduced economic growth rates. Between 1960 and 1972 the UK rate of economic growth was only 2.9 per cent per annum, compared with 5.1 per cent in the EC. Since 1973, while there has been a convergence of the UK growth rate towards that of the EC, this has been at a much reduced level of aggregate economic growth. Between 1973 and 1986 the UK rate of economic growth was 1.9 per cent per annum compared with 2.2 per cent per annum in the EC. UK growth as a percentage of that in the EC rose from 57 per cent, 1960 to 1972, to 82 per cent, 1973 to 1986. If one assumes that outside the Community the UK had continued to grow at its pre-entry rate (57 per cent of that in the EC), then UK economic growth would have been only 1.3 per cent from 1973 to 1986 (Johnson 1987). Another result in line with this has shown that the EC accounted for about 30 per cent of the UK's economic growth rate from 1974 to 1981 (Marques Mendes 1987). Since the early 1980s the UK's comparative growth rate internationally has been much improved and it is hoped that the internal market will reinforce its vibrant economy.

It is always difficult to disentangle the effects of the EC from other major changes taking place over the same period, of which perhaps the major one has been that of North Sea oil. Although this has helped to loosen the overall balance of payments constraint for the UK, its effect in pushing up the exchange rate has aggravated the trading competitiveness of manufacturing industry. Hence the expansion in sectors such as oil has been partly offset by further deindustrialization. This has limited some of the projected dynamic gains from belonging to the Community.

The faster growth of manufacturing imports from the EC and elsewhere has clearly contributed to rising unemployment in the UK. Between 1980 and 1986 UK unemployment averaged 10.6 per cent, compared with unemployment of 9.9 per cent in the EC. Weaker economies, such as the UK with its structural problems in particular regions, have tended to suffer unduly from freer trade. Furthermore, Community membership may have added three-quarters of one per cent to the UK inflation rate since 1973. Between 1960 and 1972 its inflation averaged 4.5 per cent, compared with four per cent in the EC. Between 1973 and 1986, UK inflation averaged 11.3 per cent, as against 9.6 per cent in the EC; hence UK inflation was 113 per cent of that of the Community from 1960 to 1972 and 119 per cent of that of the Community from 1973 to 1986 (Johnson 1987). The main inflationary bias has been given to food prices, since the removal of tariffs actually reduced the relative prices of industrial products.

4   Agriculture and Fisheries

Part I   The economic characteristics of agriculture

Agriculture possesses distinctive characteristics: these result in short-run fluctuations in price, while, in the long-run, agricultural prices tend to decline in real terms. The latter have necessitated movement of resources out of agriculture and into other sectors of the economy.

A free agricultural market, at the mercy of weather and climatic conditions, is likely to veer from good harvests to bad ones. The marked fluctuation in price is shown in Figure 4.1.

Reading along the supply curve: with a poor harvest, quantity

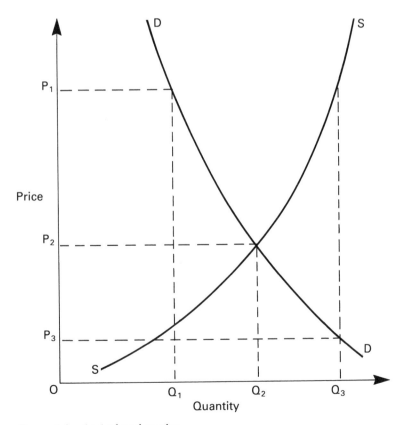

Figure 4.1   Agricultural market

OQ_1, shortages result in a high price OP_1. Quantity OQ_2 and price OP_2 provide the market equilibrium. A golden bumper harvest, quantity OQ_3, results in the low price OP_3.

A difference between agriculture and many other markets is the relatively inelastic supply and demand curves. The steep slopes of these curves magnify the range of price fluctuations.

Why is agricultural supply so unstable and unpredictable? It takes a long period of time to adjust output and the production of many joint products means that increasing output of one product in high demand may result in the surplus of another product. Agriculture, unlike many industrial sectors, is still characterized by smaller units, though farm size has risen and some sectors of agriculture aproximate to factory production, as in poultry. Resources are often trapped in farming with investment in product-specific equipment. In the short-run, farmers continue to produce as long as they can cover their low variable costs; for example, labour costs, in which there has been a much reduced labour force to remunerate. However, relative immobility has been intensified by an ageing of the farm population and a lack of better alternative jobs during a period of much slower economic growth.

Agriculture is still highly competitive, but some farmers may not be solely maximizing profits, but maximizing their satisfaction from family farming. Agriculture may respond less closely to market signals than economists would like. Some farmers may choose a target income level and to maintain this they continue to produce in an attempt to offset falling prices. Past experience has borne this out in various sectors (Capstick 1970, Ch. 4). Even with the right price signals, policy-makers find it difficult to achieve the required output level; but with the wrong price signals, which have often been given in the EC, over-production has been a major problem.

On the supply side, equilibrium is not achieved in some products. In the stable cobweb cycle a convergence towards equilibrium does not occur where supply and demand curves both have a relatively inelastic slope. In the divergent cobweb cycle, when supply is more elastic than demand, there is an explosively divergent outcome. While these lagged adjustments are based on simplified assumptions and assume that farmers never learn, the basic cycles have been well exemplified over the years in various sectors; for example, the recurrent pig cycle.

The other determinant of prices, demand, is also relatively inelastic. Both price and income elasticities are well below unity for agricultural foodstuffs; that is, a one per cent fall in price or rise in income results in a less than one per cent rise in demand. Since the 1950s, food consumption has risen only slowly in most EC countries. The population increase in the EC(12) rose only 0.7 per cent per annum, 1950–75, with a projected increase of only 0.3 per cent per annum, 1975–2000. Total food consumption in Western Europe was expected to rise by only about 0.6 per cent per annum 1975–2000 (Duchêne *et al.* 1985, p. 81). The EC's agricultural consumption, especially since the recession in the 1970s, has failed to keep pace with rising supply. Agriculture is inevitably a declining industry in terms of demand in mature, advanced economies, but paradoxically has been expanding in supply, with a sustained rate of productivity growth based on technological and biological change.

It is generally recognized that there is a need to shield agriculture from the completely free operation of market forces, though there are policy disagreements on the most appropriate measures to adopt. There is a danger that a search for stability and cushioning in the short-term can aggravate the need for long-term adjustments. The EC is now confronted by this fundamental problem of major agricultural adjustment.

Part II　The Common Agricultural Policy (CAP)

A　National historical traditions

Historically, agriculture in the major continental countries has manifested widespread protectionism. In the nineteenth century, farmers in Germany, France and Italy, resorted to protectionism and resisted change, whereas their counterparts in the UK, Denmark, the Netherlands and Belgium, modernized and reorganized their farming systems. Cheap imports of grain from the new world were impeded by high tariffs in countries such as France and Germany. In the Netherlands and Denmark imports of cheap grain were used to adapt their agriculture and they began to specialize in the production and export of high-value dairy produce and meat.

Between the wars, especially in the 1930s, agricultural policies became highly protectionist as a result of the collapse of international markets due to the Depression. Germany and Italy became concerned even more with promoting self-sufficiency. Germany realized the importance of this in reducing import dependency, since war disrupted outside agricultural supplies. In the 1940s feeding the population became the major agricultural priority. After the war, with scarce foreign currency reserves in Europe, countries continued to support domestic agriculture in order to improve their balance of payments position.

B　The evolution of the CAP

Essentially, the evolution of the CAP represented some continuity of the national agricultural policies by the major continental countries, particularly German policy, based on high prices. Since a new Franco-German *rapprochement* has been at the heart of post-war integration, then a balance had to be struck between the interests of the two countries. It was decided to adopt common policies for both the industrial and agricultural sectors. West German industry recovered strongly after 1945, based upon a liberal market approach with low tariff protection; it looked forward to increasing its share of industrial trade within the customs union and has become the dominant European industrial power. France as a large agricultural producer sought reciprocal benefits for its agriculture in the EC. The major food exporters, France, the Netherlands and Italy, sought to capture the German market, partly at the expense of non-European suppliers.

A decision to include agriculture was taken during the preliminary conference in 1955, since the removal of barriers to trade and industrial products *per se* would be insufficient, unworkable and incomplete. The Commission examined various agricultural systems before coming round to more interventionist policies; this reflected national political expediency. While efficient agricultural producers like the Dutch could have prospered with a less regulated CAP, their producers, especially of dairy products, gained substantially from higher prices.

The less efficient and high-cost countries − Germany, Belgium and Luxembourg − which were net importers, would only open up their markets if prices were set at a sufficient level to support their own farmers. To accommodate them, a range of product prices was agreed, with the first crucial prices being set for grain in 1964. Once a high price had been fixed for cereals, it became necessary to set the prices of other products at comparable levels to maintain the right inter-product relationship. One of the important products was milk; its price was raised substantially to cover high-cost producers. During the 1960s the CAP was extended to cover almost all agricultural products, with the few gaps being filled in during the 1970s (see the Common Fisheries Policy section, pp. 83–5).

C Grand objectives

The objectives of the CAP were laid down in Article 39 of the Treaty of Rome. The five aims were: to raise agricultural productivity; thereby to ensure a fair standard of living for the agricultural community; to stabilize markets; to assure availability of supplies; and to ensure that supplies reach consumers at reasonable prices. This was an ambitious list of highly desirable but sometimes conflicting principles. The consequence has been a failure to achieve some of these objectives, particularly reasonable prices; for example, many products can be purchased at much lower prices on the world markets.

Policy has been most successful in achieving the objective of secure supplies, indicated by a growing self-sufficiency in many products. However, full security of all supplies is neither desirable nor feasible, given the growing dependence on energy. It is of great importance to produce those products for which there are no close substitutes available on world markets. For other products it is prudent to buy them cheaply from the world markets, rather than becoming over-conscious about security and building up massive surpluses. These surpluses have made price stabilization very difficult and though the Community has had some success in stabilizing markets, this has been at the expense of creating even more instability on world markets.

The EC has been far more concerned with raising production than productivity (Fennell 1985), but labour productivity has increased through large-scale drift from the land and largely through greater inputs of capital. Environmentalists have become concerned about the excessive use of inputs such as fertilizers; they are also concerned about the destruction of hedgerows to create larger fields and the adverse effects on wildlife. Since the CAP was designed to benefit farmers, their incomes have risen, though the ratio of agricultural income per head to that of the economy as a whole has remained relatively constant (Van den Noort 1983). There are problems in comparing agricultural incomes closely with incomes earned in other parts of the economy since farmers' incomes consist not only of a return on labour but also on capital and land which yield capital gains; farmers also consume some of their own output. Finally, farmers do not incur the high costs of travelling to work like many industrial workers.

Apart from an uneven distribution of income, many farmers are dissatisfied on other counts; they complain that too many of the benefits are siphoned off by suppliers of farm inputs and the processors of their raw materials. Where the farmer has himself gained this has driven up the capital value of the farm, making it more difficult for new entrants to agriculture. The relatively low pay of many farm workers has led to part-time working becoming the norm in some areas. Many part-time farmers work evenings and weekends on the farm, relying on wives and elderly parents to do the real work on the farm. In West Germany, for example, the majority of farmers are part-timers, supplementing their income substantially from another job.

D   The system of common prices

While the system of common prices differs from one product to another, a general account will provide a basic picture and understanding of the main elements in the CAP pricing policy. There are four key prices: target, threshold, intervention and world prices — these are shown in Figure 4.2.

The target price (*prix indicatif*), P_x, is the internal wholesale price which should generally be obtainable, and it is important in

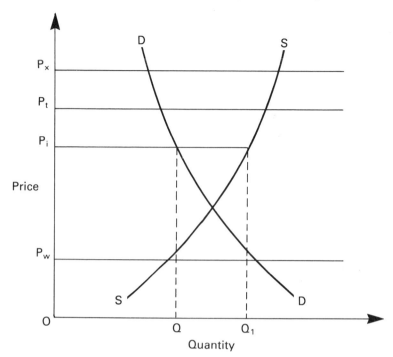

Figure 4.2 Key agricultural prices

determining other prices. This price is set for the main cereals and is based on the area which produces the lowest proportion of its own grain requirements and is the highest cost area – this is Duisburg in the heavily industrialized Rhine–Ruhr area. For some other products, slightly different price terminology is used, such as guide prices, basic prices and norm prices, though these correspond to the highest price shown in Figure 4.2.

The next price in Figure 4.2, the threshold price (*prix de seuil*) P_t, is important in relation to extra-EC trade, and more will be said about this later in relation to the world price. Other terminology analogous to the threshold price is also used, such as sluice-gate prices and reference prices, and so on. The difference between the target price, P_x, and the threshold price, P_t, is accounted for by handling charges and transport costs; for example, for grains, the costs between Rotterdam and Duisburg.

The intervention price (*prix d'intervention*) P_i, is the important support price below which prices are not allowed to fall. The EC Farm Fund (EAGGF) buys up supplies as the price falls to this level and it is obliged to buy everything offered to it at the intervention price, providing the commodity meets the quality and quantity criteria laid down; for example, quantity $Q - Q_1$ in the diagram.

The intervention price for cereals has been based at Ormes, a city in the Paris basin, which has the maximum cereal surplus, and for rice the intervention centre is Vercelli in northern Italy. The intervention storage is carried out either directly by intervention agencies or by contracts with merchants to undertake the storage, with the merchants owning the cereals. Intervention prices have resulted in very effective and high-price support for key products, such as cereals and milk. In other products, such as fruit and vegetables, the price support is at a much lower level, while some products have lacked internal support − eggs and poultry.

The world price, P_w, represents the price at which EC consumers would purchase their imports in a completely free market. The imposition of variable levies on imports raises the import price to the threshold level; this ensures that importers cannot undercut Community suppliers on price. For some products, customs duties are levied and for others in which the Community lacks indigenous supplies, such as oil and oil seeds, then a deficiency payment system is in operation (how this works is discussed in Part III, p. 80, while for more details on specific products see Fennell 1988).

The Community, with its growing surplus of intervention stocks, has had to dispose of these on the world market at price OP_w. The export subsidy used is generally described as an export refund or restitution: in Figure 4.2, $P_i - P_w$ = export restitution. A wide price gap has long existed between some Community and world product prices. In October 1986, EC intervention prices, compared with estimated representative world prices, were over twice as high for wheat, over three times as high for sugar and butter and over nine times as high for skimmed milk powder (*Financial Times* 18 December 1986, p. 25).

E Agricultural expenditure: the European Agricultural Guarantee and Guidance Fund (EAGGF)

The EAGGF or Fonds Européen d'Orientation et Garantie Agricole (FEOGA) comprises two financial sections. The Guarantee section is concerned with support prices (as outlined earlier), and the Guidance section seeks to improve the structure of agriculture. Until 1966 the Guidance section expenditure could amount to one-third of the Guarantee section; but with Guarantee sums rising rapidly a ceiling was imposed. Financial support to the farmers in the EC has escalated, and from 1982–84 was estimated at $41 billion to support more than 8.5 million farmers; the USA over the same period, however, spent $37 billion to support less than 2.5 million farmers (*Financial Times* 9 April 1986). EAGGF expenditure is shown in Table 4.1.

Guarantee spending has swamped the tiny Guidance payments. While net expenditure has been reduced by the receipt of ordinary

Table 4.1 EAGGF expenditure, 1983–88[1]

	Expenditure (million ECU)					
	1983	1984	1985	1986	1987[3]	1988[4]
EAGGF Guarantee section[2]	15 811.6	18 346.5	19 744.2	22 137.4	22 988.5	27 078.5
EAGGF Guidance section (payments)	728.0	676.2	719.6	773.5	847.1	1 157.3
Total gross expenditure	16 539.6	19 022.7	20 463.8	22 910.9	23 835.6	28 235.8
Ordinary levies	1 347.1	1 259.9	1 121.7	1 175.5	1 763.9	1 753.1
Sugar levies	948.0	1 176.4	1 057.4	1 115.5	1 438.6	1 247 8
Total net expenditure	14 244.5	16 586.4	18 284.7	20 623.9	20 633.1	25 234.9

Notes:
1 1983–85 — EC(10), 1986–88 — EC(12).
2 Net of expenditure disallowed in accounts clearance decisions (ECU 25.5 million in 1984, ECU 99.2 million in 1985 and ECU 55.3 million in 1986).
3 Budget adopted on 19 February 1987, and amending and supplementary budget No. 1 adopted on 17 July 1987 including fisheries (ECU 27.7 million).
4 Preliminary draft budget in 1988.

Source: Commission of the European Communities, *The Agricultural Situation in the Community*, 1987 Report (1988).

levies and sugar levies, these small sources of revenue have lacked buoyancy and the early ideas of a self-financing agricultural policy soon had to be abandoned.

The high level of expenditure in supporting prices can be attributed to the high prices set and to the fact that EC expenditure has replaced national expenditure on price support. For Guidance expenditure the EAGGF pays only a proportion, with the re- mainder coming from national governments and, where relevant, the individual beneficiary. It would make more sense to raise expenditure on Guidance, but while there have been movements towards this, it can only be done prudently by reining back the level of price support. If the semblance of a common policy is to be maintained, then it would be better for the Community to take over more of this Guidance expenditure and to limit the tendency of national governments to frustrate a *communautaire* policy by exces- sive aids to their own farmers − this is on the likely assumption that the EC wishes to continue with the basic principles of a common policy instead of shifting its financial costs to national Exchequers.

Guidance expenditure takes place for a wide variety of schemes and projects and like Guarantee expenditure it has a direct regional impact (Moussis 1982, p. 215). Assistance should go mainly to those in need and it is important to ensure that Guidance expenditure does not add to existing farm surpluses. The Commission proposed in 1986 to pension-off workers over 55 years of age, rejuvenating the workforce and adopting less capital-intensive production methods. However, elderly farmers do not have the energy to produce surpluses as much as younger farmers with heavy borrowing who may produce even greater quantities of unwanted food.

F   Political pressures

The political pressure exercised by the agricultural lobby is totally disproportionate to the numbers employed in farming and to its share of GDP. National agricultural interest groups have been influential in France, seeking to exploit the full potential of its large land area, with the French Farm Minister, Guillaume, continuing the passionate defence of French farming interests. Similarly, in Germany farming has tremendous political weight and the German Minister of Agriculture, Ertl, in power from 1969 to 1983, drew considerable support from farmers. In the smaller countries with fewer farmers, but with significant upstream and downstream linkages, agricultural organization is often even stronger and more effective.

Since the EC represents aggregate national interests, interest group activities have also moved upwards to the Community levels. The federation of EC farming interests is the Comité des Organisations Professionelles Agricoles des Pays de la Communauté Economique Européenne (COPA). This has lobbied strongly in the various Community institutions and its influence has far exceeded that of consumer interests.

In setting farmers' incomes each year the annual price review has generally raised prices to try to keep incomes on modern farms in line with average incomes in other sectors. Commission proposals, and more so agreements by the Council of Ministers, have tended to concede to agricultural pressures. In the highly-politicized decision-making process agricultural ministers are expected to defend their own farming interests vigorously, since they do not wish to be criticized for selling their own farmers short. Package deals have been stitched together and trade-offs made, but invariably a final agreement has only been possible by trading up the settlement. It is only financial constraints which have restored a sense of realism to agricultural policy-making by the Council, along with recent disquiet voiced by the European Parliament.

G   Agricultural problems

Low farm incomes. The CAP includes a diversity of countries with a differing level of dependence on agriculture and a wide range of farm incomes. The percentage of the labour force employed in agriculture relative to that employed in the industrial and service sectors can be illustrated, as in Figure 4.3, on a 3-variable graph.

Reading across the left-hand axis, Greece had 29 per cent of its labour force employed in agriculture; reading down the right-hand

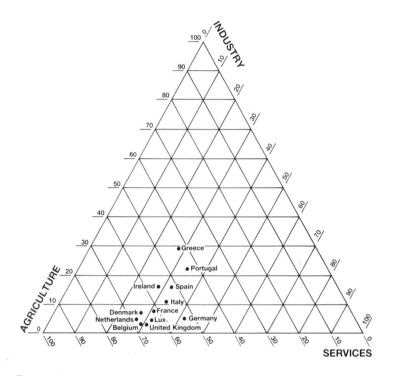

Figure 4.3   Percentage employment in agriculture and other sectors of the 'twelve' member states in 1986

axis, 28 per cent of its labour force in industry; and reading up the horizontal axis, 43 per cent of its labour force in the service sector. These graphs are useful in illustrating any 3-variable distribution which sums to 100 per cent. Other southern European countries are shown as having high dependence on agriculture.

Farm incomes are lowest in southern Europe, which has suffered from generations of poor soil conservation policies and lack of irrigation. Farmers in southern Europe have received less generous support for their produce than have their counterparts in northern Europe. In northern Europe some specialization has occurred, raising incomes for cereal growers in areas such as central France and eastern England, and also for pig and poultry producers in close proximity to ports in Holland through which animal feeding stuffs can be imported cheaply. Perhaps in the future Spain will begin to specialize − more successfully than Italy has done − in supplying fruit and vegetables to northern European markets. This is far more sensible than maintaining expensive glasshouse production in countries like the Netherlands by subsidies on heating oils.

The policy of trying to raise farm incomes has had paradoxical results, since the large number of small farmers which are most in need of welfare support have tended to receive least, whereas the smaller number of large and highly-productive farms in least need of any such support have benefited the most. The attempt to raise farm incomes by increasing farm output prices has distorted the allocation of resources and failed to tackle the problem of low income farmers effectively. More appropriate policies would be by direct supplements to labour income.

Structural policies would help to create more viable and efficient farms. Though much progress has been made in increasing the average size of farm and in better production methods, many farms are still sub-optimal. More than half of the farms in the EC are less than ten hectares (a hectare is equal to 2.4711 acres). By the end of the century there is still likely to be a third of EC farms of this modest size, even though total numbers employed in farming will continue to decline. Land fragmentation and scattered strips of land have restricted mechanization and the scope for economies of scale. Nevertheless, the optimum size of farm is still lower than the optimum unit in manufacturing industry, and well below the size of the large collective farms created in eastern Europe. But there is a danger that larger units with greater capital investment will tend to intensify production with accompanying problems of surpluses and greater environmental damage. The alternative is one of persisting with the structure of many small farms, often on a part-time basis, and perhaps seeing it as a positive rather than a negative virtue that they do not optimize output.

Farm surpluses. Agricultural output is far more variable and unpredictable than industrial output. Clearly, under-production as a result of a bad harvest would be catastrophic, particularly where countries were unable to purchase supplies on the world market. Over-production, while less of a crisis than under-production, has generated embarrassing surpluses which have tended to recur in some products. The main problem is not so much that of natural seasonal surpluses but of structural surpluses; these are the consequence of fixing prices artificially above their equilibrium level.

Technological progress has added further to the capacity of agriculture to produce in excess of demand. By use of fertilizers and other techniques, farm yields have risen since farmers found that it costs almost as much to cultivate a field to produce one tonne an acre as to produce three tonnes. These have been stimulated by high prices, though real prices for many products have actually fallen (Duchêne *et al.* 1985, p. 14). Indeed, for some years now agriculture has been subject to quite a strong cost/price squeeze which likewise has resulted in the need to raise yields. Expansionary technological forces are making the problem of surpluses a permanent feature of the agricultural landscape.

Over-production has led to massive stocks and the value of products in public storage rose to ECU 12.3 billion in 1987. The most costly stocks are of butter and skimmed milk powder. Since it is inconvenient to store fresh milk, surpluses are manifested in mountains of butter and skimmed milk powder. The actual worth of some of the stocks was only about one-third of their book value in 1986/87, since many of them had deteriorated with age (Commission 1987, p. 7). In disposing of them one needs to think less in terms of the sunk costs of acquiring them and more in terms of their opportunity costs (Chalkley 1986).

The EC(6) moved from a situation of 91 per cent self-sufficiency at its inception to one of 108 per cent self-sufficiency for the EC(10) after Greek enlargement. Furthermore, this actually understates the full rise in self-sufficiency, since UK entry into the EC depressed the Community's ratio of self-sufficiency. The EC(12) is likely to generate further over-production of some products such as wine, whilst others in marginal deficit, such as fresh vegetables, have moved into a marginal surplus. The agricultural land area utilized in Spain is second only to that in France and its potential productive capacity is substantial, as agricultural prices for Spanish producers rise to the higher levels in the EC. While the newer states may complement the northern members of the Community in some respects by importing more cereals and meat from them, in the long run the Iberian peninsula could become self-sufficient in grains. If additional surpluses do not arise, then it can only be due to the mixed blessing of inefficient farming, which is the case in Portugal.

The EC has adopted a combination of internal and external measures to alleviate the problem of surpluses. Internally, it has destroyed products such as fruit and vegetables; in addition, some denaturing of products occurred in the past, rendering them unsuitable for human consumption and fit only for animal feed. Consumers prefer the surpluses to be sold domestically and specific products, for example, butter and beef, have been subsidized for consumption by pensioners and families on low income.

The Community's external policies have consisted partly of selling off the surpluses cheaply to other countries. These have aroused almost as much emotional concern in the UK as the destruction of the surpluses, particularly when these have been exported to the Soviet Union. It is paradoxical that Soviet agriculture's main problem has been one of under-production, whereas that of the EC has been that of over-production. Other external policies are also controversial, especially the use of export subsidies to make products saleable on world markets. The only policy with any popular support, certainly on humanitarian grounds, is helping the needy people in the Third World. Yet even food aid in the long term may encourage a taste for different imported products and actually reduce the recipient's own agricultural output as prices are lowered. Products such as milk powder have higher nutritional value and are fairly cheap to store compared with butter. The EC's aid policies have been motivated by a desire to remove its food surpluses, and critics of aid believe that a policy of assisting agricultural developments *per se* may be a more effective approach in LDCs.

Distortion of international trade. The CAP has led to some alteration in the pattern of international trade. The EC's agricultural trade has gone through two phases. The first phase consisted of a massive growth of intra-trade in foodstuffs which rose more rapidly than extra-EC food imports. France and the Netherlands, more so than Italy, have increased their exports, largely to the main import markets of West Germany and the UK. But the Community market has become satiated as West Germany and the UK have increased their own levels of agricultural self-sufficiency.

The second phase was that the Community, though still a major world importer, was transformed into a major world exporter of food second only to the USA. In a few products the EC actually became the world's number one exporter (Duchêne *et al.* 1985, p. 55). However, since international trade in agricultural products represents only a small proportion of world production, major changes in the league table can occur based on rather marginal quantities. Expanding import markets for agricultural sales have opened up only slowly in Japan, the newly industrializing countries

(NICs), the Organization of Petroleum Exporting Countries (OPEC) and in Eastern Europe (Comecon). Both India and China have become net exporters of wheat and many LDCs in great need of food have unfortunately lacked the foreign exchange to translate this into effective demand. World food consumption is failing to increase at a pace necessary to absorb the surpluses of temperate developed countries.

The EC's sales in international markets are only competitive by using large export subsidies, though other countries like the USA also maintain exports in other ways. In 1985 a third of EC appropriations were for export refunds since as a once and for all transaction in many cases it is cheaper than storage. Efficient international suppliers in the rest of the world naturally resent any displacement of their own sales by the EC. They have seen the loss of many of their exports to the EC itself and this has then been compounded by displacement from other world import markets. EC exports of agricultural products to the rest of the world rose from an index of 100 in 1973 to 295 in 1986, whereas its imports from the rest of the world rose from an index of 100 in 1973 to 166 in 1986. EC policy runs counter to the whole purpose of free trade which is to create beneficial international specialization on the basis of comparative advantage. EC policy has created a further additional adverse effect of greater instability of world market prices.

Temperate food producers, such as Australia and New Zealand, have been badly affected, despite some continuing special arrangement to mitigate the worst effects on the latter. The rules of GATT for agricultural trade have been inadequate; for example, the code obliging countries to avoid export subsidies which would lead to an inequitable share of world markets has been too imprecise. The challenge by the more fair-minded exporters will hopefully lead to a more effective GATT. Australia has accused the EC of using secret subsidies at meetings of the GATT International Dairy Agreement. Both Canada and the USA have made complaints about EC exports eroding their sales of products, such as wheat. The EC's world market share of wheat rose from 12 per cent in 1979–80 to 17 per cent in 1984–85. The Iberian enlargement led to further American concern about a possible loss of its traditional exports of wheat, corn and oil seeds. It demanded compensation and at the beginning of 1987 threatened to introduce a 200 per cent tariff on a range of European goods, including gin, brandy, white wine, blue cheese and endives. A compromise was reached, averting an open trade war between the two blocs. Nevertheless, it will be difficult to reconcile the EC's concern with a managed market, and the US concern with a freer market, even though the latter does not operate a policy based on a completely open market (Josling 1986).

The CAP has had adverse global effects on poorer countries in an even more vulnerable position; for example, in South America, Argentina derives approximately three-quarters of its export revenue from agriculture and is a major producer of maize and beef. The EC took temporary measures against Argentina during the Falklands crisis but the long-term effects of the CAP have had a much more significant impact on the displacement of Argentinian products from the EC market.

Similarly, Brazil has failed to develop its export potential sufficiently to prevent a growing problem of financial indebtedness. The EC's sugar policy has been an additional factor in Brazil seeking to convert sugar surpluses into fuel to reduce its import bill for energy. Despite favourable treatment of sugar imports from the Lomé countries, the EC's own high price, and dumping of sugar on world markets, has created major difficulties for producers like Cuba, the Philippines, the Dominican Republic and Thailand – the latter also having a different complaint relating to the Community's policy on cereal substitutes. Despite sugar quotas for the EC's own producers, the CAP has shifted the price adjustment on to the residual world market. LDCs have tended to become net importers of food, not only because of the EC, but mainly because of their own inadequate agricultural policies resulting in low agricultural investment, with low domestic food prices being set in the interests of urban consumers.

H   Reforms to the CAP

Proposals for the reform of the CAP abound, but their application has often been cosmetic and fallen short of the fundamental root and branch changes which are necessary. The CAP has gradually become outmoded as under-production has given way to over-production. Reliance largely upon one policy instrument of high prices has had to be modified by a more rigorous approach, whereby prices are reduced and accompanying policies, such as income supplements, adopted. The latter is more effective, especially in improving distributional equity (Tarditi 1984). The Commission's Green Paper in 1985 recognized that a policy of continuing to lower farm prices would have to be supplemented by some income support for small farmers. In 1987 the Commission proposed that direct income aids should be applied to help 'intermediate' farms; that is, potentially viable farms. The EC Farm Fund is not prepared, however, to co-finance income for the 'social problem' farm, but is encouraging the use of other EC regional funds, and the EC has seen the importance of setting a framework for strict limits on national aids.

A policy of continuing price cuts is vital for products in surplus, and though prices could be raised for products in deficit, unfortunately more and more products are in surplus. The key product is cereals, where price reductions provide immense benefit to livestock producers who have switched to cheaper imported substitutes to feed their animals. The Commission proposed for 1988–89 a guaranteed maximum of 155 million tonnes of cereals for the EC, after which prices would be reduced. At the emergency summit meeting of heads of government in Brussels in February 1988 agreement could only be reached on a slightly larger output of 160 million tonnes, after which cumulative price cuts of 3 per cent a year would be imposed for four years. Community policy has to make clear that price reductions will be imposed cumulatively so that farmers will recognize the new signals over the coming years. Certainly the recognition that unlimited guarantees of prices and intervention cannot continue and the return of intervention buying towards its original safety-net function to deal with short-term fluctuations is welcome.

The reluctance in the past to apply the most direct and effective policy of price cuts often resulted in weaker alternatives. Co-responsibility levies, for example, have been applied to milk since 1977, but have generally been too low to be effective. They have operated on supply to reduce price, and on demand, with the levy being used in an attempt to stimulate the falling sales of milk.

Quotas have also been introduced since they seem to cause least disturbance to the existing situation. They have long been used for sugar beet and in the 1980s have been used for milk, but have been set at too high a level and production has continued to outrun consumption. In 1986 the Commission agreed on a further substantial reduction in milk quotas over a three-year period. It sought to make farmers individually responsible for keeping within their milk quotas to prevent those who were over-producing from incurring the penalties of the super levy. Quotas can be applied most easily in the case of the products mentioned where there are a limited number of factories and dairies: their disadvantage is that when rigidly set they tend to freeze the existing pattern of production inefficiently. There is a danger of being forced to extend quotas elsewhere and ending up with an even more controlled and managed system. The Commission proposed in 1987 that the sugar quota for 1988–89 should be unchanged and that the milk quota should become permanent.

Other suggestions floated have been to go beyond quotas on output and to impose them also on inputs such as nitrogenous fertilizers. Quotas on the latter would hit the operations of the larger and more efficient farms; but they would fit in with a policy of cutting output without driving the small farmer out of existence. There is certainly less scorn being shown now for a return to low-input organic farming.

The most significant proposal for important structural reform was contained in the Memorandum sur la réforme de l'agriculture dans la Communauté Economique Européene, more popularly referred to as the Mansholt Plan of 1968. Unfortunately, neither sufficient movement of labour from the land nor the significant reduction in the agricultural land area which it proposed has taken place. The latter may now be rectified by new emphasis by the Commission on setting land aside to take it out of cultivation for a minimum of five years. This could result in at least 20 per cent of arable land being retired from use by the 1990s and used for other purposes. However, its effects in cutting output may still be negated if farmers leave their poorest land fallow and simply produce more intensively on their existing land. Furthermore, if the land is used for grass and fodder crops, this will simply transfer the arable problem to the livestock sector.

Rising agricultural expenditure threatens budgetary bankruptcy with the falling value of the dollar further increasing the cost of export subsidies. The EC seems determined to maintain the principle of common financing, although this has resulted in the major agricultural importing countries contributing a disproportionate share. Any return to national financing is opposed by the major agricultural producing countries who argue that it would undermine the CAP. Furthermore, it is likely that richer member states would still choose to subsidize their agriculture heavily, but at least the support cost would be nationally apparent. The countries most affected would be those in southern Europe which lack the national financial resources necessary to support their farmers.

I   Green currencies and monetary compensation amounts (MCAs)
Why did green currencies arise? The CAP was constructed on the basis of common prices, but unfortunately the international monetary system of fixed exchange rates began to collapse in the late 1960s. In August 1969 the French government decided to devalue the franc and this was followed in October 1969 by a revaluation of the Deutschmark. Both countries wished to retain the common price system of the CAP. France was not prepared to accept the inflationary effects of devaluation on its consumers, while Germany was concerned about the adverse effects of revaluation on its farmers and their loss of exports. Therefore it was decided to retain agricultural prices at their original levels by instituting a special new system.

The system adopted is known as 'green currencies'. It might be questioned why a special procedure should apply to agricultural exchange rates and not for other products; for example, there is no 'black currency' for trading coal. The reason is that the Community has not tried to stabilize common prices for coal with an intervention system, nor has coal in recent years assumed the overriding importance of agriculture. It was decided that temporarily the difference between the new market rates of exchange and their original level (that is, green rates for agriculture) would be bridged by the use of monetary compensatory amounts (MCAs). This meant that in the case of France a negative MCA was applied, and a positive MCA for Germany.

MCAs apply to agricultural products subject to the intervention mechanism and which would otherwise suffer from currency fluctuations. Initially the MCAs were financed by national governments, but in July 1972, for trade with non-EC countries, and in January 1973, for intra-EC trade, compulsory MCAs were introduced and financed by the EC. While the joint float of EC currencies in 1973 made the system more manageable, the first enlargement of the Community brought in new countries with representative (green) rates; also, there were still problems with EC countries not able to operate in the joint float.

Any assessment of the consequences of green currencies depends upon the extent to which one considers that agriculture should be insulated from exchange rate changes. Is there something distinctive about agriculture *per se*? Whereas industrialists in trading products can choose to trade at the new exchange rates or to adjust domestic prices accordingly, farmers (without MCAs) face an immediate change in farm prices and in trading patterns. MCAs, by trying to freeze the original situation, have led to some misallocation of resources; for example, Germany's positive MCA system has enabled its farmers to sell more products abroad, reducing inroads of inherently more efficient imports from other Community countries. West German producers, benefiting from lower imported input costs, have raised agricultural self-sufficiency, much to the chagrin of countries like France.

The MCA system is extremely complex, varying between products. It mainly covered those heavily traded products for which intervention prices existed (though there were exceptions to this, with poultry and eggs being included, despite absence of intervention prices, mainly because of their dependence on cereals for which there are very significant intervention prices). The existence of MCAs added to the risks involved in trade since buyers preferred to purchase at fixed prices instead of having to carry the risk involved with an MCA; for example, the Community lost some long-term export contracts overseas by refusing to quote fixed prices.

Despite these criticisms of green currencies, they did offer some advantages, especially in the short term in maintaining price stability which would have been wrecked by floating currencies. MCAs helped to maintain a veneer of common prices, whilst at the same time conferring some freedom of manoeuvre to national governments – via devaluation or revaluation of their green currencies – to set prices to suit their own interests. The use of

MCA adjustments has sometimes facilitated agreements at meetings of Agricultural Ministers — this was because any prudent price increases could be varied by national governments for their own farmers by MCA adjustments. Nevertheless, it has been accepted that, on balance, MCAs should be phased out in the long term.

Part III   The UK and the CAP
Historically, Britain imported foodstuffs freely from the rest of the world, but during and after the Second World War steps were taken to raise the level of domestic self-sufficiency. A distinctive system of deficiency payments was introduced and made to farmers to cover the difference between the realized market price which the farmer obtained on the open market, and the higher guaranteed price. This system increased domestic production whilst at the same time enabling imports to continue relatively freely, giving consumers the benefit of low food prices. The system was financed out of general taxation, but rising budgetary costs led the government to introduce more selective policies, including guaranteed prices only for standard quantities of various products.

The UK has switched over to the Community system of farm support, though in some products, like the sheep meat regime, the UK has been allowed to operate a variant of the original deficiency payments system. But the Commission proposed in 1987 that this should be phased out as part and parcel of Community agricultural reform to limit costs.

Under the CAP, the main difference for the UK has been the fixing of a high target price as shown in Figure 4.4.

The effect of setting a high price, OP_t, induces more resources into agriculture, BC, and enables a larger surplus to be reaped by existing producers, A. Whereas under the deficiency payments system consumers purchased foodstuffs at the world price, OP_w, under the CAP there is a loss of consumer satisfaction, EF, since demand has fallen from OQ_3 to OQ_2. High prices have the unfortunate effects of raising supply and cutting demand with resultant surpluses. While the levies on imports, D, are a source of revenue they have been insufficient to finance the massive agricultural expenditure.

From the viewpoint of the UK, the import levies do not accrue directly to the British government, but form part of the Community's 'own resources'. Since the UK is still very dependent on imports of foodstuffs from outside the EC, then it contributes disproportionately in levies. Likewise, substantial levies are collected by the Netherlands, since Rotterdam is the single biggest point of entry.

Many Community countries are net exporters of foodstuffs and the total cost of subsidizing export surpluses is illustrated by the

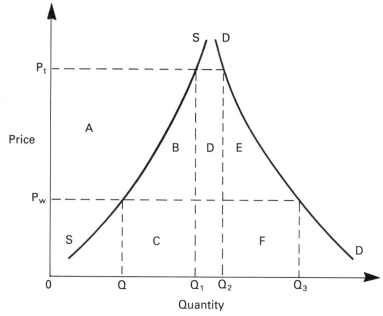

Figure 4.4   Effects of the CAP

shaded area in Figure 4.5. Whereas in any national system the exporting country would have to bear the cost of this itself, in the Community it is financed from the 'own resources' provided by all EC members. This may be logical if one believes in a 'Community', but its consequence is that the UK contributes to financing the surpluses of other EC countries – with the latter having less incentive to reduce such surpluses when they are not financing the full cost themselves.

Various estimates have been made of the budgetary costs to the UK arising from the CAP (Buckwell *et al.* 1982). In addition to the focus on budgetary costs, total costs to the UK are even higher when one adds the trade costs of buying at EC rather than world prices. Higher agricultural prices have led to a redistribution of benefits from consumers to producers and in the UK the losses have outweighed the benefits. Various studies have indicated a range of substantial costs to the UK (Whitby 1979, Buckwell *et al.* 1982, Hill 1984, El-Agraa 1985).

Much depends upon assumptions about what the scenario would be if the UK were not part of the Community. Would world prices still be lower than EC prices, and would any increase in UK demand on the world market be matched by increased supply? EC surpluses would be available on the world market, carrying export subsidies, and other world producers could probably ensure sufficiently

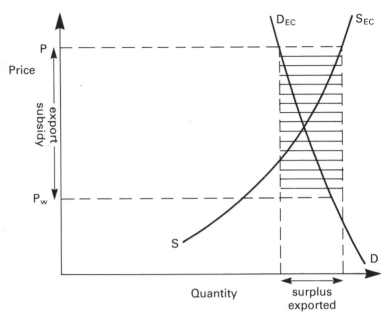

Figure 4.5   The CAP and export surpluses

abundant supplies. The UK economy would gain most in welfare from free trade (Buckwell *et al*. 1982). This would not be attractive to UK farmers and in reality such a policy seems less feasible than choosing between the CAP and some alternative system of farm support.

The CAP has had a negative effect on the UK growth rate (Marques Mendes 1987, p. 100). It has also had an inflationary effect on the UK economy and has added to the balance of payments costs by paying higher prices for food imports. Although the higher price of food has tended to dampen demand, this has again been at the expense of consumers.

The green currency system for sterling has been operated inconsistently, but in its early years was operated in the interests of British consumers. The pound floated downwards so that it fell substantially below its 1973 representative 'green' rate. Negative MCAs were applied and a widening gap opened up between the market and the green rate for the pound. Other Community countries objected to making budgetary contributions to subsidize British consumers. This in some respects was absurd, given that some of the countries with budgetary complaints about excessive contributions, such as West Germany, were benefiting in their trade from higher agricultural exports to the British market. A combination of pressures led to some devaluation of the green pound. The major change occurred when sterling became a petro-currency and the exchange rate of the pound rose above the green rate. After that time, consumers suffered but, on the other hand, British farmers have welcomed the opportunity to raise output with positive MCAs.

UK farm output has grown at a faster rate than its industrial output and British farmers have helped to bridge the trade gap left by the continuing poor performance of the manufacturing sector in the wake of deindustrialization. A high level of agricultural investment has been undertaken, raising farm incomes, despite the squeeze of high costs, price restraints and the imposition of quotas. The UK has raised its self-sufficiency, supplying more than 80 per cent of its temperate food needs, compared with just over 60 per cent in 1973. Instead of being a sizeable importer of grain, by the mid-1980s the UK had become the sixth largest exporter of cereals in the world. Cereal farmers, located largely in eastern England, have benefited substantially, more so than livestock and dairy farmers in the poorer western upland areas of the UK.

Overall, the CAP has been much criticized, particularly in the UK for its adverse effects on consumers, and some consider the policy to be a comprehensive failure (Hill 1984, p. 117). It has certainly distorted resource allocation, but its central importance in the process of integration means that policy changes are likely to be marginal rather than substantial; yet without radical reform disintegration may occur.

The Common Fisheries Policy (CFP). Fisheries are included in the definition of agricultural products and the market regime for the CAP included some market support for fish prices. France was the main proponent of such market support, being worried about the impact of free imports on its own fishing industry. The introduction of the CFP before the first enlargement negotiations with other important fishing countries resulted in major problems. Norway objected to proposals for a CFP and opted out of the EC, pointing out that the four prospective applicants had a fishing catch nearly three times as high as that in the EC(6) (Nicholson and East 1987, p. 122). For the UK, the agreement incorporated in the Act of Accession to the EC reduced its inshore fishing limit.

The Law of the Sea Conference in 1975 resulted in coastal states having resource zones extending out to 200 miles or the median line. The EC extended its own fishing limits out to that distance at the beginning of 1977. Both the UK and Ireland argued that the principle of equal access conflicted with their demands for domestic preference. But the UK was only successful in retrieving the twelve-mile limit which had existed under the 1964 Fisheries Convention. Negotiations to reach an acceptable CFP have been difficult and protracted, despite the agreement in 1977 and the revised CFP introduced in January 1983.

The concern of the CFP is to conserve and manage stocks, setting allowable catches for species threatened by over-fishing and then dividing them into national quotas. Each nation has to declare its catch and be open to inspection, but difficulties have arisen over proper verification and its enforcement in all Community countries. There are worries about too much industrial fishing by countries such as Denmark and its adverse effects on fish stocks. Market organization has tried to provide an adequate level of income for fishermen and, in addition, finance has been provided to restructure the industry.

For the UK, whereas the CAP generally yielded a golden harvest for British farmers (at least until quotas), under the CFP its fishing industry has declined. For example, between 1971 and 1980 its nominal catch of marine fish and shellfish fell, whereas that of the EC(10) rose over the same period (Macsween 1987). While the decline of the British fishing industry and its overcapacity may be attributable to other factors than the CFP, the latter's principle of free access has added to its problems.

The origins of its difficulties lay in the loss of distant fishing rights after the Icelandic victory in the cod war. International sympathies were with little Iceland which was so dependent on fishing, and it could also call upon American goodwill because of the important NATO base located there. The UK lost the valuable white demersal fish (caught near the ocean floor) which were the traditional purchase of the British consumer. The UK started to land lower priced pelagic fish (caught near the surface), greatly reducing the value of domestic fish landings. Iceland's declaration of its own 200-mile limit led to a laying-up of British trawlers with devastating effects in fishing areas like the Humber ports where much of the fish processing industry is based. Frozen fish processors began to meet the UK's traditional taste for white fish increasingly from imports.

In the revised CFP, which was based on the historic pattern of fishing for each stock, the UK had to settle for less than its percentage share of Community fishing waters. Another difficulty for the UK has been that the EC makes agreements with outside countries, so that it is all Community fishing countries which obtain reciprocal concessions. The EC has signed fishery agreements with non-EC countries, whereas national agreements by the UK, when outside the EC, would probably have led to greater national benefits on a quid pro quo basis. Agreements have been signed with countries which share joint stocks with the Community, such as Norway; also with Canada in return for reduced import duties on Canadian fish; the EC has also purchased fishing concessions from LDCs, particularly those in Africa.

The fishing industry has been whittled down in size, particularly in England, and its plight is a testimony to mismanagement when an island economy becomes a net importer of fish. Some of its problems have been common to all industries, such as rising fuel costs and overvaluation of sterling. Added to these have been the constraints of the CFP and the latest twist has been provided by Spanish entry into the EC. Despite strict limits on its fishing rights in the Community pond for its first ten years of membership, disputes with France and the UK have soon arisen; for example, over the registration of Spanish vessels in the UK eating into the British fishing quota.

5 Industrial and technological policies

Part I   Industrial problems and policies

What kind of progress has been made by the Community in developing a common industrial policy, and what form has this taken? Why is industry in the EC in general not as strong technologically, nor as efficient, as that in the USA and Japan? What can, and is, being done to remedy this? These are just a few of the questions to be examined in this chapter. It will become evident that even if the EC had not existed, it would have been necessary eventually to establish something like it, in order that European industry could enjoy the benefits of a larger market to reap economies of scale and collaborate to reduce the costs of research and development.

Industrial policy creates the conditions in which industry can flourish and its main concern has been to create a competitive and efficient industrial structure. Government intervention has sought to improve industrial performance. In addition, it has been concerned with the regional implications of industrial change and the social costs arising from this (Chapter 6 provides a fuller account). There are also social costs on the environment which are associated with industrial activities.

A Community environmental policy began only in 1973 but since that time a much greater concern has emerged about ecological issues. It is agreed that the environment needs to be safeguarded and improved, and that the principle that the 'polluter pays' should be used as much as possible. However, such a guide has some limitations since firms may have to close down if they cannot meet pollution costs. Some countries have sought to avoid giving the Community too much leeway to impose rigorous standards on them. Hence, in the SEA, it was agreed that the EC would only take action where the objectives could be achieved more effectively at the Community rather than the national level.

It is not intended here to focus on environmental issues, but rather to examine the more traditional concerns of industrial policy-makers. These have been concerned with controlling monopolies, restrictive practices and mergers. But they have had to be tempered by a recognition that large firms are necessary in some sectors to compete technologically and efficiently with American and Japanese firms. Unfortunately, European policies have often tended to support national champions, failing to recognize that the Community has opened up opportunities to develop firms on a continental scale, and to co-operate more closely.

Traditionally, monopoly has been condemned since it results in a misallocation of resources. Furthermore, because of the absence of competition, a high degree of 'X-inefficiency' may exist under the operation of monopoly. Prima facie, a strong legal anti-monopoly policy can be implemented on the basis of a highly-concentrated industrial structure: the USA has favoured such an approach. However, the case against monopoly is not always wholly conclusive, for various reasons. Firstly, in practice, oligopoly tends to prevail in most sectors rather than outright monopoly. In oligopoly, firms may either collude or compete, and both the number of firms and the kind of products being produced are influential in determining the behaviour of such firms. Secondly, large firms are able to benefit from economies of scale and are able to spend more on research and development. The EC requires companies to be of a sufficient size to compete with large international corporations. Therefore, in Europe there has been a less dogmatic policy towards large firms than in the USA. Instead of an outright condemnation of firms on the structural grounds of high concentration ratios, there has been a preference to use this as a guide, but then to go further by examining other aspects of behaviour such as conduct and performance.

Part II   EC industrial competitiveness and policies to promote technology

A   Concentration and competition policy

Concentration. Industrial concentration is reflected by the growth of large firms which have come to dominate particular industries and national economies. Absolute industrial concentration is measured from the percentage share of indicators such as employment, output, sales, etc., held by the few largest firms. Somewhat different results emerge when these indicators are used; for example, in 1985–86 Europe's three largest firms in terms of number of employees were Siemens, Philips and Unilever, each employing over 300 000 employees. When the ranking was based on stock market capitalization, then the top three firms were Royal Dutch-Shell, Daimler Benz and British Telecom (*Financial Times* 26 November 1986). Since the behaviour of giant firms is likely to be influenced by, amongst other things, the total number of firms in the industry then other measures, such as relative concentration, can take this into account. Often it is the same industries internationally which tend to be much more highly-concentrated; for example, plotting industrial concentration ratios for West Germany, France and Italy has shown certain industrial similarities (Ward 1975).

Although the extent of industrial concentration has increased in the national economies of member states, there are some factors restraining this. One of these has been the diversification of large companies into different sectors; for example, one of many firms recently involved in an extensive process of diversification in the late 1980s has been Daimler Benz. Giant companies have become much more significant in national economies, establishing themselves as conglomerates. However, their dominant share of specific industries has often been diluted by new entrants; these have either been other giant companies or − where entry barriers are sufficiently low − from the start-up of new small companies. When measuring the level of industrial concentration the most crucial determinant is the size of market. The EC's 'nomenclature des industries établies dans les Communautés Européenes' (NICE) adopted a three-digit classification − compared with the more detailed classification used in the USA (Jacquemin and Jong 1977, p. 45). The degree of concentration is greater where the market is defined more narrowly; for example, a local market for a particular kind of product such as a bottle or container is more concentrated than if one uses the whole container market at a Community level. The creation of the Community and the steps towards a single internal market provide a major constraint on local or national monopoly power. Although firms have expanded the scale of their operations in the larger market, in general the problem of monopoly is less intense at Community level.

Competition policy.   1.   Restrictive agreements. The Community has favoured free competition, through the interplay of demand and supply, since this provides the basic ingredient for efficiency. Competition policy has provided the means whereby the Community has achieved and maintained its object of free internal trade. It has tried to prevent the erection of new trading barriers and competition policy has applied not only when trade with other member states is actually effected but also where there has been an adverse potential effect. In addition to free trade, the other pillar of the Community has been to maintain open competition, based upon consumer sovereignty. Anything which appreciably distorts open competition in member states is prohibited. Only minor exceptions have been made to the open competition policy; for example, where restrictive agreements are of minor importance and are encouraging co-operation between small- and medium-sized enterprises, like that in research and development. Likewise, some exceptions have been made in the public sector with the application of state aids being permissible for particular depressed regions and industries, though the aim is to ensure that the aid is on a selective and transparent basis.

The Community in forming such a strong competition policy,

particularly against restrictive practices, has been influenced by West German practice, since the latter legislated against restrictive practices itself in 1957 (Bayliss 1985). The Commission has received firm support from the Court of Justice. Firms have to notify the Commission about any agreements and arrangements which they have made with other firms and these are generally considered invalid unless the firms concerned account for only a small part of the market or there are some benefits available; for example, in improving the production or distribution of goods, or promoting technical and economic progress; in ensuring that a fair share of the benefits go to consumers, etc. EC competition policy has been very tough and has allowed fewer exemptions than the UK's range of gateways (George and Joll 1978).

Agreements between firms have violated Article 85 – though this does not include non-binding agreements unless such concertation is followed by prohibitive practices (Mathijsen 1985, p. 170). Often some collusion is difficult to prove, like that of parallel price movements which may be quite coincidental, and have to be shown to arise from concertation which will be manifested by their repetitive occurrence. Apart from price agreements, cartels have often been established to share out markets; for example, the Dutch cement market was shared out for many years between Dutch, German and Belgian producers, leaving only a small part of the market left for free competition (Swann 1984, p. 129). The EC is opposed to such territorial market sharing and has tackled other examples of this, such as that in detergents in which Dutch and Belgian producers had agreed not to sell in each other's territory. In other practices, such as exclusive dealing agreements, these have been prohibited once geographical restrictions have been created (Mathijsen 1985, p. 178). Joint purchasing and joint selling agreements have also tended to be prohibited under Article 85.

The temptation for firms to collude during recession has been enhanced in oligopolistic markets; for example, in 1986 Shell, ICI, Hoechst and Montedipe held 65 per cent of polypropylene sales (a key product used in the manufacture of a wide range of plastics). The companies argued that between 1975 and 1983 they had lost £1000 million, but the EC showed that they were in fact operating a cartel and fixing prices. Competition policy restrains companies from getting together, though one consequence of this has perhaps been a slower downward adjustment of surplus capacity than in Japan.

2. *Dominant firm abuse*. Concern about dominant firms goes back to the days of the ECSC when France was fearful of any renewed concentration of the German coal and steel industries. In the EC, Article 86 has tackled different types of abuse by dominant firms;

for example, firms such as Commercial Solvents, which controlled materials and refused to supply them freely to other firms. Other cases of some significance have included that of Hoffmann-La Roche which was drawn to the Commission's attention by Stanley Adams, who subsequently was badly let down by the Commission. Hoffmann-La Roche dominated the market for vitamins, charging different prices in various markets, and also giving fidelity rebates which were aggregated across all products.

The concept of dominance depends upon how the product and market is defined. One important case in this respect was that of Continental Can, a large American multinational manufacturer of containers. It obtained a dominant position in the German market through a takeover, and this was followed by a takeover of a large Dutch producer. This was likely to suppress competition in both markets. The German firm had a dominant position in the market for preserved meat and fish and for metal caps for preservative jars. There was clearly more of a monopoly when the market was defined narrowly (as touched upon earlier). The Court's judgment came out against the Commission's view about Continental Can creating a dominant position, but it did provide a precedent in enabling the Commission to move into the field of scrutinizing mergers.

The Commission has long sought powers to control cross-frontier mergers and acquisitions. The competition Commissioner (Peter Sutherland) reiterated this view against anti-competitive mergers again late in 1987. A proposal was made to control companies with a joint turnover of over ECU 1 billion. However, some member states object to giving even wider powers to the relatively slow moving Commission.

The Commission under Articles 85 and 86 goes through various stages in its approach. These may include negative clearance (making sure agreements are not prohibited); where agreements do exist it obliges firms to put an end to infringements; it can issue a declaration granting an exemption. When making investigations, the Commission has wide-ranging powers to enter premises, and to examine records. For example, in early 1987 the Commission took legal and financial action against the West German government for not forcing Hoechst to admit anti-cartel investigators into one of its plants. Finally, extensive penalties or fines may be imposed and in some cases may even be extended to firms outside the EC, such as Switzerland, since the EC has claimed extra-territorial jurisdiction.

B   American and Japanese industrial challenge: inward investment
Some of the companies which have taken fullest advantage of the large EC market have been overseas multinationals. The large market and the common external tariff to outsiders have encouraged the growth of inward investment, mainly from the USA but

also more recently from Japan. J. J. Servan-Schreiber in *The American Challenge* in 1968 expressed concern, but by the mid-1970s the American challenge was being rebuffed (Heller and Willat 1975). The threat of American industrial hegemony has been reduced by the growth of large European companies, some of which in recent years have begun to invest on a large-scale in the USA itself. This trend has been stimulated by the fall in the value of the American dollar, compared with European currencies such as the Deutschmark. For example, companies like Thyssen, Renault, Hoechst, ICI, Rhone-Poulenc, BASF and Elf, etc., have all been involved in recent takeovers in the USA (*The Economist* 27 June 1987).

Countries recognize they are in keen competition with each other but if there is to be inward investment in Europe then they may as well provide the location for it instead of importing products from another country in which the new investment has been based. In the longer term there is worry about adding to the danger of over-capacity in some sectors and indigenous industry being weakened from within rather than from without. Furthermore, new inward investment has received generous subsidies in many instances and from the Community viewpoint it would be better if these were scrapped and the money redirected instead to European industry.

The main source of inward investment into the Community has come from the USA. Cumulative American investment in the EC(9) (excluding Denmark, Portugal and Greece) reached $93.15 billion by the end of 1985. In comparison, cumulative investment from Japan in the EC(9) was only $9.9 billion by the end of 1985. From 1951 to 1985 only 11.9 per cent of total Japanese direct investment took place in the EC, partly because Japanese investment was drawn more to the large and more homogeneous American market and to investment closer to home in South-East Asia (*Financial Times* 13 November 1986). Nevertheless, the recent pace of Japanese investment in the Community has accelerated, stimulated by the rising value of the yen and protectionist pressures in the Community which have threatened to cut back on Japanese exports. Japan's effect in particular sectors is now significant and inroads are being made into new sectors such as financial services. Most Japanese investment has consisted of setting-up overseas subsidiaries. In the few instances of collaborative deals the Japanese have been criticized for stripping away the technical capabilities from their partners.

The Japanese challenge has caught some of Europe's major companies off-balance. For example, Philips compared with Hitachi has had far too many factories; in 1984 it had 450 factories, whereas if it had been organized on a Japanese basis it would have had about 30 factories (Turner 1986). This has led to a new strategy at Philips of rationalization and focusing on its ten product divisions rather than the many national organizations; also, spending more on research and development and spreading the costs of this by means of joint ventures.

The Japanese move into production of goods in the EC, such as video-cassette recorders, electronic typewriters, photocopiers and microwave ovens, has been influenced by the EC's concern about the dumping of those products and its consequent imposition of controls and anti-dumping duties. For example, early in 1987 the Commission raised its anti-dumping duty on photocopiers from 15.8 per cent to 20 per cent. The most popular location for Japanese overseas investment in the Community has been in the UK, followed by the Netherlands and West Germany, while France started to adopt a very pragmatic policy in this respect during the 1980s. The Japanese themselves, for example, were shaken by the Poitiers affair in 1982 when France insisted that all Japanese VCR's had to be routed through this customs post. The need is to ensure that Japanese production in the EC does not consist simply of screwdriver factories but that there is sufficient input of national products. The EC has a ruling of 60 per cent local content measured by ex-factory prices. In the UK, for example, Nissan aims to achieve the 60 per cent mark by 1988 and up to 80 per cent by 1991.

C   EC industrial policy

Whereas the EC has a strong competition policy based upon treaty requirements, it has lacked the same legal basis for the development of an industrial policy (Butt Philip 1983). The initial approach was market orientated and generally non-interventionist. It was only in 1970 that the Community published the Colonna Report on Industrial Policy which mainly reflected a non-interventionist approach, trying to create a unified market. It was concerned with tackling various issues which included: the elimination of technical barriers to trade; the harmonization of the legal, fiscal and financial frameworks; the encouragement of transnational mergers; the adaptation of industry; greater technical collaboration, and the control of multinationals (Arbuthnott and Edwards 1979, p. 92).

During the 1960s there had been a big increase in merger activity, most of which occurred within national boundaries, and where there were transfrontier mergers far more of these were with foreign firms than with firms in member states of the Community. European mergers have been hampered by fiscal difficulties; for example, a true merger involves a legal liquidation in one country and some countries imposed liquidation taxes and capital gains taxes. Although fiscal concessions were often made, the authorities were less willing to do so when this involved the disappearance of national companies. Legal difficulties also existed with Dutch law not providing for company mergers and German law precluding mergers between German and foreign companies.

National mergers, however, have tended to create national monopolies, whilst mergers with American or Japanese companies lead to a fragmentation of European co-operation. A few major European cross-frontier links have had a long duration; for example, between the UK and Holland with Royal Dutch Shell (since 1907) and Unilever (since 1927). More recent successors to such mergers have included Agfa-Gevaert (formed in 1964): this was not a true European company but only consisted of 'Siamese twins' (Layton 1969). Some later European mergers have proved even less successful, such as the Dunlop–Pirelli merger in 1971, though this seemed to offer some complementarity in markets. Dunlop's strength lay in the Commonwealth and North American markets, whilst Pirelli's strength lay in Europe and Latin America. Their marriage was dissolved in 1981, though after that Dunlop suffered an even more disastrous performance. Unidata, the French–German–Dutch computer group which was set up in 1973 to challenge IBM, sank quickly. The eleven-year marriage of the aircraft firms, VFW of West Germany and Fokker of Holland, has also been dissolved. Difficulties have arisen in blending together different styles of management. Nevertheless, pressures on companies to combine have continued in order to obtain economies of scale and to finance the costs of R & D. The more recent internationalization of stock markets and the lowering of barriers to capital movements have stimulated further cross-national takeovers. These span the gamut of industries, even including agriculture where close Italian–French business links have been established.

A landmark in the EC's development of industrial policy was the Spinelli Report in 1973. It proposed new measures for industrial and technological policy, although these were still couched within the framework of a competition-orientated industrial policy. Among new measures were those for harmonization, freeing tenders, encouraging transnational enterprises; and help to small- and medium-sized firms to co-operate or merge. Co-operation between such firms, especially on R & D, does not fall foul of the anti-restrictive practices policy. To help small firms to find partners a Business Co-operation Centre was created.

European Economic Interest Groups (EEIGs) were first proposed in the Colonna Report, though a regulation was not finally adopted until 1985. These are aimed mainly at co-operation between small- and medium-sized enterprises; for example, in R & D. Their main characteristic is that they are non-profit seeking.

The recession during the 1970s provided a turning point towards more interventionist policies. National governments came under pressure to help industries and to avoid trading distortions many of these policies were taken over, though sometimes reluctantly, by the Community in order to co-ordinate them, and to make the assistance transparent. This is well exemplified in industries such as steel and shipbuilding. In the former, the Davignon system has operated with price and production quotas. Between 1980 and 1986 European steelmakers removed about 36 million tonnes of excess capacity. Commission proposals to dismantle quotas by the end of 1987 resulted in some strong resistance from producers. In the shipbuilding industry, national subsidies led to an agreement by the EC in 1986 to limit direct subsidies to 28 per cent of cost on large contracts, and to 20 per cent on smaller deals. Over-capacity has manifested itself in many other sectors and in the car industry, for example, over-capacity in Western Europe was still estimated to be some 3.5 million cars early in 1987.

Although the Commission has executive authority on state aids, these have proliferated. In 1970 only six cases of state aids were taken to the European Court of Justice, but by 1981 this had risen to 61 cases, of which 14 decisions were to forbid certain aids. The Commission has to be notified of state aids, but at times has been ambivalent about taking national governments to task over all their states aids. This is partly because such aids were recognized after the Copenhagen Summit in 1978 as measures enabling adaptation to competition from the NICs, albeit interim measures. The White Paper on the Internal Market 1985 proposed much tighter surveillance of aids to make member states aware of the damaging effect of their national policy in other member states.

A problem for the EC has been that national governments have often possessed stronger industrial instruments, such as those of finance, and the Community has tried to strengthen its own instruments. The fifth Medium-Term Economic Policy Programme 1981–85 proposed the introduction of 'Community preference' to help EC firms in areas like R & D. Other developments have included the founding of the European Venture Capital Association (EVCA); a European Business and Innovation Centre Network (EBN); and the Commission's own Small and Medium Enterprise (SME) Task Force. They are concerned to help small- and medium-sized enterprises in particular and these have found favourable support in the UK, where all new Community regulatory proposals have to be assessed for their impact on business.

D The EC's lag in technology

The pace of structural change has highlighted the need to replace the declining or sunset industries by new, sunrise sectors. The future lies with new high-tech sectors in which EC countries can utilize their high educational skills. Over time, the traditional down-market industries are likely to become the mainstay for the NICs. If the

EC is to remain at the forefront of major industrial powers, then policies to promote technology, comparable with that of the USA and Japan, are imperative.

New technology is a mainspring of growth and lower inflation, even though its employment-creating effects are less clear cut. Employment is most likely to increase when technology is devoted to creating and marketing successful new products, rather than to developing process technology which reduces the input of labour. Despite microeconomic readjustment and displacement of labour, the long-run impact of technology historically in aggregate has been to increase demand and employment opportunities. Japan in recent years has enjoyed much lower unemployment than the EC and those countries which lag in new technology gradually become less competitive and lose jobs. Therefore the EC has little alternative – despite the adverse short-term effects of new technology – but to encourage the transition from declining industries to expanding new high-technology industries.

The EC does not manifest a general technological lag across all industries. Indeed, in some industries the Community is strong; for example, in chemicals and nuclear power. In addition, individual countries such as West Germany are strong in specific areas such as industrial machinery, while the UK shows potential in the new area of biotechnology. The main problem for the EC is not so much technology *per se* but the managerial gap commercially in applying this technology (Sharp 1985, p. 291). The Community has lost market share in high-technology products and has a particular lag in electronics and information technology. This is serious since it affects the performance in the various sectors which use electronics which is currently a phenomenal growth industry. The EC has shown a poor performance in computers, consumer electronics, industrial automation, integrated circuits and office equipment. Its trade in telecommunications equipment has only been held in balance by some restrictions on imports. Western Europe has too few companies which are internationally competitive in information technology.

In robotics, European countries have lagged far behind Japan and a high proportion of robots in the EC are imported. Estimated numbers of robots in Japan in 1984 were approximately four times the aggregate in West Germany, France, Italy and the UK (Harrop 1985).

Those countries which are most progressive in terms of innovation capture a larger share of world markets. They are able to keep one step ahead of the NICs which use more outdated technology. What has been worrying the EC is that it has not been moving up-market at a sufficient pace, nor providing sufficient diffusion of innovation quickly enough within the economy. Apart from the pressure by the NICs in the more down-market areas, the EC has also been outpaced by Japan and it has failed to cut back on the existing technological gap with the USA.

An index of technological specialization has been constructed and this is defined as the share of each bloc in world trade in high-technology products divided by its share of world trade in manufactured products. The EC figure fell from 1.02 in 1963 to 0.88 in 1980, whereas Japan's rose from 0.56 in 1963 to 1.41 in 1980, surpassing the USA figure of 1.20 in 1980 (Heertje 1983, p. 102). The Community has a deficit on its trade in high-technology products both with the USA and Japan.

European companies have experienced an inadequate scale of operation in some sectors because of fragmented national markets, due to practices such as national purchasing policies. Yet economies of scale are important in many sectors, not only in terms of static efficiency and reducing costs of production, but also in terms of dynamic efficiency given the high threshold costs of financing R & D. For example, in telecommunications the major American companies − AT & T, Northern Telecom and ITT − plus Japanese suppliers NEC and Fujitsu, have developed built-in advantages in digital exchanges, resulting in lower costs per line.

European firms have been at a disadvantage compared with their American counterparts in fields such as patents and trade marks. In order to avoid the costly procedure of applying for separate patent protection in each country, in 1978 the European Patent Convention provided for European patent protection through a single application. This also extended to Austria, Switzerland and Sweden, though unfortunately it excluded Denmark, Ireland and Portugal. An additional defect has been that litigation has had to be conducted separately in each country. Instead of a collection of national patents, the EC has proposed a Community Patent Convention (CPC) under which a single Community patent would exist and the judgment in a Community Patent Court in one member state would be effective throughout the Community. Although Denmark and Ireland have failed to ratify the CPC, it is part and parcel of creating the internal market by 1992.

Trade marks are important in denoting the origin and quality of goods, but firms have had to make separate applications in each member state to protect them. In 1980, two proposals were presented by the EC Commission to harmonize the legislation on granting trade marks and it is planning a Community trade mark. National systems will still continue, but a Community trade mark covering the whole EC will result from a single application to a European Trade Marks Office. Various sites have been shortlisted for this office, with strong competition for its location between London and Madrid, since the latter is pressing for some institutional placement there to reflect a commitment to southern Europe.

E   Technological co-operation

Co-operation helps to avoid wasteful duplication and is appropriate in the following conditions: where high risk capital is involved; where the partners are of fairly equal size; where some standardization of the product is acceptable; and when R & D costs are high. But assessment of projects needs to be an on-going process to avoid becoming locked into non-viable commercial ventures. Some examples are given in the next section on the aerospace industry.

The launching of the European Strategic Programme for Research and Development in Information Technology (ESPRIT) in 1983 was a major development. It is centred on five main areas: advanced microelectronics, software technology, advanced information processing, office systems and computer integrated manufacture. It has been concerned with joint pre-competitive research and the EC covers up to half the costs of the exercise with industry providing the remainder. Participants have included some leading European electronics companies which have been able to increase their linkages. ESPRIT was the Community's most costly project at ECU 750 million 1984–88, followed by the large JET project whose funding from 1985–89 was ECU 690 million (Butler 1986, pp. 56–7). The Commission has sought a further ECU 2 billion for a second phase of ESPRIT to run from 1987–91; it was considered likely that there would be some further movement forward from pre-competitive research to the point of production of saleable products.

The Community has several other significant R & D programmes which includes Research into Advanced Communication Technologies for Europe (RACE) – this is complementary to ESPRIT and is trying to lay the basis for European-wide broadband communications' networks in the 1990s. Other R & D programmes include Basic Research in Industrial Technologies for Europe (BRITE), launched in 1985, which is seeking to encourage advanced technology in traditional industries. Some £80 million was allocated over four years for pre-competitive research. Other acronyms gaining currency in the new technological Community are: Forecasting and Assessment in Science and Technology (FAST); Community Programme for Education and Training in Technologies (COMETT); European Research on Advanced Materials (EURAM); a Concertation Unit for Biotechnology (CUBE); and also the Strategic Programme for Innovation and Technology Transfer in Europe (SPRINT).

Another major European research programme of a slightly different kind has been the French inspired European Research Co-ordination Agency (EUREKA). This covers all twelve EC countries plus seven EFTA countries. It was established in July 1985 to give Europe research resources on the same scale as the Strategic Defence Initiative in the USA. It was given no central Community financing but has drawn upon support from national governments. By the end of 1987 there were some 165 EUREKA projects with a total value of £2.8 billion. The UK is taking part in nearly a third of these (*Midland Bank Review*, Winter 1987). They were concerned with commercial products that have clear market applications, but with each country favouring particular projects; for example, West Germany chose several which were of environmental interest. New small- and medium-sized companies are playing a more significant role in EUREKA. Although EUREKA is separate from the Community, a small secretariat has been set up in Brussels. Essentially the co-operation is between companies to avoid a highly-bureaucratic framework, and has no joint funding or even automatic state funding. EUREKA covers many high-tech projects in an exclusively civilian sector, close to the market-place. While many of the larger companies would probably co-operate anyway, EUREKA has induced smaller companies to co-operate much more with each other. The company level approach, with mainly privately-financed schemes, provides a marked contrast with other Community-level projects such as BRITE, RACE and ESPRIT in which the EC meet 50 per cent of the cost of projects (Dinkelspiel 1987).

The Community's R & D programme is far too small since in the early 1980s it still accounted for only about 2.5 per cent of the EC's Budget, and only about 2 per cent of total public expenditure on R & D by the member states (Albert and Ball 1983). The Commission proposed a substantial increase for the period 1987–91 to enhance the EC's innovative and competitive capabilities but this was trimmed down. Ideally, by the end of the century, one would like to see EC R & D closer to half the Community Budget, and half of national public spending by member states on R & D. In the late 1980s there has been some scaling down of the R & D devoted to the energy sector so that other programmes such as information technology can take up a larger share of R & D spending. However, the major European countries with independent R & D strength and which are making large contributions to the Community Budget have become cautious about the amount and direction of R & D spending, stressing the need for this to be cost-effective. For example, the UK has sought to restrict expenditure, especially on non-commercially orientated projects – not only in the EC but also in the European Space Agency – yet these are among the few areas in the Community from which the UK derives a net benefit.

F   Case study of the aerospace industry

Nature of the problem. EC co-operation in aerospace was not called for in the Treaty of Rome and the only indirect reference was related to a common transport policy (deemed to extend to air transport). Military affairs are not the preserve of the Community, since these are dealt with by NATO. Why, then, has the EC regarded it as imperative to foster co-operation in aerospace projects? These are an essential ingredient of its common industrial and technological policy.

National aircraft industries in Europe are too small to compete effectively on their own against the USA. Their dominance has applied both to military aircraft, stimulated by massive defence expenditure, and to civil aircraft, based upon a large domestic market. Consequently, it has benefited from economies of scale with long production runs and high productivity, offsetting the higher real wages in the USA (*vis-à-vis* the Europeans). The American labour market is very flexible, tending to fluctuate in accordance with demand in terms of 'hire and fire' policies.

In 1985 the sales of the three American giants in the aerospace industry were: Boeing, $13 636.0 million; McDonnell Douglas $11 477.7 million; and Lockheed, $9 535.0 million (*Financial Times* Survey of Aerospace 26 August 1986). Some American aeroplanes have enjoyed outstanding success and profitability, such as the Boeing 727, and up to 1980 1811 were ordered. Similarly, 1069 McDonnell Douglas DC9s were ordered up to 1980. The production run of European planes has been lower, but the successful Fokker F-27 had 786 sales, and since 1969, 421 F-28s have been sold.

American firms are dominant throughout the aerospace industry from airframes to engines and from space rocketry to the simpler production of helicopters. In aeroengines, economies of scale are higher than in the production of airframes; hence the market is dominated by even fewer firms with the American companies Pratt and Whitney and General Electric being world leaders, followed by Rolls-Royce in the UK. R & D costs are enormous, with the result that co-operation is very much the key word in the industry, and an increasing amount of investment is now being put into a new prop-fan engine.

In helicopters, American firms are again dominant: Bell, Boeing-Vertol, Sikorsky and McDonnell Douglas. The European firms challenging them are Westland in the UK, Augusta in Italy, Aérospatiale in France and Messerschmitt-Bölkow-Blohm in West Germany. Not only is there a large military market but a growing civil market, as exemplified by their use in North Sea oil development.

Policy options: independence or co-operation. One example of an independent company approach has been that of Dassault in France: it created the very successful Mirage range of military aircraft. However, even this company has been forced to modify its policy in recent years. Its failure to agree on the European Fighter Aircraft (EFA) left the company to develop its own fighter aircraft, the Rafale, and it has sought to interest European countries such as Belgium and Spain in this project.

An independent policy can prove costly where the market is small and where costs rise excessively. Hence co-operation has become a byword in all parts of the industry. Nevertheless, there have been notorious examples of co-operative failures commercially. One example of this was the bilateral Anglo-French Concorde project which had both economic and political origins and the UK government also hoped that the project might be helpful in its initial application to join the European Community.

No cost-benefit analysis was ever published for Concorde, though it has been shown subsequently that the costs exceeded the benefits (Henderson 1977). The main benefits have been derived from technical 'spin-off' and from the prestige attached to the technical achievement *per se*. If some of these technical advances had never taken place — even if funds had been devoted to such research — then this 'X' element of aerospace co-operation is invaluable. Many alleged economic benefits both to employment and to the balance of payments did not materialize and there were also some significant social costs. While all investment decisions are risky, particularly in industries such as aerospace, cost-benefit analysis is essential before future decisions are taken. Otherwise there is a tendency for some political interest groups to push particular projects vigorously and unfortunately once under way they tend to acquire a momentum of their own for fear of incurring cancellation charges. The escalation of costs and the small number of planes built meant that Concorde was a major commercial mistake — though there have been others in other industries, such as the British advanced gas-cooler reactor (Henderson 1977).

Other types of co-operation have been multilateral in nature, including not only members of the EC but also some other European countries, and in addition the USA and more recently Japan. Those who support a European solution wish Europe to possess indigenous technology, seeking to exclude outsiders such as the USA. Whatever the type of co-operation, it is vital to secure a long production run to reap economies of scale. The learning curve means that the first aircraft in a series can cost four times as much as the 250th plane produced (see Figure 5.1).

Assume production is at a limited national output OQ_n on the long-run cost curve LAC_1 then average cost is OC_n. If output increased to OQ_m then average cost on LAC_1 would fall to OC_1. The small national European markets preclude production at such a low cost, though co-operation does enable the production of a

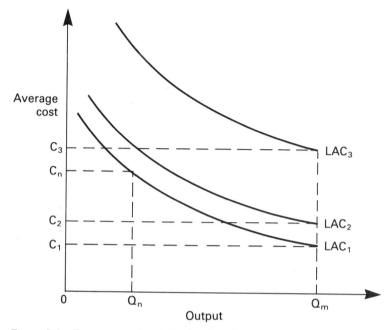

Figure 5.1 Economies of scale in the aircraft industry

higher combined output, OQ_m. Unfortunately, the long-run average cost curves are likely to be pushed to the right. This is because of the costs involved in drawing suitable partners together. They have to decide on a project which matches their different needs and often the outcome is an over-elaborate and expensive compromise. In addition the allocation of the work may not be based on comparative advantage but on an equitable distribution between the partners.

Figure 5.1 shows two different scenarios for long-run average cost: in the first of these on LAC_2 co-operation is successful in reducing average costs to OC_2. This shows the expected reduction in average costs compared with national production. However, if political and bureaucratic influence result in an escalation of expenditure and partners duplicate production, then a possible scenario is shown on LAC_3. In this situation, average costs are even higher than in the original national markets! Furthermore, it is possible that the counterfactual is not domestic production, but the purchase of aircraft at even lower cost from the USA. Some comparative estimates of alterative costs have been made for the Tornado project relative to the F-14, F-15 and F-16 (Hartley 1982, p. 180).

Additional orders for the Tornado have pushed its production to 933 planes, assuring production for Panavia until at least 1992. As

Tornado production turns down, the gap will be filled by the new Euro-fighter: the plan is for 800 aircraft in total — about 260 each for the UK and West Germany, 160 for Italy and about 100 for Spain. The industrial participation agreed was 33 per cent each for the UK and West Germany, 21 per cent for Italy and 13 per cent for Spain. A joint company has been set up to manage the venture, jointly owned by British Aerospace, Messerschmitt-Bölkow-Blohm, Aeritalia and CASA of Spain.

The success of airbus. Airbus Industrie was set up in 1970 after the signing of a Franco-German Agreement in 1969 and an earlier agreement of 1967 which had also included the UK. The latter's ambivalence about the project resulted in only Hawker-Siddeley retaining a toehold, but subsequently the UK was to rejoin the project. Other countries to participate have included the Netherlands, Belgium and Spain. The airbus was established as a grouping of mutual economic interest and in taking this form under French law it maximized co-operation and minimized the amount of disclosure and tax payment. The structure adopted conceals subsidies given, much to the displeasure of the USA. The latter claim that they infringe the rules of GATT, keeping down the price of airbuses and incurring massive losses. Airbus Industrie have defied the USA over this, pointing to Federal Defense contracts which have helped to underpin American plane makers.

In 1970 aircraft manufacturers in the EC had less than a four per cent share of the world civil market and only a 15 per cent share of the European market itself. By 1982 sales of the A-300 and A-310, as a proportion of total world commercial twin aisle jet sales, were 52 per cent and they had 350 firm orders. By the end of 1987 the A-320 had 300 firm orders from 18 airlines and it appears to be a commercial success, even though it will not make a return on invested funds until 600 aircraft have been delivered and paid for in the 1990s.

Success in aircraft production comes from producing a family of planes and airbus have plans for extending this with the A-330, a twin-engined short- to medium-range aircraft with 330 seats, and the A-340, a four-engined long-range aircraft with between 250 and 350 seats (*Financial Times* 20 August 1986 and 26 March 1987).

Airbus are even outselling Boeing on some planes and with the A-330 and A-340, by incorporating commonality of many parts, it will provide stronger competition across the product range for its American rivals. Sales of the A-330 show more market potential than the A-340 and it was suggested that airbus should co-operate on the latter with McDonnell Douglas to reduce costs and widen markets.

Part III   The UK's industrial dilemma
The UK's relative industrial decline has given way to absolute

decline in many sectors. It has concentrated too much on traditional down-market sections of production, retaining a higher share of these than of the up-market sections. For example, in man-made fibres the UK retains a higher share of international rayon production than synthetic fibre production and whereas in the former its plant size in the mid-1980s was similar to that of the USA, its plant size for synthetic fibres was only about a third of that of the USA and lower than that in Japan, West Germany or Italy. The European man-made fibres industry has sought to cut back its massive over-capacity, concentrating on higher value fibres. The UK has lost ground in textiles to West Germany, with the latter's high productivity, efficient machinery, and use of outward processing. Italy is a bigger textile producer than West Germany and has a large, successful and expanding woollen industry based on a flair for design, state enterprise and small firms operating on the fringe of the black economy (Department of Industry Investigation 1981).

It is the same story in other industries such as that of machine tools in which product innovation in the UK has been slower than by its major competitors. The UK has lost ground not only to Japan but also to Italy, which has been prominent in developing low-cost machining centres, and to West Germany; the latter's strength lies in its highly-trained and adaptable labour force (Sharp 1985, p. 287). Although the UK was to the forefront in the early application of numerical control in the aircraft industry, it has failed to develop as strongly in computer numerical control (CNC) because of weak upstream links with electronic suppliers and weak downstream links with the firms using machine tools. UK industrial strategy seems to be one of depending increasingly upon inward investment in this sector from Japan which links up with the latter's incursion into the motor vehicle industry. While the ideal would be one of indigenous industrial resurgence, this dependence on inward investment may offer the only other alternative and realistic way for the UK to recover its industrial dynamism.

Technologically the UK has been overcommitted to military expenditure, including industries such as aerospace, throughout the post-war years. The defect of this strategy is that it has resulted in a maldistribution of technological expertise, starving other important industries. New technology which might have been transferred to other industrial uses has been locked away in defence establishments. A recognition of this weakness is the government's emphasis in recent years on new technology transfer and in 1985 Defence Technology Enterprises was established in an attempt to use commercially some of the technology stored in the Ministry of Defence. Private industrial R & D in the UK has been low in comparison with its major competitors; for example, UK industry's funding of R & D was only one per cent of GNP in 1985 compared with 1.6 per cent in West Germany. While research is important, the UK has often been less successful in the crucial development for the market-place. One example of this is carbon fibre which was developed by the UK aerospace industry, yet Japan now dominates its production.

Since the end of the Second World War, total British government outlay on aircraft launch aid has been well over £2 billion. Less than 10 per cent of that expenditure has been recovered, despite the successes in Rolls-Royce engines and in aircraft, such as Vickers Viscount, with 440 being sold. The colossal expenditure involved has brought successive British governments round to the view that co-operation is essential. The dilemma is what form the participation should take and whether it is to be predominantly with other countries in western Europe or with the USA. For example, the Westland helicopter affair reflected the continuing pull of American producers like Sikorsky compared with British participation in European programmes like the NH-90.

The UK recognizes that international co-operation reduces the costs of R & D, but it has learnt from past experience, for example the expensive commercial flop of Concorde. The multilateral airbus project is more successful, though British government finance has been limited, despite new launch aid for participation in the A-330 and A-340 airbuses. The conditions for participation in co-operative projects have to meet stringent criteria. These now include regular evaluation, efficient administration, and an à la carte menu in which the UK can choose which projects to participate in.

6 Regional problems and policies

Part I Economic characteristics of regions

A Regional imbalance

The uneven pace of economic development and changing comparative advantage have resulted in spatial imbalance. Staple industries drawn in the past to locations on or near the coalfields have declined. Industrial areas with over-specialization and over-concentration on traditional industries (that is, with specialization and concentration location quotients greater than one, where one is the national average) have declined, leading to regional and urban decay. Nevertheless, the central core area of northern Europe still possesses the important attributes such as converging transport networks which are favourable to industrial development.

The periphery of the European Community is less industrialized and more rural, with a lower level of economic development. Agricultural problem areas comprise both underdeveloped areas and also developed agricultural areas in which employment has declined inexorably. There are also border areas which have experienced problems resulting from their peripheral situation, though some of these have been lessened by the creation and enlargement of the EC. France in particular has been able to open up its eastern border areas. Even its peripheral coastal regions, such as Brittany, benefited from Community enlargement, with the development of the deep-water port at Roscoff, providing a link to the south-west of England (Ardagh 1982, p. 138). Both the EC and the Council of Europe have encouraged border area co-operation, in which a better transport network has been the key to linking up regions. In 1986 France, together with Belgium and Luxembourg, put forward a proposal for border restructuring of the Longwy-Rodange-Aubange area. Even so, West German border problems with eastern Europe provide a reminder of another kind of less bridgeable frontier issue.

To what extent are free market forces able to reduce regional divergence? Neo-classical economists have argued that there is a tendency towards the equalization of factor incomes spatially, given certain assumptions such as free mobility of capital and labour, equal technology, and so on. Yet factors are not perfectly mobile, and even on the assumption that they are, labour would have to emigrate from declining regions, and capital to flow into those declining regions. In a dynamic world, as neo-Keynesians have shown, capital has often been drawn towards regions which are already prosperous since they offer higher rates of return. Capital cities have provided a magnetic attraction, since economic advantages have been consolidated by being at the heart of cultural and political influences. Multinational companies have favoured proximity to such centres for their headquarters and decision-making. Firms have obtained external economies of scale from location in large urban areas. However, there has been a tendency in recent years for pleasant medium-sized towns located on the outer fringe of such areas to attract new firms.

While dynamic growth effects may 'spill-over' to benefit the less developed regions, the latter are more likely to experience adverse 'backwash' effects, resulting in cumulative relative decline (Myrdal 1957). A polarization of resources occurs in which less developed regions experience high rates of unemployment, deindustrialization, emigration of labour – often consisting of younger and enterprising people – and a rundown, shabby infrastructure. Therefore, the free market fails to create convergence and any desirable balanced equilibrium between regions.

B   Objectives of regional policy

Countries are concerned to reduce economic and social disparities which arise from the wide differences in rates of regional unemployment. Unfortunately, however, regional policy is likely to be less effective when the overall level of unemployment is high, since this is a reflection of low demand and there are few firms wishing to expand and to relocate their activities. The absolute numbers unemployed are also high, even in the more prosperous city regions, though their percentage rate of unemployment is relatively low, with much of the unemployment being frictional and not of long duration like that in the declining areas.

A higher rate of economic growth is a precondition for reducing unemployment and raising activity rates in the depressed regions. While the automatic link between growth and numbers employed may have weakened – with capital substituted for labour – it is vital to raise the level of demand, particularly where labour supply is increasing rapidly. While aggregate economic expansion creates inflationary pressures, balanced regional development helps to alleviate this since demand can be channelled into areas with idle capital and redundant labour. This is less inflationary than pumping demand into regions of high demand which is already running up against supply bottlenecks.

Firms are concerned in their decision-taking with maximizing their private profits, but in so doing they fail to consider the social costs or social benefits which would accrue to society from a more even distribution of economic activity. The preference of firms to locate in already congested cities imposes additional social costs. By relocating in the depressed and less developed areas, social benefits could be increased. Furthermore, since many firms are 'footloose' this can be done without adversely affecting their economic performance.

Regional problems have sometimes coincided with demands for regional autonomy to meet different cultural and linguistic interests. Politically, countries have had to show a sensitive awareness to regional differences to maintain national unity. For example, in Belgium the government has tried to contain the tendency towards fragmentation between the French speaking and declining Walloon area in the south and the more prosperous area of Flanders to the north.

Part II   EC regional policy and the structural funds

A   *The case for EC regional policy*
While the case for national regional policies is well-accepted and established, is there also a case for a strong regional policy at Community level? If so, should the policy supplement national policies or replace them? The latter is what has happened with regard to the Guarantee section of the CAP. The case for an EC regional policy stems largely from the way a large free market tends to exacerbate regional problems (Holland 1976, Vanhove and Klassen 1980, pp. 227–53).

The removal of trading barriers in the customs union has led to the contraction of less efficient industries and although new industries have emerged these have often been attracted elsewhere to the 'core' areas. Newer industries perceive the advantages of maximizing sales, lowering transport costs and gaining external economies of scale by locating at the heart of the EC market. The free mobility of factors of production in the common market have tended to flow from the periphery to the core, particularly labour, though recently there has been some encouraging evidence that capital has started to flow back towards the periphery. However, weaker regions encounter difficulties in selling their products competitively, particularly when workers receive nationally-based wage rates or expect to receive rates of pay comparable to similar work being done in the prosperous areas of the Community. National collective bargaining, rather than regional or local bargaining, and also Community-wide pay comparability tends to make regional labour markets rather inflexible. In addition, the operation of national and multinational companies in charging uniform prices wherever they are located is a further source of disequilibrating activity.

Further progress towards closer integration is likely to reinforce regional problems; for example, the creation of the single internal market by 1992 will not only accelerate existing flows of trade and factors, but will also open up the Community market for services – these tend to be concentrated in the developed regions of the Community. In its external trading policy, pressure for easier access to Community markets, especially to accommodate imports from LDCs which produce more basic products, will result in an even faster contraction of traditional industries in many weaker regions.

Enlargement of the Community has brought in the peripheral European economies which has widened regional divergencies, since these are greater in countries with low levels of national income and with a high dependence on agriculture. In the EC(12), regional disparities are now twice as high as in the USA in the case of GDP and three times as high in terms of unemployment. Meanwhile, further progress towards monetary union is likely to reduce the leeway for national authorities to increase their industrial competitiveness by exchange rate depreciation. The less competitive industries, which suffer most, tend to be those located in remote regions with high transport costs. Since the EMS confers desirable monetary advantages, a concomitant of this is to tackle some of its disadvantageous regional effects by stronger EC regional policy.

B Regional policies

Different types of regional policy can be pursued, either by improving the working of market forces or intervening with positive policies of incentives to encourage relocation by private firms and active relocation of some public sector activities in the weaker regions. In addition, to try to force development towards such regions, restrictions may be imposed to curb expansion in the overdeveloped and congested areas.

Labour mobility. Unemployment and low wages result in outward migration which is pulled into other areas where jobs are plentiful and wages are higher. Up to 1973 massive labour migration occurred inter-regionally and internationally during the economic boom in the European Community. Labour emigrated from the Mezzogiorno to the north of Italy and also to the rapidly growing economies of West Germany and France. The EC became a highly-integrated labour market with freer labour mobility becoming a reality after 1968. Demand for labour became so high that the main inflow was sucked in from southern Europe where there was an even stronger 'push' element. Some of these countries – Greece, Spain and Portugal – have in the 1980s become full members of the EC, hoping to concentrate on exporting more goods to the Community instead of labour.

Some proponents of labour mobility have argued that it leads towards economic convergence between regions and countries. Areas receiving labour are able to meet their high labour demand, while areas losing labour may gain through the removal of surplus labour which was either unemployed or under-employed. In the host regions and countries, much hinges upon whether the immigrant labour supply matches the demand, or whether it leads to a dynamic growth in which demand continues to expand faster than supply, with continuing inflationary consequences. Migrant labour is exploited by low wage rates and long hours of work, since it is often weakly unionized (Castles and Kosack 1973). Businesses make higher profits from which they can finance a greater level of investment: the latter leads to the employment of both capital and labour as output rises, although some firms may prefer to continue with cheaper labour-intensive production methods.

The emigration of labour is not the panacea for regional imbalance where areas lose labour on such a large scale that they become depopulated and continue to decline. A policy of marginal labour movement is more appropriate when this creams off an over-populated area. The reduction in outward migration since 1973 is not really a good indicator of any marked improvement in regional performance, since it tends to reflect the lower demand in the core of the Community. The number of migrants living in the Community has fallen back as a consequence of repatriation, and by 1984 there were estimated to be some 3.3 million migrants living in the EC(6) and about 4.3 million in the EC(10).

Positive regional policy. Instead of reducing excess labour supply by labour mobility, a positive regional policy aims to raise the level of demand for workers. In private enterprise economies, inducements are given mainly through subsidies and tax concessions on capital, to encourage firms to expand and to relocate in unemployment black spots. A policy of subsidizing capital has enouraged a substitution of capital for labour, tending to swamp any additional output effect on the employment of labour. Often tax payers' money has been given to multinational companies which have used their bargaining power to extract maximum subsidy.

Where new firms have been attracted, these have often been branch factories of large multinational companies and in recession these have tended to be the first to face cutbacks. A lower propensity to invest during recession has resulted in a refocusing of regional policy towards greater indigenous expansion by small- and medium-sized firms with technological potential within less developed regions. This has been consolidated by attempts to link Community R & D programmes to such regions. But these policies are constrained by an existing over-concentration of R & D and innovation in the prosperous regions; also, it is difficult to develop 'leading edge' technologies in weaker regions, even though these can be applied not only to new industries but to revitalize traditional ones as well. To help weaker regions the Community has launched programmes such as Special Telecommunications Action for Regions (STAR) – with about £50 million over five years – and more recently Science and Technology for Regional Innovation and Development in Europe (STRIDE).

Proponents of interventionist planning-style regional policies advocate greater state expenditure in less developed areas; this consists of spending more on infrastructure and also of laying down specific guidelines to increase the level of nationalized industry spending in such regions. Countries in the EC have differed in their regional policy emphasis, with Italy providing one of the best examples of state enterprise (Holland 1972). In contrast, West Germany with fewer regional problems has tended to place greater reliance on market forces of labour mobility and inducements to private enterprise.

Italian regional policy has gone through several different phases in trying to tackle its problem of regional dualism, with the underdevelopment of the Mezzogiorno. The Cassa per il Mezzogiorno was founded in 1950 but was finally wound up in 1986 with its successor to be the Agenzia per la Promozione dello Sviluppo del Mezzogiorno. The Cassa had sought to improve agriculture and infrastructure and then tried to force the pace of industrialization by laying down specific targets for investment by state enterprises. State firms were instructed to make 60 per cent of their total investment and 80 per cent of their new investment in the Mezzogiorno. Italy has made positive use of its large state-holding companies as a catalyst to encourage private sector development. It succeeded in raising the percentage of national industrial investment in the Mezzogiorno from only about 15 per cent of total investment in the early 1950s to around 30 per cent in the 1970s. But too much of this investment has been in highly capital-intensive sectors yielding relatively few immediate jobs. The Mezzogiorno's private consumption per head (at just under three-quarters of the Italian national average) and its share of Italian GDP (at just under a quarter) showed little change from 1951 to 1978 (Klassen and Molle 1983).

Italy has found it difficult to narrow the gap between the so-called 'two Italies'. The research institute Svimez noted that in 1986 GNP in the north rose by 3.1 per cent, but only by 1.5 per cent in the south. Productivity per worker in southern industry was only 73 per cent of that in the north, and in southern agriculture 63 per cent of that in the north. Unemployment in the south was 18.8 per cent compared with a national rate of 11.6 per cent (*The Times* 17 November 1987). Nevertheless, there is little doubt that without a regional policy, divergencies would have been even greater, and faster emigration would have had to occur from the south. A real base has now been laid in the Mezzogiorno, despite criticisms of its industrialization without real development and an over-reliance on loss-making activities by state enterprises. Southern Italy now compares favourably with other Mediterranean countries and the changing focus of the Community towards southern Europe means that southern Italy is better placed for future development. The Mezzogiorno has been a priority for both the Italian government and also for EC aid-giving institutions.

Negative regional policy. Negative regional policy refers to measures to limit over-expansion in prosperous and congested areas. Such measures have been used by several countries, including France and the UK. At a time of economic expansion they could be justified, although generally it is better to attract firms positively to depressed regions instead of preventing them from locating at their chosen site. Since the more depressed economic conditions of the early 1970s such restrictions have had little rationale. This is because investment has fallen, and preventing firms from investing in particular areas is likely to have two effects: either the firm may postpone its investment completely, or it may decide to locate in some other region to avoid the controls − this could be in other EC countries or even in some other part of the world. A reluctance nationally to apply negative measures so strongly during recession left a gap in Community policy to control areas of over-concentration (Vanhove and Klassen 1980, p. 452).

C   The funding of EC policies

National regional policies are still more significant in many respects than EC regional policies; for example, total regional expenditure by national governments greatly exceeds that by Community aid-giving bodies. In addition, the range of regional policy measures at national level exceeds those at Community level. Furthermore, Community level funding by regional bodies has actually tended to operate via national governments. The optimum assignment of regional powers between different levels of authority is difficult to determine and the process has been likened to that of providing public goods (Armstrong 1985). It may well be that the role of national governments, both in formulating and implementing regional policy, represents the most appropriate division between the federal and the national level. It is national governments which are most knowledgeable about their own specific regional problems, and they have sought to retain their power in the Community. Even in those countries where regional power is decentralized, such as

West Germany and Italy, EC regional policy has tended to strengthen national control (Keating and Jones 1985).

The rationale of Community regional policy is to ensure that regional assistance is channelled to those regions which have the most acute problems. However, the prosperous areas are reluctant to see income transferred to weaker regions. For example, in West Germany the Finanzausgleich which provides financial compensation was challenged at the beginning of 1986 in the West German constitutional court by six German regions which thought they were either contributing too much or not receiving enough. Since regions are reluctant to accept national transfers where one might expect citizens to have some regard for the plight of their fellow citizens, then there is likely to be even less willingness to support transfers for weaker regions in other Community countries. Nevertheless, on equity grounds such transfers are justified since even the poorest areas in West Germany are still better off than the richest areas of Portugal and Greece.

A Community regional policy has had to be pursued to limit the excessive degree of support granted by countries at a national level to support their own weaker regions when such regions actually lie above the EC average on basic indicators such as employment, income per head, etc. Therefore, the Community has had to control carefully the degree of support given by countries such as West Germany to assist regions which are prosperous by European standards. For example, in 1986 the EC Commission asked the West German government for an explanation of its alleged subsidy to Daimler-Benz to build a new plant in Baden-Wurtemburg in an area not eligible for special regional assistance. The local authorities there replied that it was merely general aid to improve the region's industrial infrastructure.

The Belgian government, which was lavishing regional assistance widely to avoid cultural divisions, has similarly had to curtail the breadth of its regional assistance. Both the number of regions designated for regional aid and the level of aid have had to be reworked in such a way as to prevent non-needy areas from attracting an undue share of regional aid. EC regional policy has both co-ordinated national policies and also offered structural aid in sectors such as iron and steel, and agriculture. It then moved on, after the first enlargement, to the establishment of a specific Regional Development Fund.

D   Regional funds: an appraisal

This section examines five EC aid-giving bodies: the European Coal and Steel Community (ECSC); the European Agricultural Guarantee and Guidance Fund (EAGGF); the European Investment Bank (EIB); the European Social Fund (ESF); and the European

Regional Development Fund (ERDF). Whilst these are covered separately it should be borne in mind that some schemes have been financed jointly; for example, ERDF subsidies on EIB loans. Together, EIB loans plus ERDF grants have covered up to 80 per cent of the total costs of some local developments.

Any appraisal of these structural funds is influenced by one's judgement about the effectiveness of intervention, in particular at a Community level, and by whether one's regional priorities are industrial or agricultural. Some of the traditional industrial regions have formed an association for Régions Européennes de Tradition Industrielle (RETI: Association of Traditional Industrial Regions of Europe) to resist any further erosion of their regional assistance towards less developed areas, such as those in the Mediterranean. Over the years the operation of the various funds has been modified and improved with the establishment of clearer priorities. Furthermore, under the SEA (Article 23) a new title has been included in the Treaty on economic and social cohesion.

In 1987 the Commission proposed that budgetary resources for the structural funds should be doubled in real terms, rising from about ECU 7 billion in 1987 to around ECU 14 billion in 1992. It also proposed to concentrate the activities of the funds on five specific objectives. The first objective was to help less developed regions to catch up (that is, those with per capita GDP less than 75 per cent of the Community average); these regions cover some 20 per cent of the EC's population. It was proposed that ERDF appropriations to these regions would rise from 70 to 80 per cent. While the second objective is to assist conversion in declining industrial regions, the Commission proposed that ERDF aid for industry was to be cut back from 30 to 20 per cent of ERDF appropriations. The third aim is to combat long-term unemployment and the fourth is to facilitate the occupational integration of young people. The final objective is to speed up the adjustment of agricultural structures and to promote the development of rural areas. The EAGGF will be used for this and also contribute to the first objective of helping less developed regions. The ERDF will also contribute to these two objectives, plus that of assisting conversion in declining industrial regions. The ESF is expected to contribute to the achievement of all five objectives. The Commission's approach is based on complementing national measures, consultative partnership and in particular even greater use of programming (with a gradual disappearance of EC help to small projects). Procedures are to be simplified with better co-ordination and a reuse of dormant commitments (Commission July 1987).

The European Coal and Steel Community (ECSC). The coal industry's fortunes have fluctuated very much in the post-war period, with initial expansion to fuel Europe's industrial recovery giving way to contraction as greater energy choice emerged between different fuels in a competitive multi-fuel situation. The EC has pursued a low-cost energy policy – unlike that in agriculture. In the 1960s as the Community enjoyed super-economic growth it imported cheap oil on a large scale and also found it cheaper to purchase coal from some low-cost world suppliers. The EC recognized that it had to be as competitive as possible with other countries which were using cheap oil, such as Japan. While the energy policy chosen appeared judicious at that time from a macroeconomic perspective, at the microeconomic level it resulted in massive regional and structural decline in coal-mining areas. Whereas these could be tackled satisfactorily when there was buoyant growth in the economy, by reabsorbing displaced workers into new industries, the decline became far more difficult to cushion during the 1970s and the 1980s.

Even at the macro level, the decision taken to rely on the import of oil led to problems as oil prices were raised by the OPEC cartel and balance of payments positions deteriorated in EC countries. The rather insecure and now high-cost oil imports moved the Community to a greater recognition of the benefits of indigenous energy supplies. Meanwhile, a slowing down in the rate of economic growth created by the energy crisis has reduced the overall demands for energy inputs. Oil prices have been volatile and with the weakening of the OPEC cartel prices have again become more competitive – this is desirable at the macro level for oil importers, but is detrimental to the future of the coal industry in the Community.

The ECSC has made loans to both the coal and the iron and steel industry to finance investment projects, schemes for conversion and housing modernization and improvement (at a very low rate of interest); also, grants have been made to assist the redeployment of workers. The ECSC has been able to finance its expenditure partly from a levy imposed on sales of its products. Cheap and large loans are also available to firms prepared to move into coal and steel regions.

Unlike the coal industry, the steel industry experienced a longer period of economic expansion until the early 1970s when it was hit very badly by the depression. Traditional steelmaking areas operating old-fashioned small-scale plants and in close proximity to local sources of ore have been closed down. New giant plants have been constructed, many at coastal sites, since competitors such as Japan led the way with tremendous cost advantages accruing from economies of scale. Conversion has become very important to try to create and transform undertakings capable of reabsorbing redundant workers. To redeploy workers emphasis has been given to resettlement allowances and to financing the acquisition of vocational training skills. Under the Davignon Plan the EC steel industry has been greatly restructured and slimmed down to enhance its competitive efficiency. For example, in 1986 just under 63 000 workers in the ECSC were affected by restructuring.

The European Agricultural Guarantee and Guidance Fund (EAGGF). This fund was developed to administer the CAP and because of the high price support most of the expenditure has consisted of guaranteeing prices, with only a small proportion being concerned with guidance expenditure. CAP expenditure helps all farmers and not only those smaller farmers in very peripheral regions. It is therefore neither an efficient agricultural policy nor an effective regional policy. However, efforts have been made to link the EAGGF more closely to regional policy and one indication of this was in 1974 when 150 million EUA were transferred from the Guidance section of the EAGGF to the ERDF (Vanhove and Klassen 1980, p. 422). The larger farms in the EC operating in regions with favourable conditions have gained most, especially those involved in grain and dairy production which have received very high price support. Although structural measures have been developed very much to favour those in southern Europe, expenditure on this has had to be curtailed because of the undue weight given to the Guarantee section of the Fund.

Structural measures have generally given farmers a minimum of 25 per cent of the total cost of projects for modernization of farms, rationalization, improvement of processing and marketing; help with movement of workers from the land, plus help to mountain and hill farming in less favoured areas (and the latter scheme was strengthened further in March 1987). Also, restructuring aid has been extended to the fishing industry. The Commission has proposed a focus on particular priorities in order to avoid spreading resources too thinly and the reform of the structural funds is assisting this policy (Commission August 1987).

While policies to assist declining sectors such as agriculture are vital, they can only cushion its decline. They cannot maintain, let alone increase agricultural employment in the future. Hence there is a need to develop related ancillary activities, such as food processing, plus other activities to increase handicraft, industrial and service employment in rural areas. Thus the EC has moved forward with integrated development programmes, particularly in the Mediterranean. This is sensible since reliance on the CAP price support policy has little effect on some Mediterranean areas, such as Andalucia in Spain, with its landless labourers and many unemployed workers (Duchêne *et al.* 1985, p. 184).

The European Investment Bank (EIB). The EIB has been empowered to provide loans for projects which fall into the following categories: for developing less developed regions; for modernizing or converting undertakings, or for developing fresh activities; and for projects of common interest to member states.

The Bank's subscribed capital was doubled to ECU 28 800 million from 1 January 1986. Italy's subscription was raised from that date to 19.127 per cent — the level each subscribed by Germany, France and the UK. However, most of the Bank's funds are raised on international capital markets at keen terms because it has a secure and high credit rating. The EIB is a very important source of long-term loans and has occasionally provided a guarantee for raising loans. Its loan terms depend upon the conditions prevailing in international capital markets and also on the projects themselves. Loans to industry are normally for a period of seven to twelve years and up to 20 years for infrastructure projects. Borrowing is at a fixed rate of interest and is a very useful source of funds for risky projects (Vanhove and Klassen 1980, p. 413). Repayment of the loan may also include a period of grace before any repayment of the principle needs to be made.

The Bank has been of greater significance in terms of total lending than some of the other much heralded and better known funds. Table 6.1 shows the extent of EIB lending, of which nearly 90 per cent has occurred within the EC rather than in conjunction with the EC's European Development Fund.

An appraisal of the EIB's activities, especially from the viewpoint of a regional dimension, would point to some of the following deficiencies. The Bank is not concerned solely with regional imbalance but with other functions (as laid down at the beginning of this section). It has financed common projects of joint interest to Community countries, such as the airbus project. Much of this expenditure on new industrial investment often occurs outside weaker regions. Although the EIB is concerned with financing improvements to the infrastructure, again much of this occurs in developed regions; for example, the EIB has agreed to lend ECU 1.4 billion for building the Channel Tunnel, resulting in more investment in the south-east of England. If one wished to focus financial assistance purely on the problem regions then the multi-purpose role of the Bank would have to be diminished. For those who favour a more interventionist and subsidized approach to regional development, the EIB would appear to be too much of a commercial institution, providing repayable loans and not grants (except when supplemented by a small subsidy from the ERDF).

The EIB is never a source of the whole finance for a project, but provides up to half of the cost, with the borrower having to obtain the remainder from other financial institutions. The Bank's lending,

Table 6.1   EIB Financing, 1959 to 1986

	Amount in ECU	%
Loans from EIB own resources and guarantees[1]	**46 490.5**	**87.3**
within the Community	42 142.8	79.1
outside the Community	4 347.7	8.2
Financing provided from other resources[2]	**6 746.9**	**12.7**
(accounted for in the Special Section)		
within the Community, from the resources of the New Community Instrument (NCI) for borrowing and lending[3]	5 463.6	10.3
outside the Community from member states or Community budgetary funds	1 283.3	2.4
Grand total	**53 237.4**	**100.0**
within the Community	47 606.4	89.4
(of which guarantees)	(622.1)	(1.2)
outside the Community	5 631.0	10.6

1   Loans in Portugal and Spain have been recorded as being outside the Community until the end of 1985.
2   Excluding Euratom loans and loans on special conditions made available under the Lomé Conventions as described by the Commission of the European Communities.
3   The New Community Instrument has operated since 1979, through which the Commission transfers money to the Bank for specific purposes.

Source: EIB Annual Report (1986) Luxembourg p. 23.

now approaching World Bank levels, was focused initially upon large projects. Some of these have been extremely capital-intensive, with the consequence that apart from workers employed in the initial building work, they have failed to mop up surplus labour. It has also been argued that too much finance has been canalized into polluting industries, such as the motor, chemical and nuclear power industries (Lewenhak 1982). With the benefit of hindsight, society is now much more conscious of the environmental externalities associated with these industries. But in any energy investment a difficult choice has to be made between coal, oil, gas and nuclear power, with none of them being completely immune from some undesirable environmental impact.

The emphasis on financing large projects gradually diminished after the introduction in the late 1960s of a global loan system for allocating funds to financial intermediaries to on-lend to medium-sized firms. These intermediaries can be of many types but are mainly banking institutions. As such they are concerned primarily with the application of normal banking principles, especially with the capacity to repay loans. In some respects, from the perspective of promoting regional employment or steering funds to key sectors, they may be the wrong people to act as intermediaries. However, at least global loans were a step forward and a recognition that financing big projects *per se* was a mistake.

Large projects in 'growth-pole' locations have not only provided few jobs, but often added to over-capacity, with the same vulnerability to decline as many traditional industries. Smaller and medium-sized firms in contrast have offered more potential for stable indigenous growth. By the mid-1980s over half of all the Bank's industrial investment was under the global loan system. However, this again has not been as effective as expected in creating jobs and it has been suggested that more of its loans should be switched from manufacturing to the growing service sector (Pinder 1986).

The EIB is undoubtedly attractive to borrowers in countries which would have to pay high domestic interest rates and pay off loans over a short time period. But while EIB loans can make investments look more favourable, it is a market-based institution and can only respond when there is a demand from borrowers. In a recession when investment intentions are gloomy and pessimistic, investment is low and yet it is precisely at this time that investment needs to be stimulated. Despite innovations by the EIB in its lending policy, investment is demand-determined and has tended to fall away during recession. Some borrowers faced repayment problems, exacerbated by exchange rate changes – to alleviate the latter governments have provided some element of protective compensation for borrowers. The British government felt that this had become too costly and though it was retained for loans to the public sector, it announced in 1985 that it was no longer willing to cover exchange risks on small loans: this policy change is somewhat inconsistent with the overall strategy of helping small businesses.

The European Social Fund (ESF). The ESF has been in operation since 1958 and a full coverage of all its activities will not be given here, but merely signposts indicating the Fund's changing direction and emphasis. Originally it was not a proper instrument of regional policy, but a major turning point in its activities occurred during the 1970s. In 1971 the Fund was reformed, with increased finance, and even greater changes were brought about in 1974 with the Council's adoption of the Commission's Social Action Programme. Its priorities were to create full and better employment; improvement of living and working conditions; and participation by employees in the process of decision-making. There was in addition a statement of many other proposals in producing a worthy list of desirable social developments (Shanks 1977).

Implementing new developments was difficult against the background of a worsening economic climate. The incidence of unemployment has risen, in particular affecting young people seeking to join the labour market for the first time, but also the duration of unemployment is even greater among older workers as long-term unemployment has become well entrenched. Hence the ESF now targets its expenditure increasingly on these two groups. In addition, the Fund provides assistance to other groups: migrant workers; the disabled; women returning to employment and often requiring re-training; and workers adversely affected by new technology. The latter is a major preoccupation of the Community and to improve technological performance and to mitigate any adverse labour market consequences, the ESF now insists that all its training projects are not only to have a vocational orientation, but must include a minimum amount of time devoted to new technology.

The ESF has recognized the regional dimension of its activities by allocating 44.5 per cent of its funds in the EC(12) to super-priority regions, while remaining expenditure also focuses mainly on areas of high unemployment and areas facing problems of readaptation. The areas most adversely affected are those depressed areas such as southern Italy and also whole countries such as Greece, Portugal, the Republic of Ireland and Northern Ireland.

It can be seen then that the ESF is concerned with a very narrow interpretation of social policy. It focuses mainly on employment/unemployment and training, rather than the usual extensive concern of social policy with health and social welfare. In transferring resources, many of these in the early years went to West Germany which was actively carrying out vocational training and resettlement, but in more recent years resources have been channelled increasingly towards the poorer countries, such as Italy. For example, the distribution of ESF financing in 1986 continued to favour Italy, with a share of 21.72 per cent. The shares of other countries were: UK 16.23 per cent, France 14.82 per cent, Spain 13.93 per cent, Ireland 9.40 per cent, Portugal 8.76 per cent, and Greece 5.60 per cent.

The share of EC expenditure devoted to the ESF is still far too small. In 1985 it faced demands for almost ECU 5 billion, but it had resources of only ECU 2.5 billion, and in the event less than ECU 2.2 billion was actually committed to new schemes. In 1986 Iberia began to take a large slice of the Social Fund, putting together acceptable proposals far more quickly than had been anticipated by officials in Brussels. The funding to both the ESF and ERDF could be expanded significantly – if only agricultural expenditure could be reduced. Indeed, there may be a case for merging the two Funds and co-ordinating their operations more closely. This is because the Social Fund's pursuit of supply-side labour market measures can only be really effective if the ERDF succeeds in raising the level of regional investment demand; then the highly trained and retrained workers can be reabsorbed into the labour market. The ESF currently finances the running costs of schemes and not the capital costs, whereas the ERDF finances subsidies to capital costs of investment.

The main problem in the EC is the high level of aggregate unemployment and its uneven distribution which adversely affects the welfare of its citizens. Measures such as Community-wide finance and payment of unemployment benefits would be a significant step forward. Certainly, Community problems have deepened and extended beyond some concerns in the ESF about whether workers are deriving sufficient job satisfaction, or are participating enough in their firms − too many workers are without any jobs and the Social Fund is overwhelmed by applications, often delaying the payments paid to applicants.

Those who regard the EC as a Community, rather than as a market, and seek an upward equalization of social standards must be rather disappointed by the limited progress which is being made. At a time of high unemployment, when the need for social policy has grown, the meagre resources provided have failed to match these needs. Furthermore, many draft directives on social policy have been blocked in the Council by member governments opposed to active social intervention at Community level.

The European Regional Development Fund (ERDF). There was no explicit call for a common regional policy in the Treaty of Rome and it was only after the decision taken to enlarge the Community that the ERDF was finally established in 1975. Its allocations have grown from ECU 257.6 million (or 4.8 per cent of the EC Budget) to just over ECU 3 billion (or nearly 9 per cent of the Budget) in 1986. The ERDF (or FEDER − Fonds Européen de Développement Regional) has been assisted in its operation by two Committees upon which national officials have sat: the Regional Policy Committee and the Fund Committee.

The ERDF covered some 60 per cent of the EC's land area and some 40 per cent of its population. It has provided grants for industry, services and crafts and much of its investment has focused on infrastructure, such as transport, energy and water engineering projects. This is shown in Table 6.2.

ERDF grants are normally half of the investment costs and up to 55 per cent for projects of exceptional regional significance. For projects with a large investment cost, the rate of grant available falls and generally lies between 30 and 50 per cent. The regions eligible for assistance were those designated by national governments, and ERDF funding was concentrated very heavily on a small number of

Table 6.2   ERDF financing in the EC, 1975–85

Type of investment	Amount granted (in m ECUs)	%
Industry, services and craft	2 481.52	17.7
Infrastructure	11 347.78	81.0
Studies	43.63	0.3
National programmes of Community interest	133.98	1.0
Total	14 006.91	100.0

Source: Commission of the European Communities, ERDF in Figures 1975–85 (1985), p. 4.

regions, especially in Italy and the UK; for example, from 1975–86 the three Italian regions – Campania, Sicilia and Calabria – received some 20 per cent of the ERDF expenditure quota. By 1986 five of the ten most assisted regions were located in the Iberian peninsula (Commission, ERDF Report for 1986, p. 43).

The system of fixed national quotas for ERDF expenditure was considered to be advantageous to Italy and the other new members of the Community which experienced severe regional problems. However, these quotas meant that the ERDF lacked sufficient discretion in allocating its finance and some critics have emphasized its disadvantages; for example, '*FEDER possédant une caractéristique unique parmi les instruments de la Communauté qui handicapant son actions: l'attribution aux Etats membres de certains quotas*' (Moussis 1982, p. 221). In 1979 some amendments were made which allowed the Community to introduce specific regional development policies, of which one of the most significant was the concept of a small non-quota section of 5 per cent of ERDF finance which could apply outside the nationally-designated areas. This provided a very limited degree of additional flexibility, but was a significant step by the EC in trying to wrestle regional policy away from tight national control (Keating and Jones 1985, p. 37). This led the Commission to propose an enlargement of the non-quota section to 20 per cent of the ERDF and it also sought to concentrate the quota expenditure on a smaller number of regions defined according to Community criteria; but these proposals were very controversial.

Eventually, agreement was reached on a system of flexible quota guidelines. Instead of each country being given a fixed percentage quota, this is now based on a minimum and maximum limit. The lower limit constituted the minimum which a country was entitled to receive and the upper limit was the maximum it could attain. The total minimum expenditure was set at 88.63 per cent so that the Commission had discretion over the small remaining marginal expenditure up to 100 per cent of the ERDF's funds. Countries

Table 6.3   ERDF national shares – 1986 percentages

Country	Lower limit	Upper limit
Italy	21.62	28.79
Spain	17.97	23.93
UK	14.50	19.31
Portugal	10.66	14.20
Greece	8.36	10.64
France	7.48	9.96
Ireland	3.82	4.61
Germany	2.55	3.40
Netherlands	0.68	0.91
Belgium	0.61	0.82
Denmark	0.34	0.46
Luxembourg	0.04	0.06
Total	88.63	117.09

Source: ERDF Twelfth Annual Report for 1986, p. 5.

submit many applications so that they can attract some of the 12 per cent marginal expenditure. Obviously the theoretical maximum set at 117.09 per cent of the fund in 1986 was unattainable. Table 6.3 shows the range of national shares in ERDF in the enlarged Community.

Spain is now second only to Italy in its ERDF entitlement, with nearly 75 per cent of its national territory and 48 per cent of its population in assisted areas. Portugal is fourth in its entitlement and has shown an ability to put together viable projects for all its regions eligible for assistance (with the exception of Lisbon). This yielded some $189.7 million, compared with $107.8 million from the ESF and $32.9 million from the EAGGF (*Financial Times*, Survey of Portugal, 12 March 1987). Furthermore, if the amount of aid received was expressed per head, then countries such as Portugal, Greece and Ireland would move up the league table of national shares and others such as Italy and the UK would move down.

ERDF expenditure has grown and between 1975 and 1986 it created and maintained nearly 764 000 new jobs and most of these were newly-created jobs (Commission, ERDF Report for 1986, p. 75). The ERDF has moved to a preference for financing programmes rather than individual projects and it expects at least 20 per cent of a nation's share of Fund expenditure to be spent on programmes. It was hoped that this would improve co-ordination and coherence, reducing the time and effort spent in assessing each individual project. The programme approach increases the role of the Comunity in regional policy. Programmes are either Community programmes or national programmes of Community interest. There are also integrated development operations bringing all loans and grants together to concentrate on particular areas; finally, there are integrated Mediterranean programmes.

While the ERDF has moved in the right direction, its financial resources are still far too small and only a fraction of those spent by member states (Armstrong 1985). The magnitude of agricultural expenditure has curtailed the finance available for the ERDF. In addition, it was easiest to reach a political compromise which gave all countries some shares in the Fund's allocation − however small − diluting the limited finance available. EC regional expenditure should also add to regional expenditure by national governments, but unfortunately instead of it being additional, it has often been substituted for some national regional spending. Nevertheless, governments like to claim that in considering their spending plans they make allowance for the inflow of EC funds and without them suggest that their regional spending would be even lower.

Part III   UK regional experience
The UK has suffered from three particular problems. As the first European country to industrialize it has also become the first to deindustrialize. Its over-commitment to staple industries and their subsequent decline has resulted in deindustrialization with very severe effects on traditional regions. The second problem is that the rate of economic growth in the UK has been considerably lower than in other EC countries in the post-war years. Although during the 1980s the UK's relative rate of economic growth *vis-à-vis* its continental neighbours has greatly improved, much of the growth has been in the tertiary sector. Thirdly, the UK economy lies on the periphery of the Community's core area. Whereas the UK's location was central for trade with the Americas, the reorientation of trade towards the central areas of the Community has inevitably intensified the problem of regional imbalance.

The North-South divide has become very pronounced in the UK. The south-east and East Anglia were the only regions in the UK with GDP over £5000 per head in 1985 and an unemployment rate of under 10 per cent of the working population. If the depressed Inner City London boroughs were excluded, then the two nations' division would be accentuated further. Most of the traditional manufacturing jobs have been lost in the North, while most of the service jobs have been created in the South. For example, the sun-belt area stretching down the M4 corridor from Cambridge to Bristol reflects a growing concentration of high-technology sectors such as electronics. Some infrastructure demands in the South are high and government needs to monitor the regional implications of its own expenditure. Its dilemma is that if it does not maintain the attractiveness of the south-east by improving communications such as the Channel Tunnel then even that region may decline below the

European average. A synthetic index based on GDP and unemployment for the EC(9) from 1977–81 indicated that most UK regions had fallen below the EC average of 100. The UK's most prosperous area, Greater London, reached a level of 72 per cent of Hamburg, whilst its poorest region, Northern Ireland, was only 23 per cent of Hamburg.

Regional performance is closely related to national performance, with the more prosperous regions tending to lie very much in West Germany and the poorer regions in the UK, Ireland and southern Europe. EC regional funding is at best a palliative, though in Ireland is more significant when calculated per head of population. For the UK both the limited total regional funds available and their insufficient concentration on its problems have reduced the effectiveness of EC policy. UK regions now receive even less as a consequence of southern enlargement and its rural areas, which are above the EC's new GDP per head level; for example, the Scottish Highlands and Islands, seem likely to suffer. The UK's depressed industrial areas will also be squeezed eventually. The UK even has problems in its capital city where depressed conditions have led to riots in Brixton and Tottenham, yet under EC regional policy capital cities have been exempt from aid (except Dublin).

Given the magnitude of regional problems in the UK it seems paradoxical that instead of the government increasing the level of regional expenditure it has actually reduced it since 1979. It has been critical of the costs of regional policy in redistributing employment rather than creating many new jobs. The assisted areas have been reduced to cover a smaller percentage of the working population and after a move away from automatic investment grants to selective grants in 1984, it was announced finally in 1988 that automatic grants were to be scrapped. This greatly reduces the distinction between developed and intermediate areas, though new schemes are available to help small companies in development areas. It has been argued that the direction of governmental policy in the UK could be further improved by better co-ordination and by giving depressed English regions their own regional development agencies with wide powers (Armstrong and Taylor 1987).

Given the inadequate level of UK regional funding, depressed regions have had to tap EC regional funds. However, a full comparison of EC regional transfers shows a predominantly agricultural imprint, so that between 1973 and the end of 1986 the UK received £8632 million from the EAGGF, compared with only £1600 million from the ESF and £1519 million from the ERDF. A regional breakdown of ERDF commitments 1975–86 shows that Scotland received nearly a quarter of these, with 15 per cent each going to Wales and to the north of England, nearly 14 per cent to north-west England, and 10 per cent to Northern Ireland (Commission, ERDF Report for 1986). In 1986, UK receipts from the ERDF were £298 million, from the ESF £335 million, but from the EAGGF receipts were £1385 million (HMSO 1987).

To maximize the return from Community funds it is necessary to submit as many sound and well-conceived projects as possible. Applications have been rejected where they have not been fully documented or failed to meet the formal conditions on assisted areas, costs, number of jobs created, and so on. Awareness of the ERDF is high and in the UK applications for infrastructure projects are made via the Department of the Environment and private sector applications are made via the Department of Industry. However, the House of Lords has concluded gloomily that 'the Regional Fund caused very little to happen that would not have happened anyway, and that the principle of additionality was largely disregarded in practice' (Select Committee 1984).

The ESF has been a less well-known source of regional support — applications are made via the Department of Employment. In some ways the ESF offers fertile ground for applications since there are no national quotas — unlike the ERDF. In 1985 the UK submitted over 2200 applications to the ESF and the Fund is heavily over-subscribed. Applicants may be safer to ask for only 25 per cent of their expenditure to be covered to be sure of receiving this rather than asking for over 50 per cent.

The government squeeze on public expenditure has encouraged local authorities to establish direct links with the EC; more so than in France with its more centralized system (despite some steps to decentralize in the 1980s). Local authorities can use ERDF grants as a substitute for loans on which they would have to pay interest. While there are additional costs involved in seeking EC finance, those authorities which have appointed liaison officers, particularly in designated areas, have been most successful in tapping Community funds. This indicates that the employment of additional staff putting together viable programmes, would be worthwhile as long as the inflow of EC funds exceeded the additional costs of employing them.

EC regional funding may at times appear something of a charade, with complaints about slow receipt of funds. Nevertheless, local authorities, especially those in areas unscheduled for national regional assistance, would probably prefer to have closer direct links with Brussels than with London. But there is no guarantee that their programmes would be approved by a larger bureaucracy dealing with regional affairs in Brussels because of limited funds and the excessive number of claimants. In conclusion it is important that receipts from EC funds are fully maximized and in order to improve the Community's image areas need to be made aware of the specific contribution by the EC.

7 Monetary integration

Part I The characteristics of the international monetary system: fixed and floating exchange rates

The growth of trade between countries requires a system for currency exchange and essentially the choice is between some kind of fixed or floating mechanism. In the early post-war years the international economy opted for a system of fixed exchange rates, after the traumatic experience of the 1930s. This new international mechanism was very much an Anglo-American creation and led to the setting up of the International Monetary Fund (IMF). It was based upon a fixed exchange rate system in which the dollar was fixed in relation to gold and the dollar as the pivot of the system was fixed in relation to other international currencies. Where countries experienced disequilibrium, financial assistance was forthcoming from the IMF, and when countries reached a position of fundamental disequilibrium they were expected to adjust their exchange rates.

The fixed exchange rate system served the international economy well in providing the certainty and stability which was needed by traders and investors. It provided a 'known element' in an uncertain world where there are too many variables. Nevertheless, it ran into specific difficulties since there was a misinterpretation of IMF rules and countries in fundamental disequilibrium sought tenaciously to defend the parity of their currencies. The countries with balance of payments deficits were reluctant to accept the political consequences of devaluing their currencies. They had sizeable reserves trying to ward off speculation, but usually succumbed eventually. Problems were compounded by the lack of equivalent pressure on countries with balance of payments surpluses to revalue their currencies, and though one country's balance of payments deficit is matched by another country's balance of payments surplus, the countries in surplus did not rush to revalue for fear of making the task of their exporters too difficult.

The international monetary system was undermined by growing balance of payments deficits in the USA and a greater reluctance by other countries to hold dollars. This led ultimately to a crisis at the beginning of the 1970s with the break from gold and the devaluation of the dollar. Massive speculation and increasing divergence between national rates of inflation and economic performance brought the fixed exchange rate system to a state of collapse. Thus in the early 1970s the international economy moved over, with great euphoria, to a regime of floating exchange rates.

Floating the exchange rate seemed to offer an additional policy instrument, instead of being a policy target of economic management, enabling countries to pursue their own domestic economic policies. It was assumed that any balance of payments deficit/ surplus would be adjusted automatically by appropriate exchange rate changes. It was assumed that markets were more likely to arrive at the 'right' exchange rate than were governments in administering a fixed rate − even if the latter were fixed at the correct level to begin with, the reluctance to alter it meant that it soon became the wrong rate of exchange. Countries would no longer need to hold massive reserves to defend their exchange rates, so floating exchange rates could help to alleviate the shortage of international liquidity. To the extent that there were uncertainties about exchange rates, then for a small cost traders and investors could protect themselves in forward markets.

Like most fundamental changes, the claims made were far in excess of what could be delivered by a floating exchange rate. While firms can protect themselves against exchange rate fluctuations, the uncertainty and costs are a particular handicap to smaller firms in international trade. The system has been characterized by marked instability of currencies which have fluctuated wildly in the short-term and in the long-term have still failed to settle at the correct levels. Smaller countries have found it difficult to withstand the sheer volume of capital movements as speculative capital has flowed in and then out of their currencies. In countries with depreciating currencies, a nominal fall in exchange rate was not translated into the same effective exchange rate fall since it stoked up inflationary pressures. This resulted inevitably in the need for other policy instruments to be used, negating the very freedom which floating exchange rates were supposed to confer to domestic policy-makers. In countries with appreciating currencies, such as West Germany, this has not markedly affected its trade performance, partly because its specialization has been in exporting goods such as capital equipment where price is less important than the technical capacity of machines which are well-designed, reliable and delivered on time.

Floating exchange rates have failed to live up to their expectations and imposed significant costs. These include adjustment costs of temporary misalignments; greater uncertainty in trading products which has contributed to a slowdown in capital formation; a rise in protectionism by countries whose exchange rate has been pushed up too far; and an additional increase in world inflation. Furthermore, any substantial degree of national monetary autonomy has been something of a 'myth' (Tsoukalis 1986). Yet the great overhang of mobile capital has precluded a full return to international fixed exchange rates, though it has led to suggestions for a tax to dampen excessive capital mobility. What has occurred has been an attempt to create some exchange rate stability between the major blocs, and in particular within the EC via the EMS. In other words, to try to obtain internationally the best of both worlds from a blend of flexible and fixed rates.

Part II   Economic and Monetary Union (EMU) and the European Monetary System (EMS)

A   The characteristics of optimum currency areas
An optimum currency area (OCA) is a group of countries linked together through fixed exchange rates. Major academic contributions were made in this field during the 1960s and 1970s. They provided a useful background to consideration of the viability of EMU, even though this goes further than OCAs in seeking common economic policies and ultimately a common currency (Coffey 1977, p. 4).

The ability to create and maintain an OCA is based essentially upon the extent to which there are forces leading to convergence within the area, without necessitating an adjustment of the exchange rate. A key criterion used to justify an OCA was that of factor mobility (Mundell 1961). His pioneering theory is open to criticism on the grounds that the direction of factor flows is ambiguous, since capital may flow more to the dynamic region while labour may be relatively immobile and reluctant to move from the depressed region. Impediments still remain to the free mobility of labour in terms of linguistic difficulties, lack of skills and shortage of finance, etc. Although the EC has free labour mobility, much of the immigration has arrived from non-EC countries.

A subsequent contribution stressed the importance of 'openness' in the economy (McKinnon 1963). Highly open economies which are very dependent on trade will be able to rely on fiscal and monetary policies without needing to alter their exchange rate. Highly open economies have a high marginal propensity both to import and to export products. Where a balance of payments deficit exists then deflation can rectify this, with only a small amount of deflation being required to restore a balance of payments equilibrium since much of the cut-back in expenditure will be on reduced imports. Countries will also prefer fixed exchange rates and eschew floating exchange rates where currency depreciation is highly inflationary (and workers do not have money illusion, so that wage inflationary pressure is sparked off again). However, note that for stronger countries fixed exchange rates are more inflationary than allowing the exchange rate to appreciate in value.

EC countries have become much more open with the removal of intra-Community trading barriers and intra-EC imports and exports as a percentage of GDP more than doubled between 1960 and 1985.

Intra-trade is particularly high for the Benelux countries, though lower for the UK. From the latter one may infer that the UK was correct not to join the EMS exchange rate mechanism, though in fact its growing trade with the Community means that there is not now a large difference between UK intra-trade with the EC compared with that conducted by other countries, such as Italy and France, with the Community.

Another criterion for an OCA which has been enunciated has been that of diversification (Kenen 1969). Highly-diversified economies will be able to manage without having to rely on exchange rate changes, since if demand in one export sector falls, the effect will be small — assuming again a high mobility of labour and capital into other sectors. Although in a depression most export industries might be affected seriously, the larger economies in the Community are sufficiently diversified to withstand this, more so than the smaller economies. It can be seen in examining individual EC economies that some countries may be prime members of an OCA on particular criteria, but not on others (Presley and Dennis 1976). For example, the Benelux countries are highly open, but they are much less diversified than the economies of the larger member states of the Community.

A far more important problem which has beset economies has been that of inflation and it has been argued that a similar national propensity to inflate should be used as the main criterion for an OCA (Magnifico 1973, part 2, pp. 43–81). Inflation rates diverge since countries have different preferences and a different trade-off between unemployment and inflation. In any kind of monetary union some of the countries have to sacrifice their preferences, either conforming to one preference — usually that of the dominant country — or agreeing on a common objective between themselves. Greater problems arise where countries have different trade-offs, since even if they were to agree on the same unemployment preference, countries with Phillips curves closer to the origin, such as West Germany, have lower inflation. Institutional labour market practices partly underlie its lower wage-pushfulness; for example, its industrial unions and system of co-determination (*mitbestimmung*).

Since the Phillips curve trade-off has partly broken down it has been argued that any success in reducing unemployment can only be temporary; hence, governments have little choice except to aim for price stability. This led to more persuasive views on the prospects for EMU (Presley and Dennis 1976). However, the monetarist approach of controlling the rate of growth of the money supply to create lower and convergent inflation has run into problems in defining and controlling money supply satisfactorily.

Where the four criteria for an OCA exist, then the case for EMU is strong. The USA provides a shining example to which the EC aspires, in which the dollar totally fulfils the true functions of money across a large geographical group of states. Furthermore, it has been argued that any misgivings one might harbour about abandoning the independent use of one's own exchange rate is misplaced where a complete union exists; that is, with economic policy co-ordination, a pool of foreign exchange reserves and a common Central Bank (El-Agraa 1985). However, where workers do suffer from money illusion, where only a pseudo-union exists (i.e. incomplete EMU) and where different trade elasticities exist, then it may still be argued that a multiplicity of currencies provide the most flexible adjustment to tackle regional disparities.

B   The case for monetary union

Monetary union comprises the essential ingredients of fixed exchange rates and the integration of capital markets. The case for monetary union is closely tied up with the CAP since changing exchange rates results in changing prices and incomes for farmers (see Chapter 4 on agriculture and in particular the section on MCAs which were introduced to try to insulate agriculture from the consequences of these exchange rate alterations). Just as agriculture and monetary integration are closely linked, likewise other chapters show how monetary union needs integration in other spheres such as regional and budgetary policies.

Although MCAs helped to hold the CAP together, they resulted in various complications, misallocating resources by encouraging further high-cost production in countries such as West Germany. France was particularly upset to see West Germany adding further agricultural gains to its existing large industrial benefits. The issue of MCAs was a source of disruption in the general cosy relationship between Schmidt and Giscard d'Estaing in March 1979.

Apart from the connection between EMU and the CAP, there are positive financial benefits which accrue from having greater fixity of exchange rates. They provide stability, facilitating the flow of goods and capital. They also provide economies in the amount of reserve holdings since these are pooled. When one moves on from fixed exchange rates to the eventual outcome of one EC currency, then money can fully perform its function as a medium of exchange by eliminating the costs of money conversion. If the currency becomes a key currency, which is highly likely, then, like the dollar, benefits arise from seigniorage. Thus holders are prepared to hold that currency without pressing to exchange it, enabling the union, if it wishes, to run a balance of payments deficit.

By 1979 the EC had become increasingly disenchanted with the volatile system of floating exchange rates. It was also very concerned about the need to offer some alternative to the increasing problems afflicting the dollar. Apart from the traditional concern about the dominance of the dollar and dollar 'imperialism', which has often been expressed by countries such as France, there was growing recognition over time that the USA's economic situation was deteriorating. The USA shared the problem of many other countries in terms of rising costs of imported energy, and a high propensity to import goods from countries like Japan. But what constitutes a special and continuous long-term burden to the USA is its very high defence expenditure. The likelihood of a continuing balance of payments deficit in the USA makes holders of dollars keen to switch into other reserve currencies. Other national currencies have been reluctant or unable to fulfil this role; hence countries such as West Germany, fearful of a rush from dollars driving up the mark in an excessive and unstable way, have sought to develop a common EC monetary position.

C The winding road to EMU

EMU was not mentioned explicitly in the Treaty of Rome and it did not provide for fixed and immutable exchange rates, though Articles 103–109 did set down the principles of unrestricted currency convertibility, abolition of restrictions on capital movements, and the co-ordination of economic policy. To facilitate the latter, a Monetary Committee was established in 1958 and a Short-Term Economic Policy Committee in 1960. In 1964 there was formed a Committee of Governors of Central Banks, a Budgetary Policy Committee and a Medium-Term Policy Committee – these committees were later merged into a new Economic Policy Committee.

While exchange rates remained fixed there was little point in initiating EMU and it was only when pressures built up in the late 1960s for exchange rate adjustments that the issue assumed some urgency. The devaluation of sterling in 1967 was followed in 1969 by the devaluation of the French franc and the revaluation of the Deutschmark. There was concern to prevent countries from resorting once again to protectionist measures, since France, for example, had introduced import controls in the immediate aftermath of the 1968 crisis.

In 1965 and 1969 both P. Werner and R. Barre came up with proposals for monetary reform, with the latter proposing amongst other things, a system of monetary support and financial assistance to help economies experiencing balance of payments deficits. Both of these personalities were to be influential over the next few years in shaping EMU, after the decision to introduce it which was made at the European Summit in late 1969, under the leadership of Brandt and Pompidou.

While member states were persuaded of the benefits of EMU

there were significant differences in perspective and to reconcile these a working party was established under P. Werner. The differences were largely between France and Germany, but alongside the French were Belgium and Luxembourg, while the German view was shared by the Dutch and sometimes by the Italians. These different perspectives have been given the label 'Monetarist versus Economist'. The monetarist position was to favour a commitment to fixed exchange rates and pooling reserves along the lines of the second Barre Plan, published in March 1970. The competing economist strategy was not to rush ahead with monetary union since this was 'putting the cart before the horse' before economic co-ordination had been achieved. The West German approach was enshrined in the Schiller Plan in March 1970. This detailed plan divided up the progress towards EMU into clear stages and it was only in the final stage that a common currency was to be introduced. West Germany has been concerned to persuade other countries to reduce their excessive rates of inflation since under a fixed exchange rate system it felt that it was importing inflation from others. A greater co-ordination of macroeconomic policies, in particular to reduce wide national disparities in rates of inflation, has been an ongoing concern of West Germany.

The Werner Committee had to resolve these different perspectives, coming up with a compromise described as one of 'parallelism' (Kruse 1980, pp. 70–5); that is, parallel advance on both fronts in co-ordinating economic policy and moving forward by narrowing exchange rate margins, integrating capital markets and finally establishing a common currency and a single Central Bank. In March 1971 EMU was born and a stage-by-stage timetable was over-optimistically drawn up for its full achievement by 1980.

The main outcome was the creation of the 'snake' in 1972. Already the international monetary order had been shaken by the devaluation of the dollar and the Smithsonian Agreement in December 1971, after which there was a widening of the margins of currency fluctuations which had existed during the post-war period. The original ±1 per cent margin (a band of 2 per cent) was now widened internationally to ±2¼ per cent (a band of 4½ per cent). EC countries themselves decided to limit the range of their own member currencies to a band of 2¼ per cent, hence the band for the snake was half the width of the 4½ per cent 'tunnel'.

In preparation for the first enlargement of the Community, the UK, Denmark and Ireland were to be included. However, in June 1972 speculation drove both sterling and the Irish pound from the snake and the tunnel, followed a few days later by the Danish krone – though Denmark was able to rejoin the scheme later that year. Italy withdrew from it at the beginning of 1973, and in spring 1973 the international fixed exchange rate mechanism collapsed and was replaced by one of floating exchange rates. Although the snake continued between those EC countries which were able to participate, the system floated in relation to other currencies, and thus the snake ceased to be 'in the tunnel'. Between 1973 and 1978 there were widespread currency realignments and further departures from the snake; for example, by France on two occasions, 1974 and 1976, and Sweden, which had participated, withdrew in 1977. These have been described quite aptly as '*les vicissitudes du serpent monétaire*' (Moussis 1982, pp. 60–4).

The official target to achieve EMU by 1980 was dropped, but that did not prevent a plethora of new reports making further suggestions and recommendations. In 1974 Fourcade made a French proposal for a larger snake, a boa, which would have wider margins and allow countries to withdraw and re-enter the system. In 1975 a study group chaired by Marjolin reached the pessimistic conclusion that the prospects for EMU had been destroyed by discordant economic and monetary policies. Yet reports continued to circulate, with a group of prominent economists in 1975 suggesting the issue of a parallel currency, the Europa, for private use. A Belgian proposal by Tindemans in 1976 sought to strengthen the snake and suggested that a parallel currency might help. It also recommended greater co-ordination of economic policies, though it fell short of any target or deadlines for EMU. This was followed in the same year by a Dutch proposal (Duisenberg chairing the Council of Ministers) that European currencies ought to come closer together and that economic co-ordination might be improved by the creation of 'target zones'.

Despite adverse economic circumstances, a series of reports and favourable public opinion provided continued momentum; for example, Eurobarometer surveys recorded public opinion in favour of a European currency. There was highest support for a European currency to replace weaker national currencies in countries such as Italy, than in those with stronger currencies, such as West Germany. Although the ambitious goal for EMU was postponed, the Community made a renewed and modest start again via the EMS.

D Political initiatives to launch EMS membership

The political initiative for the EMS was taken by Roy Jenkins in his capacity as President of the EC Commission. He argued in a speech in Florence in October 1977 that in the new situation of high inflation and high unemployment, the EMS could help to alleviate both macroeconomic problems. This reflected the new economic analysis starting from lower inflation and from which would come lower unemployment. This approach differed from the original Phillips curve analysis in which inflation was inversely related to the level of unemployment.

The Community was in much need of redirection and the choice of EMS was timely and appealed to West Germany, and Jenkins courted their support in his speech at Bonn in December 1977. His ideas were well received since it was clear that the dollar faced major problems and there was an international currency vacuum which could only be filled by a West German monetary initiative. In the past, West Germany had accepted American monetary initiatives and American hegemony, showing a marked absence of responsibility for the international monetary system. EMS provided it with a historic opportunity to take the leading role (Strange 1980). West Germany would gain very much, both at an international level and also domestically from greater currency stability. There was concern in Germany about the damaging effects of over-valuation of the Deutschmark which were eroding its export competitiveness and it hoped that in EMS it would be able to depress the value of the mark. Chancellor Schmidt became a major instigator of EMS, but he had to contend with some internal scepticism; for example, there was concern about West Germany becoming more prone to inflation in EMS, whereas with the floating Deutschmark currency appreciation dampened inflation. There was also worry about the degree to which West Germany would have to support weaker currencies and weaker economies. Nevertheless, on balance the EMS seemed favourable and by co-operating with other EC countries it hoped to reduce the pressure on key currencies such as the mark and the dollar.

The next crucial step was to engage the support of Giscard d'Estaing in France, since Franco-German co-operation has formed the heart of Community developments. Politically, France wished to remain shoulder to shoulder with West Germany in the first division of world powers, rather than heading the second division. It offered France an opportunity to avoid a continual slide in the value of the franc, while a stronger franc would help the French to pursue an effective anti-inflation strategy. It was naturally important to enlist other countries into membership of EMS, though if that proved impossible then at least the range of credit facilities to support weaker members would not be dispersed so widely. It would be those weaker members which would enter the lower division of a two-tier Community.

Weaker countries, such as Italy, responded positively to avoid confirming its position in the second tier. Since Italy had taken the decision to become a founder member of earlier bodies like the ECSC at a time when its steel industry could have been swamped by more competitive imports, it recognized the benefits of being in at the beginning of any new developments – in particular if special arrangements could be made. It managed to secure a wider margin of ± 6 per cent for the lira, having guided the lira downwards to an undervalued level ready to enter the EMS. Italy also hoped that strict monetary obligations inherent in the system would be more effective than internal exhortations for restraint in dampening inflationary pressure. While Italy would have welcomed a fundamental restructuring of the Budget and the CAP to provide a greater transfer of resources, after a pause for reflection it joined the EMS.

The entry of the three major EC countries into the EMS was accompanied by the smaller countries which joined fully into the system. They were enthusiastic since small countries often manifest an even greater dependence upon trade as a percentage of GNP, and with high imports currency depreciation created inflationary instability. The Dutch have shared a close identity of interest with West Germany. Belgian influence was reflected by personalities such as Tindemans and van Ypersele who sought to reconcile the perspectives of different countries in a search for compromise and agreement. Denmark was also concerned with monetary discipline, though often less successful in actually achieving low inflation and currency stability.

The Irish decision to join the EMS manifested a resurgence of political confidence in seizing the opportunity to break free from its historic satellite currency link with sterling. In the past the Irish punt has been dragged down by successive devaluations of sterling, but there was now concern that the punt might appreciate in relation to sterling, adversely affecting Irish trade. In practice, the opposite has occurred and since 1979 the punt has depreciated against sterling. Whilst this has favoured Irish trade, the pattern of its trade has diversified towards other EC countries. Ireland has welcomed this and felt that in the traditional currency arrangements of the British Isles its economic fortunes were tied too closely to the slow-growing and inflation-prone UK economy. The balance between the two economies was maintained very much by the drain of free factor movements and by high interest rates in Ireland. In joining the EMS Ireland gained financial assistance, confident that if or when the UK decided to join, it would have illustrated its political and monetary independence from the UK. Having benefited so much from the CAP, it saw little to be gained by acceding to British requests for the EMS to be linked with agricultural and budgetary reform.

E EMS: the mechanics of operation and the ECU

The design and mechanics of the EMS differ from those of its predecessor, the snake, in various ways. A most important and central new creation is the ECU which has now replaced the earlier units of account which were used by the Community. The ECU is composed of a fixed amount of each Community currency in its 'basket', whose individual percentage share is based on the country's respective GDP, trade and short-term credit quotas. While the weight of ECU currencies in the basket is fixed, changes in market exchange rates have resulted in an increasing weight of appreciating currencies, such as the Deutschmark, and the falling weight of depreciating currencies, such as sterling. To avoid the risk that the ECU might become over-dominated by the strongest currency in the basket, arrangements were made for the shares of the ECU basket to be re-examined if the weight of one currency changed by 25 per cent or more; it was also agreed that the composition of the basket would normally be re-examined every five years. The composition of the ECU is shown in Table 7.1.

Table 7.1   Composition of the ECU

| | Amounts of national currencies | | % share of currencies in the basket | |
	In the original ECU basket	In the revised ECU basket 24 Sept. 1984	13 March 1979	September 1987*
German mark	0.828	0.719	32.98	34.9
Pound sterling	0.0885	0.0878	13.34	11.9
French franc	1.15	1.31	19.83	19.0
Italian lira	109.0	140.0	9.50	9.4
Dutch guilder	0.286	0.256	10.51	11.0
Belgian franc	3.66	3.71	9.63	9.1
Luxembourg franc	0.14	0.14		
Danish krone	0.217	0.219	3.06	2.8
Irish pound	0.00759	0.00871	1.15	1.1
Greek drachma	—	1.2	—	0.8
Total			100.0	100.0

*The Economist, 19 September 1987, p 86.

Source: European Documentation, The ECU, March 1984, Luxembourg.

The drachma has now been incorporated, with a very low share of the ECU, but a high rate of inflation in Greece has been an obstacle to its participation in the exchange rate mechanism. In the future, if Portugal and Spain can reduce their rates of inflation, then the EMS is likely to accommodate them. The peseta would account for a significant element in the ECU and the Spanish Prime Minister, Felipe Gonzalez, has driven down its rate of inflation so that Spain can then participate in the EMS.

The ECU, the exchange rate mechanism and the divergence indicator. Each currency participating in the EMS has a central rate expressed in ECUs; this was derived from the rates ruling in the snake, while for others it was based on those existing on 12 March 1979. From these central rates a grid of cross-parities is derived for each pair of currencies in the system. Around these parities margins of ±2.25 per cent are allowed, and for weaker currencies, such as the Italian lira, a wider margin of ±6.0 per cent was agreed. Intervention occurs to enable currencies to operate within these parities. There was much discussion about whether the intervention should be based on the bilateral grid or on the deviation of a currency in relation to the ECU. There were various technical objections to the use of the latter (van Ypersele and Koeune 1985, pp. 48–9). Some concern, for example, was expressed that the divergence of one currency against the ECU would not necessarily be accompanied by the divergence of another currency in the opposite direction and this would make it difficult to decide which currency to use for intervention purposes. It was decided therefore, after the 'Belgian compromise', to use partially an ECU-based divergence indicator from which there would be a presumption to act, but that the bilateral grid would provide the automatic intervention. Thus the Central Bank, in the currency which had appreciated to its full margin, would buy the currency of the weak country which had depreciated, and the latter's Central Bank would sell the strong currency.

Both the ECU and the innovation of the divergence indicator constitute major differences from the earlier snake system, with the ECU having proved more important than the divergence indicator (Zis 1984). The maximum divergence spread of a given currency against the ECU is ±2.25 per cent and the divergence is set at 75 per cent of this spread. Some observers may be puzzled as to why the variations are not precisely three-quarters of this, which can be explained since each country's currency is a fixed part of the ECU basket. The formula to calculate the divergence limit is ±2.25 per cent multiplied by $(1 - w)$ where w is the weight of the currency for which the divergence spread is being calculated. The greater the weight of the currency, the smaller is its maximum spread. Thus, West Germany has the lowest percentage divergence limit. When the Deutschmark was 37.38 per cent of the ECU then the market ECU rate of the mark rose by $2.25 \times (1.00 - 0.3738)$ of this, that is, by 1.40895 per cent. The divergence indicator is three-quarters of this, that is, 1.0567. Italy has the widest divergence limit because of the ±6 per cent applied to the lira.

In general, a currency will reach its divergence threshold before reaching its bilateral limit against another currency; but it is possible for it to reach its bilateral limit first when two currencies are at opposite poles, and all the other currencies are fairly stable. When a currency crosses its divergence threshold the authorities are expected to correct the situation by various policies: these include diversified intervention in different currencies to provide a better spread in the burden of intervention between EMS currencies; also, domestic policies, in particular interest rate changes, plus other measures such as incomes policy. Finally, changes in central rates may be made, but to ensure that these do not occur too frequently and are not carried out unilaterally, extensive financial assistance is provided so that countries can fulfil their EMS obligations. This financial assistance was more extensive than that available under the snake, in spite of Germany's attempts to limit the amount. Short-term finance was made available for 45 days, compared with 30 days under the snake. In the EMS short-term financial support was offered for nine months and medium-term financial assistance for a period of between two and five years. Measures were also introduced to strengthen the economies of weaker member states. While the full demands of Italy and Ireland, in particular for large grants, could not be met, it was agreed that loans would be made available which could receive interest rate subsidies from bodies like the EIB.

The financial support available is derived from countries depositing part of their gold and dollar holdings with the European Monetary Co-operation Fund (EMCF) and the countries concerned are credited with ECUs. It was intended that the EMCF would be turned within two years into the EMF and that there would be full use of the ECU as a reserve asset and means of settlement. However, the transition to this second phase had to be delayed.

The ECU's attractiveness to users. The ECU carries out some of the functions of money, even though there are no ECU notes or coins circulating in member states. Belgium made a start in 1987 by actually minting an ECU coin. Other progressive steps have been suggested, such as the issue of a limited amount of ECUs to be used by tourists and migrant frontier workers to save them the costs of currency conversion; also, that perhaps ECU postage stamps could be introduced.

The ECU offers many benefits in its usage, not merely as a standard measure for the operation of the Community, but also for private sector activities. Indeed, the private sector has made wide use of the ECU, with some multinational companies, such as the French company Saint-Gobain, drawing up their financial accounts in ECUs and others invoicing customers in ECUs, to reduce exposure to adverse exchange rate movements; for example, about $1 billion worth of Italy's exports were invoiced in ECUs in 1986.

Both savers and borrowers have recognized the advantages of operating through ECUs instead of national currencies. They receive a more stable return, avoiding the unforeseen effects of volatile changes in national exchange rates. Money placed in ECUs earns a weighted average of member countries' interest rates. Savers can open ECU accounts for fairly small amounts in Belgium and Luxembourg, though West Germany initially restricted the opening of such accounts; it was opposed to any kind of index-linked savings, classing the ECU in that category. By 1987 West Germany showed some inclination to relax its opposition to ECU accounts, provided other countries in return would ease their controls on the movement of capital. Savers living in strong currency countries will receive a higher interest rate in ECUs (though they may have to accept some depreciation against their own currency). Savers living in weaker currency countries and investing in ECUs will be protected more against losses by depreciation. Some savers in Belgium, Italy and France have become keen on ECUs.

The ECU offers advantages to borrowers and it has grown to become one of the major bond-issuing currencies, along with the dollar, Deutschmark, sterling and special drawing right (SDR). The composition of the SDR basket has been simplified, but is so dominated by the dollar that the ECU has been favoured by investors looking for a dollar alternative. By using ECUs, borrowers in weak currency countries are able to raise capital abroad more easily and at a lower interest rate than at home.

F Evaluating the performance of the EMS

Any evaluation is limited by the difficulty of determining what the situation would have been like without the EMS; also, there are many facets of the EMS. In addition, much depends upon which end of the exchange rate spectrum one prefers, since if the aim is exchange rate fixity, then some would argue that the system has been too flexible, with over-use of adjustment in central rates (Padoa-Schioppa 1984). Nevertheless, the general experience of currencies operating outside the EMS has been one of far greater volatility in exchange rates.

Overall, the EMS has been recognized as being fairly successful, despite early misgivings by those who preferred monetary union to take place through the introduction of a European parallel currency (Zis 1984, pp. 59–60). After the two devaluations late in 1979 of the Danish krone, along with a small revaluation of the West German mark, no currency realignments were necessary in 1980. Circumstances were favourable, partly because weaker currencies, like the lira, had entered the EMS at low central exchange rate levels, and with a wider margin for the lira. Italy survived without having to devalue until October 1981. West Germany continued to control its inflation with greater success than other countries, though the rise in oil prices severely affected its balance of payments, creating a massive external deficit in 1980. Apart from the Deutschmark weakening in

1980 against the EMS currencies, it also weakened against the dollar; this helped to take some of the speculative pressure off the mark as buyers purchased dollars. Indeed, the longer-term problems have arisen when the dollar has weakened, and investors have switched into the mark, driving up its value. In the medium- and long-term, the lower rate of inflation in West Germany has caused pressure for further revaluation *vis-à-vis* other EMS currencies.

Table 7.2 shows the changes in EMS central rates. Between 1981 and 1983 five currency realignments occurred; these mainly affected the franc and lira in devaluations and to a lesser extent the Danish krone and the Irish punt. These currency realignments resulted in agreed changes which were conducted quite swiftly and without major panic of the kind which had existed under the fixed exchange rate system of Bretton Woods. The alignments also resulted in more symmetry, with the stronger currencies also experiencing revaluation at the same time. The main revaluations have been to the West German mark and to a lesser extent to the Dutch guilder. The exchange rate adjustments have usually been accompanied by internal domestic policies to make the currency changes more effective and conducive to the maintenance of durable equilibrium.

There were no EMS currency alignments in 1984 and only one in 1985 − a significant depreciation of the Italian lira. April 1986 marked the ninth alignment in EMS, triggered mainly by weaknesses of the French franc, since French inflation had reduced the competitiveness of its manufactured goods. France had sought a larger devaluation than that eventually agreed upon; a collective package emerged in which there were accompanying currency readjustments, with the usual revaluations of the Deutschmark and the Dutch guilder. Italy's decision not to devalue the lira aroused some misgivings by Italian businessmen fearing loss of competitiveness and rendering the Italian lira potentially more vulnerable.

The French franc and the German mark came under strong

Table 7.2   Changes in EMS Central Rates

	Dates of realignments										
	24/9 1979	30/11 1979	22/3 1981	5/10 1981	22/2 1982	14/6 1982	21/3 1983	21/7 1985	7/4 1986	2/8 1986	12/1 1987
Belgian franc/											
Lux. franc		0.0	0.0	0.0	−8.5	0.0	+1.5	+2.0	+1.0	0.0	+2.0
Danish krone	−2.9	−4.8	0.0	0.0	−3.0	0.0	+2.5	+2.0	+1.0	0.0	0.0
German mark	+2.0	0.0	0.0	+5.5	0.0	+4.25	+5.5	+2.0	+3.0	0.0	+3.0
French franc	0.0	0.0	0.0	−3.0	0.0	−5.75	−2.5	+2.0	−3.0	0.0	0.0
Irish pound	0.0	0.0	0.0	0.0	0.0	0.0	−3.5	+2.0	0.0	−8.0	0.0
Italian lira	0.0	0.0	−6.0	−3.0	0.0	−2.75	−2.5	−6.0	0.0	0.0	0.0
Dutch guilder	0.0	0.0	0.0	+5.5	0.0	+4.25	+3.5	+2.0	+3.0	0.0	+3.0

Source: *Financial Times*, 29 May 1986, updated to 1987.

speculative pressure in January 1987, resulting in another realignment of the EMS. This became necessary because a weakening of the US dollar led to a flow of money towards the Deutschmark. The French government suggested that it was mainly a German problem and this was reflected by the revaluation of the Deutschmark by 3 per cent (along with the Dutch guilder), whilst leaving the French franc unchanged. West Germany bowed to speculative pressure, preferring the anti-inflationary effects of revaluation, to reducing interest rates or increasing domestic expenditure. To limit the full manifestation of French weaknesses, other countries which preferred to revalue in January 1987 had their requests refused. A growing balance of payments deficit by some countries with West Germany may well turn the system even further towards a crawling peg mechanism in the future.

There has been some loosening of exchange controls under EMS during the 1980s. These were the first significant movements since 1962 when the EC removed foreign exchange restrictions linked to trade and individual change in residence, but not those dealing with share placements, short-term investment and individual investment across borders. While the UK, West Germany, Denmark and the Netherlands have no exchange controls, Italy and France are gradually coming into line. In November 1986 EC Finance Ministers agreed on a package obliging members to remove exchange controls on long-term credit and on buying and selling unlisted securities, unit trusts and other mutual funds. A full removal of control on capital movements is now the target for 1992. However, there is a danger that fully-mobile capital flows − given continuing divergencies in economic performance − could destabilize the exchange rate mechanism.

The resort to currency realignments in the EMS has been less frequent than critics predicted and they have been agreed collectively, so all the onus has not fallen solely on the weaker countries facing devaluation. There has been more stability in the exchange rates between EMS countries than of other currencies such as sterling and the dollar. There has also been greater similarity in the level of interest rates and some consensus on the need to bring down the rate of inflation. Whilst the EMS may still not have created a sufficiently low and converging level of money supply and inflation rates, policy is moving in the right direction. The average growth rates of monetary aggregates have fallen since 1979 and inflation differentials have narrowed (Healey 1988). Between 1980 and 1986 the average rate of inflation in the EMS group fell steadily from 11.3 per cent in 1980 to 2.5 per cent in 1986.

Unfortunately, it seems unlikely that unless low inflation really does succeed in securing a faster rate of economic growth and lower unemployment, countries will be able to resist pressures to reflate.

The average unemployment rate in the Community remains stubbornly high and some countries would prefer to see the priority being one of reducing unemployment instead of further controlling inflation. Yet the freedom to pursue such an independent policy is constrained within the EMS. There is recognition that it is only economic convergence which can create the conditions for long-term stability between Community exchange rates. Unless this can be achieved, the Deutschmark will remain the preferred currency to hold, whereas if other countries could achieve a similarly low rate of inflation, then the pressure to appreciate would be taken off the Deutschmark.

Various recommendations have been made on ways to strengthen the EMS: these could include some indicator of convergence measures, rather like the divergence indicator, with an expectation that the Commission would be obliged to issue warnings to members to take appropriate action. More concrete developments have actually included a restatement of the objective of EMU in Article 20 of the SEA. In addition, in September 1987 European Finance Ministers agreed on new measures to defend currencies in the EMS, before the weaker ones reached their floor. They also agreed on an increase in the short-term credits available to defend currencies, to extend the repayment period and to allow greater repayments in ECUs rather than West German marks. Much of the recent initiative has come from France, trying to push West Germany towards further evolution of the EMS with, for example, proposals for a Community Central Bank; but West Germany is reluctant to see a weakening in its own Central Bank and any threat to its price stabilization policy.

Part III   UK ambivalence towards the EMS

There are some similarities between the UK's attitude to the formation of the EMS and the formation of the EC in the 1950s. The UK thought that there was a distinct possibility of both ventures foundering, and therefore it avoided the risks inherent in being a positive founder member. Thus sterling, though part of the ECU, did not participate in the exchange rate mechanism. Evidence suggests that the UK's policy approach has been shortsighted since both the EC and then the EMS 'took off' successfully. The UK belatedly joined the EC and presumably will join the EMS exchange rate mechanism at some stage. To join later always implies reluctance, a lack of real commitment and a loss of political goodwill. Furthermore, it appears an anomaly to belong to the EC and not to belong fully to the EMS exchange rate mechanism. On balance the EMS does not seem to manifest such adverse features as those associated with other aspects of sectoral integration which the UK has entered into, such as the CAP. However, perhaps the UK regards EMS as presaging a looser form of à la carte integration.

The UK attitude to the EMS was to lay down such stringent bargaining conditions for its membership that there was little likelihood of them being accepted. For example, the list of conditions in the Green Paper on the EMS in 1978 may have been desirable, but there was no prospect of satisfying them all. The UK had doubts whether the weaker countries which had dropped out of the snake would be able to stay in. With the UK's tendency for wage inflation to outstrip productivity, it felt there was a need for exchange rate depreciation as a crucial policy instrument. There was a desire not to operate under an overvalued exchange rate, necessitating the imposition of deflationary domestic policies. In practice, however, non-participation in the EMS exchange rate mechanism actually resulted in an overvalued exchange rate during the early 1980s!

The Labour government, already split in the past on the issue of the EC, simply lacked the confidence, support and vision to move forward in the process of European integration. It tried to link the introduction of the EMS to budgetary reform, though any progress on both fronts simultaneously was difficult. The UK also expressed concern about any adverse effects of the EMS on the dollar, seeming to show even more concern about this than the Americans themselves. Nevertheless, there was general hostility to the EMS from other quarters in the UK; for example, the National Institute of Economic and Social Research agreed with most economists who had submitted evidence against the EMS to the House of Commons Committee which examined this in November 1978. Of even more emphatic influence was the opposition of the Treasury, though it had participated through Mr Cousins in the detailed discussions with Dr Schulmann and M Clappier, the German and French representatives, about the precise construction of the EMS (Ludlow 1982).

The Labour government underestimated the unstoppable political momentum by the West German and French leaders towards the establishment of the EMS. They had become increasingly disillusioned with the UK's attitude and it was really only a desire of France to reduce the excessive weight of the Deutschmark in the ECU which helped to prevent the UK's total exclusion from the EMS. The UK settled for an intermediate position opting out of the exchange rate mechanism. Yet by joining this the UK could have prevented the currency split with Ireland; it could have pressed to join with wider margins, like the lira; and also have benefited from the financial aid available.

Mrs Thatcher and the EMS. While the reluctance of the Labour Party to embrace the EMS was understandable, the lack of enthusiasm of the Thatcher governments requires a somewhat different explanation. The predilection of the Conservative government for market forces was applied to the foreign exchange market, taking the view that the market was more likely than intervention to create the right exchange rate for sterling. The government removed exchange controls, resulting in an outflow of capital, and this appeared judicious in an attempt to restrain the rising value of sterling (as a petro-currency); even though the combination of both effects was to have a devastating impact on UK unemployment. The Thatcher government also decided initially to introduce a medium-term financial strategy in which it sought to achieve its anti-inflationary strategy by using monetary targets instead of by using an exchange rate target. However, by 1986 the UK had started to move away from its main reliance upon money supply targets; this was because of the problems in attaining them successfully. Their defects are that more deposits are now held outside the banking system; also, the development of sophisticated corporate financial transactions means that a single act of borrowing may often be counted several times. Hence there was some recognition that instead of a money supply target there could be gains from pursuing an exchange rate target, yet the UK still did not join the EMS exchange rate mechanism.

A major obstacle to UK participation is the distinctive nature of the economy as a significant oil producer − though the Netherlands has not found near self-sufficiency in energy any barrier to membership of the EMS. But the UK's dependence upon world oil prices has made sterling a volatile petro-currency which fluctuates widely and might have difficulty in being contained within the EMS. A continuous fall in world oil prices − brought about by the failure of OPEC to maintain a cohesive cartel − would lead to a long-run decline in the value of sterling. There is concern about the opposite effect of a change in oil prices on sterling and the Deutschmark, with a fall in oil prices leading to a rise in the Deutschmark. Both sterling and the Deutschmark have been used as reserve currencies, with the Deutschmark tending to eclipse sterling nowadays.

Any durable participation of the UK in the EMS is dependent on the UK reducing its rate of inflation towards the lowest West German level on a permanent basis. Much depends, therefore, upon the willingness of the UK to pursue the same preference of low inflation, and also its ability to achieve this successfully. Under Conservative governments, economic policy has brought down the rate of inflation to a level compatible with its membership of the EMS. Given this, it is surprising that the UK has postponed entry into the exchange rate mechanism for so long. In addition, more recently sterling has been observed to shadow the Deutschmark and close co-operation has occurred with the Bundesbank. Furthermore, it was understood that a secret target zone for the movement of sterling against the Deutschmark had been agreed between the two countries around the time of the Group of Five meeting in Paris in February 1987. The central target rate for sterling was believed to be about 2.90 Deutschmarks and assuming an EMS-style flexibility of 2.5 per cent around this, then action was necessary to prevent sterling rising much above 2.97 Deutschmarks. The successful managed float of sterling against the Deutschmark was finally breached in March 1988 when sterling was uncapped, amidst disagreement between Mrs Thatcher and the Chancellor of the Exchequer over interest rate policy.

The timing of entry into the EMS exchange rate mechanism is crucial and any fall again in the sterling/Deutschmark rate to just under 3 Deutschmarks to the pound would seem to provide a favourable base to maintain UK competitiveness without worsening its unemployment problems. The UK could then either peg sterling at this level, maintaining the nominal rate of exchange from a strong anti-inflationary position, or it could crawl downwards to maintain the real exchange rate over time. The government's worry, despite its own propaganda, has been whether the economy was sufficiently strong, since, if not, it would suffer a loss of face through devaluation of the pound soon after its entry into the EMS. Furthermore, the UK, in general, probably has less to gain from belonging to the EMS exchange rate mechanism than countries such as West Germany which conduct far more intra-EC trade. The Treasury and the Civil Service Committee in 1985 felt that enough doubts remained for the UK to stay outside and to maintain the status quo.

The arguments surrounding the EMS are finely balanced but UK entry into the EMS exchange rate mechanism would offer several advantages. For example, it would restore monetary integration with Ireland; it would also make the EMS more attractive to other European countries, such as Norway. The UK would have less need to run such excessively high nominal and real interest rates, particularly if the UK opted for a wider exchange rate margin like the lira. If the pound were weak, EMS members would be committing themselves to defend the exchange rate. EC countries themselves, both politically and economically, believe that the Community would be strengthened by full UK participation in the EMS. They fret about the costs which they are bearing to create real exchange rate stability, whereas the UK is left free to choose its own rate of inflation, with the nominal sterling exchange rate being adjusted to restore its real exchange rate.

Some financial commentators, such as Samuel Brittan of the *Financial Times*, would welcome the discipline which the EMS will continue to impose on the UK to keep down its rate of inflation.

Furthermore, if the UK fails to join the EMS exchange rate mechanism when the time is right with a low inflation rate and a low exchange rate (brought about by a fall in oil prices), then prospects of joining under better conditions in future may be even less auspicious. The government has recognized that one day the UK will go into full membership, though the Chancellor of the Exchequer late in 1987 would still not make a prediction about the timing.

Pressure on the UK to join has increased, with the inclusion of monetary articles in the SEA and the proposals for full capital liberation. Jacques Delors, as President of the Commission, threatened that progress on this front could not occur if some countries would not conform to the monetary discipline of the EMS. Since the EMS has operated to some extent like a crawling peg system, and has been more accommodating than the EMU, UK reservations about the EMS seem exaggerated. The latter has fallen short of the preconditions laid down by the Werner Report about completely eliminating exchange rate margins and locking parities together irrevocably — that is a much more distant prospect.

8 Fiscal policy: taxation and the Community Budget

Part I Fiscal policy issues

The term fiscal policy covers a wide range of public finance issues relating to both taxation and government expenditure. One of its main concerns has been with the allocation of resources since public goods have to be provided collectively. However, in recent years most EC countries have become concerned about the excessive size of the public sector, cutting the public sector borrowing requirement and trying to make room for the growth of the private sector. Even those countries which could indulge in high public expenditure in the past from energy revenue, such as the Netherlands and the UK, have had to moderate the level of public expenditure.

The concern of fiscal policy with macroeconomic stabilization has been the outcome of Keynesian economics. However, over recent years a scepticism has emerged about the effectiveness of Keynesian demand management policies when the outcome was invariable large budget deficits − such policies proved highly inflationary. Successful economies, such as West Germany, have been run along more orthodox lines, being less preoccupied with Keynesian macroeconomic stabilization policies, giving greater priority to monetary policy, within which at a microeconomic level freely competitive market forces could operate. West Germany is the dominant economy in the Community and the pivotal force, so that economic policy in the EC is influenced very much by the German example.

National governments have traditionally used fiscal policy to create a more equitable distribution of income by designing progressive taxation in terms of ability to pay, whilst trying to ensure that on the expenditure side benefits go mainly to the poor. Such policies have not always been successful, with often high marginal tax rates existing not only for the higher paid groups, but also for some of the low income groups because of the poverty trap. Meanwhile, expenditure policies have often included indiscriminate subsidies going to all groups, not only the poor.

This chapter will focus on tax harmonization and in particular on the role of the Community Budget. Given the functions of national budgets, is the role of the Community Budget to carry out these same functions? What kind of activities does it carry out? Has it a macroeconomic stabilization role? How has it affected the distribution of income? Deciding on the appropriate level of activities is difficult, even within a country; for example, the balance between national and regional provision, with West Germany tending towards the latter sub-national level represented by the Länder. It is an even more difficult problem for the EC since its federal nature could be enhanced with a larger budget, but those countries contributing disproportionately to its finance remain lukewarm. Nevertheless, there is scope for transferring some activities currently financed at a national level to the Community level.

Part II   Tax harmonization and the Community Budget

A   The rationale of fiscal harmonization
Fiscal harmonization is bound up with the achievement of the customs union, the Common Market and the Economic and Political Union. The first phase of removing customs frontiers remains incomplete when tax barriers still exist. The phase of freeing the movement of factors of production is also inhibited by different taxes. Finally, as more positive integration has occurred in different sectors, further tax harmonization has become necessary. For example, in agriculture, differences in Value Added Tax (VAT) in the early 1980s meant that farmers in the UK and Denmark, unlike those in other member states, could not claim back a percentage of VAT which had been paid on factors of production.

The different excise duties levied on products such as wine and tobacco (plus tobacco monopolies in France and Italy) have distorted competition. Despite proposals to harmonize these, substantial differences have existed since each country has been reluctant to relinquish its choice on the appropriate level of national taxation for these products on health grounds; there are also different tax yields according to the different patterns of consumption. Countries' revenue requirements vary and are higher where these have to satisfy high public expenditure.

The aim of the Community is not to standardize everything, but to harmonize taxation as a means of achieving other Community objectives. But countries, having relinquished some important national economic policy instruments already as a consequence of integration, such as tariffs, quotas and free exchange rates, are naturally wary of any erosion of an independent fiscal policy to manage their economies. Nevertheless, tax harmonization has assumed added urgency since this is part and parcel of financing the Community Budget and progress towards integration in other areas, such as the EMS and the internal market, is facilitated by a large redistributive Budget to help poor countries.

B   Types of taxes
The EC has sought to promote the harmonization of three taxes; VAT, excise duties and corporation tax. It has not proposed to

harmonize income tax, since labour is less mobile than capital; hence, direct taxation provides the major independent policy instrument for national governments to use in managing their economies. However, it is intended that the overall fiscal stance between countries will be co-ordinated.

Value Added Tax (VAT). Value added tax or *taxe sur la valeur ajoutée* has been applied in France since 1954. The Neumark Report in 1963 recommended VAT and it was decided to introduce this as the sales tax for the Community by a Council Directive in April 1967. It was proposed that other member states which were operating different systems would change over to VAT by 1 January 1971; but extensions were necessary for Belgium and Italy and the latter did not introduce VAT until early 1973. It became tied up inextricably with Italy's other tax reforms and both the Mezzogiorno and export industries opposed VAT since under the existing turnover tax large rebates were possible. Other countries were much keener to introduce VAT, for example West Germany, even though their cumulative multi-cascade tax benefited exporters by generous rebates.

The disadvantages of cascade taxes (that is, taxes on total value), compared with VAT, were that they encourged vertical integration of production by firms purely to minimize their tax payments. For example, assume three stages in a firm's activities with the value of the product (excluding tax) at the end of the stages being £1000 (stage 1), £2000 (stage 2), and £3000 (stage 3). Assume a 10 per cent cascade tax was applied at each stage; hence tax payments would be £100 (stage 1), £200 (stage 2) and £300 (stage 3), making the total tax payable £600. To reduce the tax bill, businesses engaged in vertical integration in order to pay only £300 tax on the total value of £3000. VAT is neutral with regard to the structure of economic activity. The tax is paid not on the total value at each stage but on the added value; hence, a 10 per cent VAT would yield £100 (stage 1), £100 (stage 2) and £100 (stage 3), that is, £300 VAT payable. Only in the case of the business being integrated is the cascade tax and the VAT bill the same. Without such integration a cumulative cascade tax yields more than VAT; in the example used, a 5 per cent cascade tax would have yielded the same as a 10 per cent VAT.

The replacement of cascade taxes by VAT has removed the incentive for the kind of integration which offered no economic gains apart from saving tax. Cascade taxes in encouraging integration increased monopoly structure (even though the latter is more likely to occur with horizontal than with vertical integration). 'Le remplacement des taxes cumulatives à cascade par la taxe à la valeur ajoutée a eliminé la source principale des discriminations au sens des articles 95 et 96 du traité CEE' (Moussis 1982, p. 319).

A distinct advantage of VAT for the tax authorities is that it is difficult to evade since businesses have to make sure on invoices that tax has been paid at the previous stage of production so that their own tax payment is correct. VAT is also more favourable to fair trade than cascade taxes since the latter were often generously rebated for export, providing exporters with a hidden subsidy because of uncertainty about the exact amounts of tax which had been paid at each stage. With VAT the taxes rebated are clear and VAT is applied at the destination by the importing country. Unfortunately, this means that a fiscal frontier still exists. If VAT was harmonized then exports could take place smoothly from the country of origin.

The use of jurisdictional terms such as 'destination' and 'origin' are worth clarifying, though fuller details can be found elsewhere (Robson 1980, pp. 90–6). Where the destination principle is applied on all products in the country where they are consumed, both domestic and imported products face the same tax, while domestically-produced goods for exports are exempt from the tax. Under the origin principle, the taxes are imposed on the domestic production of all goods whether exported or not, and not imposed on imports. Apart from the existence of a fiscal frontier with the destination principle, this is preferable where VAT rates have not been harmonized.

VAT is a general tax levied at all stages of production and distribution covering services (when the services affect the final price of goods) and consumer goods. Several Directives have been introduced, such as the Sixth Directive in 1977 which was important in introducing a uniform basis for VAT. This sought to establish a common list of taxable activities and a common list of exemptions. This was necessary since the collection of the EC's own resources from VAT receipts to finance the Community Budget can only be equitable if all countries have the same basis of assessment. Hence the VAT payable to the EC Budget is based on a common notional structure, but has allowed countries to continue with their own existing VAT rates and their existing derogations.

The difference in the rate of VAT charges and also in the number of rates used in particular countries is shown in Table 8.1.

Denmark has had the highest standard rate of VAT − equal to nearly 10 per cent of its GDP − while Italy has been one of several countries which has had a luxury rate of taxation, setting this at 38 per cent. Greece has also chosen three rates of VAT, though it delayed their introduction initially because of its primitive book-keeping methods and worries that it would raise Greek payments to the Community Budget. However, VAT replaces nearly half of the 500 indirect taxes existing in Greece.

Progress in harmonizing both the number and level of VAT rates

Table 8.1   Rates of VAT in member states as applicable in October 1986 (%)

Member states	Reduced	Normal	Superior
Belgium	6 and 17	19	25 and 23
Denmark	—	22	—
West Germany	7	14	—
Spain	6	12	33
France	5.5 and 7	18.6	33.3
Greece	6	18	36
Ireland	0 and 10	23	—
Italy	2 and 9	18	38
Luxembourg	3 and 6	12	—
Netherlands	6	20	—
Portugal	8	16	30
UK	0	15	—

Source: *Science et Vie Economie*, February 1987.

has been constrained by two particular problems: firstly, member states when using VAT as part of their economic policy are sometimes concerned about any inflationary effects from raising VAT – France has in the past suspended this on the retail sale of beef to keep down the rate of inflation. Secondly, countries differ in the extent to which they wish to define and tax products as luxuries or essentials. The latter may carry only low rates of VAT, be zero rated or exempt from VAT. Those that are zero rated are generally treated better than those which are exempt, since the latter are only exempt at their particular stage of production and they will have been charged VAT on the goods which have been bought in for processing or for resale.

The Rogalla Report by the European Parliament in 1983 called for a standstill on any further widening of tax rates and a dual rate of VAT. Lord Cockfield's proposals in 1987 were to approximate VAT in two bands; a lower band between 4 and 9 per cent and a standard band which is likely to be between 14 and 20 per cent. While countries may apply for exemptions, the ultimate goal is the removal of fiscal frontiers by 1992. Instead of collecting the tax at the frontier, the authorities will collect it later, internally, when tax declarations are made.

Excise duties. The five main excise duties are on beer, wine, spirits, tobacco and mineral oils. These account for most of the excise receipts, though there are variations between member countries; for example, Denmark has a high and important excise duty on cars, whilst Italy has numerous minor excise duties on products such as sugar, coffee, salt and matches. The imposition of excise duties can be based on the value, weight, quality or strength of a product.

Excise duties are levied on products with a low price elasticity of demand, and the excise duty is usually shifted forward to the consumer. They represent a significant revenue-raising element for governments since the five main excise duties account for up to 25 per cent of consumer spending.

Excise duties both reflect and influence patterns of production and consumption; for example, wine producing countries tend to have no or only very low excise duties. Members of the EC(6) have tended to have lower excise duties, not only on wine but also on other alcohol and cigarettes, than those of the northern European entrants to the EC (the UK, Ireland and Denmark). There have been very wide differences in excise duties, in particular between highly-rated Denmark and the much lower rate in France. They reflect different governmental approaches to matters such as health, and in addition can be sources of tacit protectionism. Excise duties levied on mineral oils have widespread effects since they are important inputs for many industries.

In 1978 the EC changed the system for tobacco, abolishing duties on raw tobacco leaf, and a new sales tax was introduced at the manufacturing level, combined with a specific tax per cigarette as well as VAT. But in general, rates of excise duties have varied more widely than VAT rates and unlike the latter, excise duties are normally imposed in one operation at an early stage in the production process. It was suggested that some consideration might be given to replacing excise duties by special VAT rates (Prest 1983). Recent proposals by Lord Cockfield have been to harmonize excise duties at common rates and these would have major repercussions; for example, Danish prices would fall across the board, hitting government revenue heavily. Greece, on the other hand, would experience massive price rises for some products, such as cigarettes and spirits. The retail price changes which would occur in the EC(12) are shown in Table 8.2.

Corporation tax. Corporation tax is a tax levied on company profits. Three different systems have been used in EC countries: the Classical system in which there was complete separation of corporation tax and personal income tax; a split-rate or two-rate system; and a partial imputation system with a tax credit. The Neumark Committee in 1963 favoured the split-rate system used in West Germany. Another report, the Van den Tempel Report in 1970 favoured the Classical system which existed in the Netherlands, Luxembourg and the UK (though in 1972 a White Paper proposed the French partial imputation system with a tax credit). In 1975 the Commission proposed to go down the path of a partial imputation system with a tax credit.

The rationale for harmonizing corporation tax is that capital is

Table 8.2 Retail price changes from proposed excise duty harmonization (%)

	Petrol (super)	Popular cigarettes	Spirits	Wine	Beer
Belgium	17	25	1	− 9	5
Denmark	−19	− 44	− 50	− 45	− 37
France	− 9	70	6	11	18
West Germany	19	2	5	13	12
Greece	− 5	170	145	13	8
Ireland	− 4	− 10	− 41	− 64	− 51
Italy	−29	36	118	13	0
Luxembourg	32	51	26	3	14
Netherlands	0	18	− 1	− 10	− 6
Portugal	− 3	90	107	13	10
Spain	19	120	90	13	18
UK	15	− 6	− 37	− 47	− 37

Source: European Commission, from the *Financial Times*, 16 July 1987.

highly mobile and countries with lower rates of corporation tax than others will attract capital; also, if the lower corporation tax were reflected in lower prices, then it would affect not only capital markets but the goods market as well. The 1975 draft Directive did not propose a standard rate of corporation tax though, among other things, it suggested that both the corporation tax and tax credit rates should lie within a band between 45 and 55 per cent. While most rates fell within this band, there were exceptions, with a high rate of tax on distributed profits in West Germany and a very low rate of corporation tax in Italy. The differences in the tax credits have varied even more widely and only the tax credit rates in Belgium, France and Ireland fell within the range proposed by the Commission. The EC has made little progress in implementing its various draft Directives and as with other forms of tax harmonization governments are reluctant to harmonize when it involves sacrificing their own distinctive system and the flexibility which they believe it provides.

C The Community Budget

Relationship to national budgets. The Community Budget differs from national budgets in two respects. The first of these is that the Community Budget is relatively small in size and Community expenditure has been barely one per cent of the EC's GDP − 0.987 per cent of the GDP of the EC(10) in 1984. EC budgetary expenditure has been little more than the Budget of the largest Land in West Germany. This under-development of the Community

Budget is in marked contrast to the high and much increased levels of national expenditure as a percentage of GDP – up to some 45 per cent of their GDP. The key functions which one normally expects to be conducted in a federation, such as defence, are excluded from the Community. Defence lies in the province of national governments and organizations like NATO.

The second important difference is that national budgets are functional budgets whereas that of the EC is an accounting type of budget which is expected to balance – despite difficulties in achieving the latter. Some borrowing facilities exist and these are extensive for the ECSC and Euratom and for the EC they include the EIB, the Community loan instrument since 1975 and the new Community instrument since 1978. The Budget itself is concerned mainly to raise revenue to balance its financial expenditure and it is not engaged in macroeconomic Keynesian stabilization policies of running budgetary deficits to stimulate demand in order to reduce persistently high levels of unemployment. While a case could be made out for the EC to run deliberate budgetary deficits, some governments consider this to be undesirable because of its inflationary consequences. The Community Budget finances specific sectoral activities and exogenously determined factors have influenced the large agricultural expenditure. Indeed, it will be shown that the EC's major preoccupation in recent years has been to contain pressures towards budgetary imbalance.

Budgetary receipts. The separate budgetary arrangements for the ECSC, Euratom and the EEC were brought together into a General Budget after their merger in 1968. Both Euratom and the EEC were initially dependent for their receipt on national contributions and a key was constructed to determine these, based on national income and the degree of involvement in different activities. This was a reasonably fair system, but the Community decided in the mid-1960s to introduce its own direct sources of revenue. It started to use both customs duties and agricultural levies on imports from outside the Community. Customs duties and agricultural levies for the EC are collected at important entry points; ports such as Antwerp and Rotterdam, and then handed over to the Community. The most open economies with high imports from extra-EC sources therefore contribute disproportionately to these revenue sources.

The EEC was influenced in its desire to have its own direct source of revenue by the ECSC which has imposed levies on coal and steel production. It was decided to introduce the crucial new element of a percentage of VAT to raise the Community's revenue receipts and provide sufficient own resources. These have developed at an earlier stage in the evolution of the EC than in other unions, such as the USA or the German Zollverein. Own resources provide the EC with some independence, although it still depends on member states to collect the revenue for which they have received 10 per cent of the revenue collected – the Commission in 1987 proposed the elimination of this refund.

VAT tends to be a regressive tax, certainly when compared with the progressive nature of income tax. Although with VAT, higher income countries which consume more tend to pay more than others, one has to bear in mind that VAT is excluded on investment and exports, both of which are usually higher in more successful economies. This has led to some criticism about the wisdom of relying so much upon VAT as the EC's main source of revenue (Brown 1985, pp. 312–13). Furthermore, reliance on VAT has grown and it became necessary to raise the VAT ceiling from one per cent to a maximum of 1.4 per cent from the first of January 1986, and there was some pressure to have this raised again to 1.6 per cent in 1988 to finance the EC's growing commitments.

VAT is the major revenue source, outpacing customs duties and levies on agricultural imports which are insufficiently dynamic sources of revenue, because the EC has concluded a wide range of agreements with outside countries and negotiated tariff reductions in GATT. These sources of budgetary receipts are shown in Table 8.3.

A search has been underway for additional revenue sources for the EC, such as those from excise duties. But progress in the field of taxation has been slow in an area where unanimous voting has been required. The most significant proposal by the Commission has been to introduce a fourth revenue source linked to GNP. This would be provided from the difference between each country's GNP and its actual VAT base. The proposed ceiling would be set at 1.4 per cent of GNP (Commission August 1987). It would represent a significant increase in EC resources since GNP tends to be more progressive than VAT and is intended to include Italy's 'black' economy. Since the EC will continue with VAT at one per cent on its base (including zero-rated products), this compromise of using both VAT and a return to GNP represents the usual Community fudge.

Budgetary expenditure. A small amount of expenditure goes on financing staff and administration, but the bulk of it finances common sectoral policies. The most significant area of expenditure has been on agriculture as shown in Table 8.4. Its claims on the Budget have become even larger when the dollar has fallen in value since the latter has increased the cost to the Community in disposing of its agricultural surpluses on the world market. The search for agricultural solutions has continued somewhat elusively, although some ingenious proposals have been made; a fighting fund to get rid

Table 8.3   Budgetary receipts of the European Communities (million UA/EUA/ECU)[a]

| | ECSC levies and other | European Dev. Fund contributions | Euratom contributions (research only) | Miscellaneous and contributions under special keys | EC Budget | | | | Total EC | Total |
| | | | | | Own resources | | | | | |
					Miscellaneous	Agricultural levies	Import duties	GNP contributions or VAT[bc]		
1958	44.0	116.0	7.9	0.02				5.9	5.9	173.8
1959	49.6	116.0	39.1	0.1				25.1	25.2	229.9
1960	53.3	116.0	20.0	0.2				28.1	28.3	217.6
1961	53.1	116.0	72.5	2.8				31.2	34.0	275.6
1962	45.3	116.0	88.6	2.1				90.2	92.3	342.2
1963	47.1		106.4	6.7				77.4	84.1	237.5
1964	61.3		124.4	2.9				90.1	93.1	278.7
1965	66.1		98.8	3.5				197.6	201.1	366.0
1966	71.2	40.0	116.5	3.9				398.3	402.2	590.0
1967	40.3	90.0	158.5	4.2				670.9	675.1	913.9
1968	85.4	110.0	82.0						2408.6	2666.0
1969	106.8	130.0	62.7	78.6				3972.6	4051.2	4330.7
1970	100.0	170.0	67.7	121.1				5327.3	5448.4	5746.1
1971	57.9	170.0			69.5	713.8	582.2	923.8	2289.3	2517.2
1972	61.1	150.0			80.9	799.6	957.4	1236.6	3074.5	3305.6
1973	120.3	150.0			511.0	478.0	1564.7	2087.3	4641.0	4911.3
1974	124.6	220.0			65.3	323.6	2684.4	1964.8	5038.2	5312.8
1975	189.5	311.0			320.5	590.0	3151.0	2152.0	6213.6	6623.1
1976[d]	129.6				282.8	1163.7	4064.6	2482.1	7993.1	8433.7

1977	123.0	410.0	283.0	1 778.5	3 927.2	2 494.5	8 483.2	9 016.2
1978	164.9	147.5	217.2	2 283.3	4 407.9	4 975.8	11 884.2	12 196.6
1979	168.4	480.0	230.3	2 143.4	5 189.1	7 039.8	14 602.5	15 251.0
1980	226.2	555.0	1 055.9e	2 002.3	5 905.8	7 093.5	16 057.5f	16 838.7
1981	264.0	658.0	1 219.0	1 747.0	6 392.0	9 188.0	18 546.0g	19 468.0
1982	243.0	750.0	187.0	2 228.0	6 815.0	12 197.0	21 427.0	22 420.0
1983	300.0	700.0	1 565.0	2 295.0	6 988.7	13 916.8	24 765.5h	25 765.5
1984	408.0	810.0	1 060.7i	2 436.3	7 960.3	14 594.6	26 052.4j	
1985	453.0	710.0	2 491.0k	2 179.0	8 310.0	15 218.0	28 198.0	29 361.0
1986	439.0	800.0	96.0	2 699.0	9 700.0	22 679.0	35 174.0l	36 413.0
1987			276.0	3 297.0	9 762.0	23 342.0	36 677.0m	

Notes:

a UA until 1977, EUA/ECU 1978 onwards.

b GNP until 1978, VAT from 1979 onward.

c This column includes for the years to 1970 surplus revenue from previous years carried forward to following years.

d As a result of the calculations to establish the relative shares of the member states in the 1976 budget, an excess of revenue over expenditure occurred amounting to 40 543 573 UA. This was carried forward to 1977.

e Including surplus brought forward from 1979 and balance of 1979 VAT and financial contributions.

f Including surplus of ECU 82.4 million and balance of 1979 VAT carried forward to 1981.

g Including surplus of ECU 661 million.

h Includes surplus of ECU 307 million.

i Includes ECU 593 of repayable advances by member states.

j There was a small deficit in 1984 in respect of EC budget due largely to late payment of advances by some member states.

k Includes non-repayable advances by member states of 1981, ECU 6 million.

l Budget adopted on 10 July 1986.

m Preliminary draft budget 1987.

Source: Commission of the European Communities, *European Economy*, Annual Economic Review, 1986–7, No. 29, July 1986, p. 167.

Table 8.4   Budgetary expenditure of the European Communities (million UA/EUA/ECU)[a]

	ECSC operational budget	European Development Fund	Euratom[b]	EC General Budget						Total
				EAGGF[c]	Social Fund	Regional Fund	Industry Energy Research	Adm. and others[d]	Total EC	
1958	21.7		7.9					5.9	5.9	35.5
1959	30.7	51.2	39.1					25.2	25.2	146.2
1960	23.5	63.2	20.0					28.3	28.3	135.0
1961	26.5	172.0	72.5		8.6			25.4	34.0	305.0
1962	13.6	162.3	88.6		11.3			81.0	92.3	356.8
1963	21.9	55.5	106.4		4.6			79.5	84.1	267.9
1964	18.7	35.0	124.4		7.2			85.9	93.1	271.1
1965	37.3	248.8	120.0	102.7	42.9			55.5	201.1	607.2
1966	28.1	157.8	129.2	310.3	26.2			65.8	402.2	717.3
1967	10.4	105.8	158.5	562.0	35.6			77.5	675.1	949.8
1968	21.2	121.0	73.4	2 250.4	43.0			115.3	2 408.6	2 624.2
1969	40.7	104.8	59.2	3 818.0	50.5			182.7	4 051.2	4 255.9
1970	56.2	10.5	63.4	5 228.3	64.0			156.1	5 448.4	5 578.5
1971	37.4	236.1		1 883.6	56.5		65.0	284.3	2 289.3	2 562.8
1972	43.7	212.7		2 477.6	97.5		75.1	424.3	3 074.5	3 330.9
1973	86.9	210.0		3 768.8	269.2		69.1	533.8	4 641.0	4 937.9
1974	92.0	157.0		3 651.3	292.1		82.8	1 011.9	5 038.2	5 287.2
1975	127.4	71.0		4 586.6	360.2	150.0	99.0	1 017.8	6 213.6	6 412.0
1976	94.0	320.0		6 033.3	176.7	300.0	113.3	1 392.2	7 952.6	8 366.6
1977[e]	93.0	800.0		6 667.6	55.3	400.0	167.0	1 303.9	8 483.2	9 376.2

1978	159.1	394.5	9 552.3	256.5	254.9	266.8	1 430.8	11 884.2	12 190.8
1979	173.9	480.0	10 765.0	527.0	499.0	288.0	2 368.0	14 602.5	15 256.4
1980	175.7	508.5	11 596.1	502.0	751.8	212.8	2 994.9[f]	16 057.5	16 741.7
1981	261.0	658.0	11 443.0	547.0	547.0	232.0	4 060.0	18 546.0[g]	19 465.0
1982	243.0	750.0	12 792.0	910.0	2 766.0[h]	346.0	4 613.0	21 427.0[i]	22 420.0
1983	300.0	752.0	16 331.3	801.0	2 265.5	1 216.2	4 151.5	24 765.5[j]	25 817.5
1984	408.0	810.0	18 985.8	1 116.4	1 283.3	1 346.4	3 387.4	26 119.3[k]	27 337.3
1985	453.0	710.0	20 546.4	1 413.0	1 624.3	706.9	3 932.4	28 223.0[l]	29 386.0
1986	439.0	800.0	23 104.0	2 533.0	2 373.0	762.0	6 402.0	35 174.0[m]	36 413.0
1987			24 077.0	2 589.0	2 495.0	1 055.0	6 461.0	36 677.0[n]	

Notes:

[a] UA until 1977, EUA/ECU 1978 onwards.

[b] Incorporated in the EC Budget from 1971.

[c] This column includes for the years to 1970, substantial amounts carried forward to following years.

[d] Including the European Parliament, the Council, the Court of Justice, the Court of Auditors and the administrative part of the ECSC Budget.

[e] In 1977 appropriations for the Social Fund carried forward from 1976 and subsequently cancelled amounted to 227 716 611 UA while total expenditure for 1977 amounted to only 172 439 999 UA giving the net figure shown here.

[f] Including surplus of ECU 82.4 million carried forward to 1981.

[g] Including ECU 1173 million carried forward to 1982.

[h] Including ECU 1819 million UK special measures.

[i] Including ECU 2211 million carried forward to 1983.

[j] Including ECU 1707 million carried forward to 1984.

[k] There was a small deficit in 1984 in respect of EC Budget due largely to late payment of advances by some member states.

[l] There was a cash deficit in 1985 of ECU 25 million due to late payment of advances by some member states.

[m] Budget adopted on 10 July 1986 – includes cost of refund of ECU 2685 million to UK.

[n] Preliminary draft budget 1987 – includes cost of refund of ECU 2366 million to UK.

Source: Commission of the European Communities, *European Economy,* Annual Economic Review, 1986–7, No. 29, July 1986, p. 166.

of stocks; EAGGF expenditure to be modified from a system of financial advances by the EC to one of reimbursement by national governments which would be recompensed later by the Community; automatic stabilizers to trigger action such as price cuts whenever spending passes a given limit. Other Commission proposals to tax oils and fats have been condemned because of their effects on both consumers and outside suppliers, such as the USA.

Despite encroaching bankruptcy, there are pressures to increase spending in desirable areas, to raise the profile of the Community and to offset uneven distributional effects of the Budget. Although expenditure on the Social Fund predated agricultural spending, the introduction of agricultural spending by the EC in 1965 swamped that of the Social Fund (which constituted a higher proportion of the Budget in 1965 than in subsequent years). Non-agricultural expenditure can only be expanded either by taking steps to cut agricultural spending, or by increasing the overall level of Community expenditure. Then the Social Fund could be increased – perhaps even to finance unemployment benefits – and the Regional Fund could make a real impact, rather than a cosmetic one, on the magnitude of EC regional problems.

There are particular obstacles impeding the redirection of budgetary expenditure. Those countries, especially agricultural ones, benefiting from the existing pattern of expenditure, are reluctant to see these eroded. Agricultural countries benefit substantially in terms of total receipts and the smaller countries, such as Ireland and Denmark, have fared particularly well in terms of per capital receipts. Such a redistribution of income on welfare grounds may be justified for Ireland, but not for Denmark. Other small countries, like Belgium and Luxembourg, have also gained significantly from being the host to Community institutions, though part of their income does not accrue to their own citizens but is repatriated by EC employees. While precise distributional effects of the Budget are uncertain and the President of the Commission, Jacques Delors, refused to publish net budgetary transfers for fear of encouraging '*juste retour*', some estimates have been made and published elsewhere, as shown in Table 8.5.

The Community is divided in its approach beween the Commission, Parliament and the southern European members which generally favour more expenditure, especially non-agricultural expenditure. On the other hand, the UK, West Germany and more recently France, which pay most towards financing the Community, want to limit their excessive expenditure. Increasing the level of expenditure would enhance the Community's role, making agreement easier, though there are strong constraints on expansion. Governments are concerned about a rising proportion of budgetary expenditure as a percentage of Community GDP, even though this

*Table 8.5   EEC Budget transfers, 1985 (figures in m ECU: + net benefit, −
net payment*

	GDP per head as % of EC(12) average	Before British rebate	After British rebate
Denmark	153	+ 400	+ 300
Luxembourg	142	+ 300	+ 300
West Germany	138	−3100	−3500
France	126	+ 500	0
Holland	112	+ 500	+ 400
Belgium	108	+ 600	+ 500
UK	91	−3000	−1000
Italy	86	+1200	+ 800
Ireland	66	+1200	+1100
Greece	38	+1400	+1400

Note: Spain and Portugal joined in the EEC only in 1986. They will probably be small net-budget beneficiaries, so worsening all other's positions.

Source: *The Economist*, 20 June 1987.

is far below the minimum proposed by the McDougall Report. National governments involved in making cutbacks in domestic expenditure to make room for the private sector − which they perceive to be the basis of success of their major competitors in the USA and Japan − find it hard to acquiesce to more expenditure at Community level. Furthermore, such expenditure, even when initiated to remedy the adverse distributional effects of the Budget, is sometimes wasteful and on inappropriate objectives.

The EC wishes to plan its future development on the basis of adequate, stable and guaranteed resources. In February 1987 Jacques Delors unveiled to the European Parliament proposals for a new source of revenue linked to GNP, permitting a significant increase in the Community Budget up to 1992. While the rate of increase in spending would be no greater than from 1980–86, there would be more spending on structural funds to create greater cohesion, as a quid pro quo for progress in the internal market. But expenditure on agriculture will still remain too high, even though it is intended that its share of the budget will fall to a half, while regional and social spending will double to reach about a quarter of the Budget.

The role of the institutions in the budgetary process. The Commission has continued in its role of providing new initiatives for further integration, with an accompanying need to finance such developments. The Commission prepares preliminary draft budgets which are examined by the Council of Ministers. There is a special Budget

Council which is composed of Ministers from national Finance Ministries and it reaches its decisions by qualified majority voting. The Council of Ministers usually trims back budgetary expenditure and then passes on the draft Budget to the EP.

The EP has tried to increase its powers, particularly in the budgetary field. It has been given the last word on so-called 'non-compulsory expenditure' — this differs from 'compulsory expenditure' that is necessary to carry out the provisions of the Treaty. Thus, non-compulsory expenditure relates largely to EC spending on regions, social policy, energy, industry, transport, and so on. Compulsory expenditure is mainly on agriculture, especially on Guarantee spending and some Guidance spending. The Council therefore still controls the bulk of expenditure and even on the non-compulsory expenditure (NCE) there is a limit by which this may be raised by the Parliament. The three objective criteria used to determine the maximum NCE are: the trend in GNP (in volume terms), the average variations in the budgets of member states, and the trend in the cost of living during the preceding financial year. The maximum rates fixed annually for NCE varied from 14.6 per cent for 1975 to 8 per cent for 1985.

Since 1979 the elected EP and the Council have been locked in a struggle almost every year over the size and shape of the Budget and their respective powers. Parliament has succeeded in raising annual expenditure marginally, even though its room for manoeuvre is mainly confined to NCE. For example, after Parliament's first reading of the Budget, the Council's second draft was some 10 per cent higher both in 1985 and in 1986.

Parliament and Council clashed quickly in 1979 when the latter failed to obtain the qualified majority necessary to reject the EP's increase in the Regional Fund. The conflict between the two institutions became even more intense in 1980 when the EP rejected the Budget for the first time, by 288 votes to 64. Clashes continued in the early eighties over contentious issues such as the CAP and the British Budgetary rebate. The Fontainebleau Summit in 1984 in tackling the latter appeared to have settled the Budgetary problem, paving the way to greater progress. In practice it failed to do this completely and there has been continuing budgetary turbulence.

Expenditure claims have tended to overstretch resources and at the end of most years since 1984 it has not been possible to agree satisfactorily on a Budget for the forthcoming year. For example, at the end of 1984 the proposed Budget for 1985 was rejected by the EP on the grounds that it only contained sufficient funding for agriculture for a period of ten months and not twelve months' expenditure. Another dispute emerged between Council and Parliament in 1986 and that time the EP denounced the Budget on the basis that it only contained enough money for ten members and not for an enlarged Community of twelve members. This dispute was referred to the Court of Justice and its judgment in March 1986 came down in favour of the Council having the final say in fixing the maximum rate and disappointed the EP by nullifying its powers other than at the margin. However, the Council was not wholly satisfied, since in June 1986 the Advocate General condemned the Council's dictatorial behaviour. The Advocate General, Mancini, recommended that if agreement could not be reached between the Council and Parliament, the matter should be referred to the President of the Court of Justice for a decision. The Court's judgment in July 1986 prohibited both Council and Parliament from establishing a *de facto* situation unilaterally. The consequence of its judgment is that the Council and the EP must negotiate and achieve a result. They have to agree on a maximum rate of increase of resources, otherwise the Community is forced to survive under a system of provisional twelfths (the previously monthly funds).

Disagreements have been resolved by the use of creative accounting, with terms such as 'negative reserves' (to which appropriations not used by the end of the year would be transferred). Early in 1987 yet another subtle proposal was made by the Budget Commissioner, Henning Christopherson, to stick to the 8.1 per cent agreed maximum growth in non-farm spending; but, to find some extra cash by pushing this to 8.149 per cent, by ignoring small changes which did not alter the first figure after the decimal point!

Conflicting interpretations have arisen since the Council had adopted accounting policies based on a stricter application than the EP, which has reflected the spirit of an evolving and expanding Community. Budgetary discipline provides a constraint on such developments and Euro-conflict has arisen over finance and the exercise of power. The EP has tried to exercise its budgetary influence on the Council in different ways; it has played on the divisions between the Council of Ministers dealing with budgetary and agricultural affairs; it has sought to exploit national divisions in the Council so as to muster a blocking minority, but has found it harder to get the qualified majority to increase the non-compulsory spending which Parliament favours. The EP has also continued to challenge the interpretation of what is compulsory and what is non-compulsory expenditure, trying to switch more elements into non-compulsory spending – even though a classification of these elements was agreed in 1982.

To monitor budgetary procedures, the Court of Auditors operates along with the Parliament's Committee of Budgetary Control. They are concerned to ensure that money is spent effectively to avoid waste and certainly greater attention needs to be given to getting value for money from EC expenditure.

Part III   Taxation in the UK and the problem of the Community Budget

Taxation. Before the UK joined the EC its tax system was distinctive in showing a greater reliance on direct taxation than other countries (particularly France and Italy), whilst its indirect taxation was based mainly on purchase tax across a wide range of consumer goods. This was levied at a wholesale stage and charged as a percentage of the wholesale price, originally at two rates, though both the rates and the number of them increased. Purchase tax came under criticism for its adverse effects on the performance of particular sectors, such as the motor industry. The problems of manufacturing industry and its excessive taxation in relation to services led to the introduction of the selective employment tax (SET) in 1966 – this was a tax on the employment of workers in the service sector.

VAT offered the advantage of replacing these taxes by a single sales tax levied at the retail stage. But a disadvantage was that it proved more costly to collect VAT since purchase tax had been collected from under 100 000 taxpayers. A seven-fold increase in tax officers was needed to collect VAT from more taxpayers. When the Richardson Committee first examined the replacement of purchase tax by VAT in 1964 they actually concluded that purchase tax was preferable to VAT. In 1973 the UK altered its system (as it did in other areas, such as its agricultural deficiency payments), not so much because of major defects but as measures to harmonize within the EC. After 1979 the Thatcher government increased the rate of VAT from 8 per cent to 15 per cent, with offsetting reductions in direct taxation as part of its new supply-side policy. Nevertheless, the government has shown some sensitivity to Community proposals to harmonize VAT as part of the creation of a full internal market, since this would affect British zero-rating on a wide range of goods and services such as food, housing, etc.

Budgetary problems for the UK. Budgetary problems have been a source of continual friction and strain in the UK's membership of the Community. Although in other EC countries few citizens consider that their own country benefits most from the EC, in the UK a large majority perceive not only that the UK benefits least but also contributes most (Hewstone 1986). Problems have arisen with regard to both revenue and expenditure.

On the revenue-side the UK has a highly open economy (especially in its trade with the rest of the world); it has contributed disproportionately to the EC's revenue in the form of customs duties and levies on agricultural imports. While the pattern of UK trade has changed, with greater imports from the Community, this has not really solved the problem. If the UK imports more foodstuffs from the EC, obviously no import levies are payable, but the UK simply substitutes higher trade costs for higher budgetary costs. In other words, instead of importing low-cost foodstuffs from the rest of the world and paying an import levy to raise the price to the level prevailing in the Community, the UK pays the high price directly to import from a Community supplier.

The choice of VAT as the major source of Community revenue is also unfavourable to countries with high consumption and low investment and which have imports in excess of exports. From a UK perspective, some additional source of revenue may have been preferable, such as a tax on imports of oil. But this would have resulted in the Community having an energy policy similar to its agricultural policy and given the criticisms of the latter it would not be desirable to advocate yet another high price policy. Furthermore, if the tax were imposed not on oil imports but on oil production, then the UK would actually suffer disproportionately. If a tax on oil (and other energy sources) were introduced, then from the viewpoint of conserving energy it would be better to tax consumption. While the latter would be a useful Community tax measure, unfortunately it would still not solve the UK's budgetary problems. In practice it is difficult to find additional revenue sources which are good taxes and which also result in a lower budgetary contribution by the UK (Denton 1983).

As a small agricultural producer, the UK has not been able to secure a net budgetary inflow from the overdeveloped level of CAP expenditure. Although a system of '*juste retour*', in which every country receives exactly the same as it contributes, cannot be recommended, a system in which low income countries are net contributors to the Budget is a very perverse outcome. It has proved extremely difficult to develop other common policies which are as favourable to the UK as the CAP is to the more agricultural countries. Although new areas of expenditure could be opened up, it is necessary to ensure that the Community is the appropriate level to conduct these policies instead of the national level. Expenditure by the EC on defence, social expenditure and so on would particularly suit the UK. Changes like this would be fundamental and to date have been mainly piecemeal, since politically the EC has found it necessary to retain the expensive CAP and this has constituted an unfortunate restraint on expanding expenditure in other areas.

Budgetary dialogue with the UK. When it joined the EC the UK accepted that it would contribute to the Budget in accordance with a fixed percentage key, beginning at 8.78 per cent in 1973 and increasing to 19.24 per cent in 1977. The Labour government became concerned that this would represent an undue burden on the UK, since its relatively slow rate of economic growth meant that its share of Community GNP was likely to decline; this happened, more so when measured using current exchange rates rather than rates designed to reflect purchasing power parity of currencies. The government focused upon reducing UK contributions, since it was dubious about being able to change Community expenditure in a way more favourable to the UK. It pressed forward with a renegotiation and agreement was reached at the Dublin Summit in 1975 for a payback system for countries which oversubscribe to the Budget. It applied to gross contributions and a complex formula was established for a sliding-scale reimbursement. Despite a favourable referendum vote in 1975, the UK's budgetary terms worked out badly.

Budgetary problems soon resurfaced and were brought to a head in 1979 by the new Conservative government, again at a Summit in Dublin. The UK pressed for a cut of £1 billion in its contribution, but the maximum reduction offered was £350 million. The government tried, relatively unsuccessfully, to increase Community expenditure in the UK, for example with proposals for greater Community aid for investment in the coal industry. Budgetary confrontation resulted in stresses and acrimony, deflecting the Community's attention from much needed developments in other areas. Although the UK appeared to have a strong case in pointing to the inequities in the Budget, its pleas were frustrated and France constantly argued that the only concessions could be lump sum, degressive and temporary (Butler 1986).

Early in 1980 the UK was offered a better deal after linking the Budget discussion to the setting of agricultural prices. On average between 1980 and 1982 the UK received a refund of about 70 per cent of its net budgetary contribution. The British government agreed at the Brussels Summit in March 1984 that its contributions would be redefined to exclude the counting of levies and customs duties in its search for some permanent solution. It appeared that this had been achieved at the Fontainebleau Summit in 1984 and in return for agreement to raise the EC VAT contribution, the UK obtained guaranteed rebates every year at just under 60 per cent − whereas the earlier rebates received under the 1980 agreements had been for absolute financial amounts (Denton 1984). The Fontainebleau agreement in its technically complex calculation of rebates to the UK created a special position which was resented by other countries. While West German contributions to the British rebate have been reduced, West Germany is still concerned about this, plus the fact that rich countries such as Denmark continue to be net beneficiaries from the Budget.

The resolution of the basic budgetary problems still falls short of the UK's aspirations, being inequitable to the extent that a country with a relatively low income per head remains a net contributor. Between 1973 and 1986 the UK's total budgetary imbalance with the EC was −£7785 million. However, some improved settlement had to be reached eventually to avoid an impasse so as not to distract the Community from new progress towards southern enlargement. It was recognized that the UK had a genuine grievance, but its tactics upset other member states in demanding the return of its own money and threatening established pillars of the Community, such as the CAP. British policy continues to be based on keeping tight budgetary finance to encourage agricultural reform; it has been adamant about better husbandry before sanctioning further expansion in expenditure. This attitude resulted in deadlock at the European Summit in Copenhagen in December 1987, since the UK's compensatory offer was less than that reached at Fontainebleau, though the use of the additional GDP base was welcomed. Fortunately, greater progress was possible, with a new agreement at the emergency European Summit in Brussels in February 1988.

9 Worldwide trading links

Part I External background

Although the EC has been concerned very much with the process of internal integration and with fostering intra-trade, it has had to institute a common external policy towards the rest of the world. The EC is a giant in world trade and has created a distinctive preferential system in its extra-trade arrangements. It has focused its closest links with key areas with which the major ex-colonial powers such as France and the UK have had historic links. It was natural that the EC would seek to consolidate these links in using trade and aid to exercise its political influence in strategic areas such as the Mediterranean and Africa. They are important sources of supplies of energy and raw materials which need assistance such as foreign investment from the Community to develop more rapidly.

The Community's external policy has become intertwined with its policies in other sectors. For example, the consequences of the CAP have resulted in outside countries seeking to preserve their exports to some extent by reaching special trade arrangements with the EC. Outsiders have also sought to reduce the diversion of their manufactured exports caused by the common external tariff (CET). Modifications to the latter represent the Community's most potent weapon in dealing with outsiders. EC preferential agreements have multiplied to such an extent that very few countries are subjected to the full CET. However, an open trading policy has accelerated the decline of the Community's traditional industries, with related regional problems in those areas affected by imports. The EC has recognized the need to expand the new high-tech industries, but some countries such as France have made progress towards this conditional upon using the EC's common commercial policy in a more protectionist way to outsiders (Pearce and Sutton 1986).

This chapter examines some of the EC's worldwide trading connections. How beneficial are these special trading arrangements to the Community and what have been some of their effects on other countries? It pinpoints those areas which have special arrangements with the Community: EFTA, most of the Mediterranean and in particular those countries in Africa, the Caribbean and the Pacific (ACP). Most emphasis is given to the ACP since EFTA has been covered in Chapter 1 and Mediterranean enlargement is developed in more detail in the next chapter. This hierarchical ranking has resulted in a 'pecking order' of outside links, some of which, like the Mediterranean agreements, have been condemned for being against both the latter and the spirit of GATT (Pomfret 1986).

*Table 9.1   EC(12) – exports and imports by main country groups (%)**

	Exports				Imports			
	1963	1973	1980	1985	1963	1973	1980	1985
EC(12)	48.4	56.1	55.8	54.7	43.1	53.2	49.4	52.9
EFTA(6)	13.4	11.3	11.0	10.0	9.0	8.3	8.6	9.3
Eastern Europe	3.0	3.8	3.5	2.8	3.4	3.1	3.7	3.9
United States	7.3	7.6	5.6	10.1	11.8	8.7	8.6	8.0
Japan	1.0	1.4	1.0	1.2	0.9	2.1	2.6	3.4
Developing countries	22.3	17.0	21.3	18.4	25.8	21.3	25.1	20.4
of which: OPEC	4.1	3.9	8.1	6.0	8.6	8.9	13.8	8.4
NICs	5.6	5.1	4.5	3.9	5.4	4.9	4.4	4.8
Rest of world	4.6	2.8	1.9	2.8	5.9	3.2	2.0	2.1

* Because of different data sources, some figures may deviate slightly from some of those in other tables.

Source: UN COMTRADE Data Base in A. Utne, *Efta Bulletin*, No. 4, Vol. XXVII, October–December 1986.

The geographical distribution of EC trade is shown in Table 9.1. More than half of EC trade was intra-trade by 1973, and its major external trading partners are the USA, EFTA and the developing countries.

Part II   The EC's preferential and non-preferential links

A   The EC's non-preferential links with developed countries

The United States. The EC and the USA have enjoyed very close links since the USA has generally supported EC integration, but their harmonious relationship has deteriorated in recent years. Friction has arisen in specific economic sectors such as that of agriculture, currently on the GATT agenda at the Uruguay Round, and the USA announced in 1987 that it wanted an end to all farm subsidies by the end of the century. In other industries such as steel, the Americans have opted for import controls, arguing that European imports have been highly subsidized (Hine 1985, p. 234; Tsoukalis 1986, p. 23).

In relation to eastern Europe the EC has adopted a less hostile view than the more distant Americans. The USA has been prepared to use trade sanctions as a way of putting pressure on the Soviet Union. Through the Co-ordinating Committee on Multilateral Export Controls (COCOM) security-related exports are controlled. The attempt by the USA to control exports of high-technology products to eastern Europe by its many business subsidiaries and by European companies operating under licence in the EC, has resulted in disagreements between the EC and the USA. The USA has likewise objected to Community countries subsidizing export credits and loans to eastern Europe.

Political/military differences have become more apparent, in particular under President Reagan. While they remain allies with common interests, the traditional close coupling between the two blocs is now questioned much more widely than in the past. Economically, the US faces massive budgetary and trade deficits, and the latter is likely to be cut only by reduced expenditure abroad, continued depreciation of the dollar and by further protectionist sentiments; these are likely to work against EC interests.

Japan. Japan began its trade dialogue with the Community in the early 1960s, although only bilateral deals were reached. The imbalance in trade has arisen since imports from Japan rose from under one per cent of EC imports in 1963 to 3.4 per cent in 1985, whereas EC exports to Japan showed only a minor increase from one per cent in 1963 to 1.2 per cent in 1985. While the virtue of a multilateral trading system is that it is unnecessary to achieve bilateral balance with each country, the EC and Japan agreed in 1983 to a voluntary export restraint (VER) on various sensitive product. VERs by the mid-1980s were applied to just over a third of Japanese exports to the Community. Despite these, Japan's trade surplus with the EC has continued to widen, reaching $16.7 billion in 1986.

The trading problems can be attributed not only to Japanese non-tariff barriers (NTBs), but to the Community's own deficiencies. These include low capital investment in high-tech sectors and weaker marketing: for example, in the mid-1980s there were only some 2000 European businessmen in Japan, whereas Japan had some 33 000 businessmen in Europe.

Comecon. Comecon is the acronym which is usually used to describe the Council for Mutual Economic Assistance (CMEA) which was founded in 1949. It was a means of ensuring Soviet hegemony in eastern Europe and its main membership consists of the USSR, Bulgaria, Czechoslovakia, the German Democratic Republic (GDR), Hungary, Poland and Romania. The aim of Comecon, like that of the EC, is to promote integration of trade in order to prevent wasteful duplication in production. Thus the Soviet Union supplies much of the energy, raw materials and aircraft, while other countries such as Hungary supply buses, and the GDR supplies electronics. Disagreements have arisen over specialization and Romania has pressed ahead, despite objections by the Soviet Union, with industries such as petrochemicals.

Compared with the EC, Comecon is a more inter-governmental and less supranational organization. The satellite states have preferred this, given the weight of the USSR. Factor mobility has also been less in Comecon and although capital has flowed from the USSR to countries such as the GDR and labour has moved from Poland to the GDR, these movements have been less easy than in the EC.

In 1986 53 per cent of Comecon trade was intra-trade and most of its members have conducted more than half of their trade within the bloc. One exception to this has been Romania, which has significantly reorientated its trading pattern with the West. The GDR is of particular significance in this context because it has a special trading relationship with West Germany. An inter-zonal trading agreement was signed in 1949 to provide free trade between the two parts of Germany and to try to reduce the isolated status of West Berlin. The latter has been a pawn in the struggle between East and West, and West Berlin's incorporation into the EC has been a source of friction. For example, it held up various agreements on fishing with the USSR and on the inclusion of socialist African states in Lomé. The intra-German trade has been unsupervised by the Community, and EC countries, apart from West Germany, have preferred to regard the GDR as an outsider. There has been some concern by them about imports from the rest of eastern Europe being channelled through the GDR. These intra-German links are very important, though there is no prospect of them superseding those with the Community, since the latter can absorb far more exports than the GDR.

Comecon's original autarkic view of trade eventually gave way to the realization that trade was a means of economizing on resources and of obtaining sophisticated products from the West. By 1986 12 per cent of Comecon trade was with the EC, though only 3 per cent of EC trade was with Comecon. Trade has been stimulated since the Community has granted most favoured nation treatment to eastern European countries, enabling them to benefit from tariff reductions (Yannopoulos 1985, p. 30). However, the links between the EC and Comecon have been bedevilled by a variety of limiting factors. Both systems are based on competing philosophies and they have been loathe to recognize each other legally, though under Gorbachev steps have been set afoot to give a belated formal recognition to the Community. The links have been mainly on a bilateral level between individual countries, or between the EC and eastern European countries, in areas such as fisheries, in which countries like the USSR have entered into negotiations with the Community (Lodge 1983). The EC has not wished to legitimate Soviet hegemony in eastern Europe by its actions.

The trade of Comecon with the Community has been inhibited by the new protectionism, though apart from products such as textiles and clothing, etc., their exports have suffered less from discriminatory trade agreements than from their own internal and fundamental deficiencies. For example, Comecon countries have lacked a proper pricing policy for their products, often underpricing them to obtain Western currency, and partly to undermine Western markets — this has resulted in numerous anti-dumping cases against eastern Europe. They have also faced problems in exporting agricultural products because of the CAP, though in some respects agricultural exporters fared better than those selling industrial products because of the generally poor quality of the latter and severe competition from the NICs. The import needs of Comecon for industrialization have generally exceeded their export capabilities. Currency convertibility led to bilateral deals involving different forms of counter-trade; the latter involved complex and rather inefficient forms of trading.

The desire of eastern Europe to catch up with the West has led to massive borrowings to finance their industrialization. This resulted in major indebtedness because of rising interest rates and economic recession which reduced the propensity of Community countries to import from Comecon. Poland was the first country to experience problems in servicing its massive external debt and by the early 1980s its hard currency debt ratio to hard currency exports approached 500 per cent. The root cause of the Polish crisis has been lack of incentive and poor morale (Drewnowski 1982). Rescheduling Polish debts has become necessary, accompanied by massive cut-backs. The Polish crisis has led the West to recouple trade policy to political and human rights issues.

B   The EC's preferential trade relations

EFTA. The EC has accorded primacy to its trading links with EFTA which lies at the apex of its trading hierarchy. Special arrangements had to be made for EFTA countries after the departure of the UK and Denmark into the EC in 1973. Free trade exists in industrial goods, with a single trade document being used. The Community has tended to run a balance of payments surplus in its trade with EFTA. In 1985 EFTA accounted for about 10 per cent of the EC's trade, whereas for EFTA the Community is far more important and 56 per cent of EFTA's trade was conducted with it in 1985. Nearly three-quarters of this EC–EFTA trade consists of manufactured goods. While EFTA is more important as a group than in terms of individual countries, some of the latter are still significant, since the Community sells more goods and services to Switzerland and to Sweden than to Japan, more to Norway than to Canada, more to Finland than to China (*The Economist* 21–27 November 1987).

The Mediterranean. The importance of the Mediterranean to the Community has grown from the initial preferential trade links which

France conducted with its former North African colonies in Morocco, Tunisia and Algeria. Algeria has the largest population and income per head of the three countries, drawing much of its revenue from oil exports. The agreement with these three Maghreb countries is separate from the Community's agreements with other countries in Africa under the ACP. Economically, countries like Tunisia have responded more positively to Community preferences than others such as Morocco. Morocco has also shown concern at Iberian enlargement of the Community, with estimates that this may cost Morocco some 2 per cent of its GDP (*Financial Times* 13 July 1987). In July 1987 Morocco surprised the Community by applying for membership, though this is impossible since membership is only open to European countries. Unfortunately, the Community appears to have got itself into a zero sum game in which trade concessions to certain countries are at the expense of others.

The signing of an association agreement with Greece in 1961 established a precedent, after which it became difficult to reject other preferential applications and one was soon signed with Turkey in 1963. Greece has carried its association to full membership and this is discussed in the next chapter, along with Turkey's application.

At first the Community was much preoccupied with internal integration, but its preferential agreements with African countries (under Yaoundé and later Lomé conventions), and the Maghreb (Morocco, Algeria and Tunisia), and Greece and Turkey, led to other preferential agreements in 1970 with Spain and Israel. The Community has a free trade agreement with Israel and the latter has gained significantly from this. To maintain a balance with Arab countries, co-operation agreements have been signed with the important Mashreq (Egypt, Lebanon, Syria and Jordan).

The proliferation of Mediterranean agreements in the early 1970s also included an association with Malta after 1970 and with Cyprus after 1972, and customs unions exist for free industrial trade with these two islands. Both have recorded good rates of industrial growth, though Malta has been in a better position to raise its exports to the EC and has attracted inward investment, especially in industries such as clothing (Pomfret 1986, pp. 68–75).

Yugoslavia also signed a non-preferential agreement so that by the 1970s the only Mediterranean countries lacking in special relations with the Community were Albania and Libya. The complicated pattern of individual agreements required some rationalization and after Commission proposals in 1972 the Community sought to replace individual agreements by a more global approach to the Mediterranean. The Community has identified this area as one of strategic importance and has used its commercial policy to exercise political influence – whereas the USA has used its naval presence. The EC draws its oil and other raw materials from the area. The Mediterranean countries themselves have perceived economic advantages in securing access to the EC market to stimulate their own industrial development and agriculturally to offset some of the protectionist nature of the CAP. The EC has brought the Mediterranean into its orbit, though the extension of its influence in the area infringes GATT. It provides a poor example to other countries such as the USA which could also start to make greater use of preferential agreements as part of its own foreign policy (Pomfret 1986).

The general view was that the effects of preferential agreements would only be marginal, since tariffs have been lowered by GATT. However, preferences have had a substantial impact on particular products where EC protection has been high, such as agriculture and textiles. The more outward-looking Mediterranean countries have been the ones to benefit most and they have provided an attractive source for multi-national inward investment. Hence, it was a logical development for countries such as Spain to move to full membership of the Community.

The southern enlargement of the Community has aggravated its relations with outsiders such as the USA and other Mediterranean countries. The countries producing similar products to those of the new entrants are the ones most vulnerable to displacement. New entrants to the Community not only add to its immediate problems, but dynamically the effects of higher Community agricultural prices are likely to increase supply, further threatening outside Mediterranean countries. The EC since enlargement has increased its self-sufficiency in many products, and imports from 'foreigners' seem likely to bear the brunt of future protectionism.

ACP countries: problems of trade and aid. ACP countries, as LDCs, are characterized by low income per head and over-dependence on agriculture. Most endure a precarious agricultural existence and some have suffered badly from drought in recent years. Many of the younger skilled and more mobile people have often been forced to emigrate from arid African countries to take advantage of opportunities elsewhere in countries like Senegal or the Ivory Coast.

The oil exporting countries have naturally benefited from the rise in oil prices (including ACP countries such as Nigeria, Congo, Gabon, Trinidad and Tobago). Other ACP countries which are oil importers have suffered and also their exports to OPEC have not consisted of sufficient industrial products to increase sales there significantly.

Apart from exogenous shocks, many LDCs have been moulded by their colonial inheritance. For example, high wages in the public sector, plus a legacy of minimum wage legislation, have distorted resource allocation. Overseas multinationals have further reinforced the bias against investment in the indigenous private industrial sector. High wages militate against labour-intensive employment (yet labour is the abundant factor), and also generate inflationary pressure. ACP countries have tended to experience higher wage costs and inflation than many of the NICs in Asia.

LDCs require financial aid to fill both their savings-investment gap and their gap in foreign exchange. They can see the benefits from aid, even though they prefer to earn their living in the world to a greater extent by engaging in trade. Indeed, the latter is of far greater significance, since aid under Lomé has been equivalent to only about 3 per cent of ACP exports to the EC (Stevens 1984).

Aid has created some problems with regard to debt servicing and over-dependence on donor countries. The EC Pisani Memorandum in 1982 noted that 'below a certain effectiveness and relevance, aid becomes an evil for it nourishes illusions and encourages passivity'. This is a very controversial issue since many development economists still maintain that the benefits exceed the costs and that the quality and quantity of aid should be improved. About 15 per cent of EC(10) aid has been channelled through the Community. EC aid has been criticized on the grounds of its small size – in relation to keeping up with inflation and the growing membership of the ACP – and bureaucratic documentation which has resulted in slow disbursement. Although in principle the ACP are responsible for selecting aid projects, the EC has used its financial powers to influence the choice and implementation of projects (Stevens 1984, p. 16).

EC association with the ACP. Links with LDCs were not provided for in the Spaak report in 1956 but were proposed subsequently by France and included in the EC, since France regarded its colonial territories as a natural extension of France itself. It was also a means of ensuring that some of the financial costs of aiding overseas territories would be shouldered between EC countries. A European Development Fund (EDF) was established to channel aid to the associates and over the first five years it was agreed that France and Germany would subscribe the lion's share equally.

France has been very successful in charging high prices for its exports to the associated countries. Where French production costs have been above the world price this has had the adverse effect of diverting trade towards less efficient French producers. Close francophone co-operation has been maintained in Africa, helped by monetary union between France and the West African and Central African states. The large-scale presence of French advisors and a tendency to tie aid to French exports enabled France to supply 40 per cent on average of francophone imports beween 1975 and 1982 and to enjoy a massive trade surplus with francophone Africa (Barclays Bank Review 1983). Trade with associates has tended to provide a 'significant balance of trade surplus for the EC which has helped it to offset trade deficits with countries at a higher level of economic development such as the USA and Japan.

From Yaoundé to Lomé. By the early 1960s many of the overseas territories had been given independence and a new basis of association signed at Yaoundé in 1963 came into effect in 1964. It covered 18 associated African and Malagasy states (AASM), and was later joined by Mauritius in 1971. Under Yaoundé I expenditure was 730 million units of account and under Yaoundé II from 1969–75 918 million units of account were spent. The aid was generous since most of it was given in grants and much of it went to heavily populated countries like Zaire (the ex-Belgian Congo). Some of the interior states, for instance, Chad, are very backward and much in need of aid, whereas many of the coastal states in Africa enjoy greater scope for trade (Cosgrove 1969).

Yaoundé was essentially neo-colonial, with no pretence of economic equality between the EC and the African associates. Trade relations were based on the reciprocity of trade advantages. However, under Lomé, countries succeeded in ending the process of having to grant reverse preferences (Coffey 1975). The first agreement at Lomé (the capital of Togo) in 1975 was between the EC and 46 ACP countries; it was considered an inspiring and exemplary step forward towards a more balanced relationship with LDCs. Yet this is something of a facade since the ACP countries are so much more dependent upon the EC for trade and aid, whereas the ACP constitutes a much less significant trading partner for the Community. Nevertheless, the fact that the Caribbean and Pacific could form a joint group with the Africans was remarkable and their co-operation has created a group with some bargaining power and an ability to speak with one voice.

Nigeria, the Ivory Coast and Zaire account for nearly half of total ACP exports to the Community. The EC is much less important for the Caribbean countries for whom the USA is a greater trading partner. Poverty is endemic since about 40 per cent of ACP countries recorded no growth in income per head during the 1970s and by 1984 only 16 Lomé countries had an income per head of over a thousand dollars. Their dilemma is which path to take in development since the formation of horizontal regional trading blocs separate from vertical links with the Community is very appealing. Unfortunately, intra-trade between LDCs is low and disagreements have arisen over the location of industries. This has not been an insuperable problem in all horizontal trading blocs, but continuing difficulties have forced LDCs into traditional trade links with the Community.

A second and third Convention were signed at Lomé, based upon the same principles of duration and legality as the first agreement. Although they manifested improvements in some areas, the Community in recession could never match the aspirations and needs of the ACP. In Lomé II, in which agreement was finally reached on 31 October 1979, the EC exploited the divisions and lack of leadership in the ACP (Long 1980, Ch. 2). Negotiations were further protracted during Lomé III since the ACP was tied up with negotiations relating to the reduced funding from other international agencies at that time.

The financial endowment of ECU 3.5 billion under Lomé I was increased to ECU 5.5 billion under Lomé II and ECU 8.5 billion under Lomé III. However, under Lomé III 1985–89, this had to cover 66 states, compared with 46 states under Lomé I (see Table 9.2).

Most of the financial aid has been in the form of outright grants, or loans on very soft terms. The role of the EIB has been enhanced in Lomé III, particularly in providing risk capital. Apart from its financial endowment, Lomé III has a significant chapter on encouraging the greater flow of private investment to the ACP.

Lomé III has broken new ground in its provision for greater cultural and social co-operation. It has also placed considerable

Table 9.2   Lomé III – financial endowment for 1985–89 (mECU)

Grants to individual ACP states	4306
Emergency aid	210
Aid for refugees	80
Interest rate subsidies for EIB loans	210
STABEX	925
SYSMIN	415
Special loans	600
Risk capital	600
Loans from EIB	1100
Total	8500 ·

Note: **ACP states:** Angola, Antigua and Barbuda, Bahamas, Barbados, Belize, Benin, Botswana, Burkina Faso, Burundi, Cameroon, Cape Verde, Central African Republic, Chad, Comoros, Congo, Djibouti, Dominica, Equatorial Guinea, Ethiopia, Fiji, Gabon, The Gambia, Ghana, Grenada, Guinea, Guinea Bissau, Guyana, Ivory Coast, Jamaica, Kenya, Kiribati, Lesotho, Liberia, Madagascar, Malawi, Mali, Mauritania, Mauritius, the People's Republic of Mozambique, Niger, Nigeria, Papua New Guinea, Rwanda, St. Christopher and Nevis, St. Lucia, St. Vincent, São Tomé and Príncipe, Senegal, Seychelles, Sierra Leone, Solomon Islands, Somalia, Sudan, Suriname, Swaziland, Tanzania, Togo, Tonga, Trinidad and Tobago, Tuvalu, Uganda, Vanuatu, Western Samoa, Zaire, Zambia, Zimbabwe.

Source: M. Blackwell, Lomé III, *Finance and Development*, September 1985, p. 33.

emphasis on developing services such as tourism and maritime transport. Concessions have been made within the existing framework to increase imports from the ACP in sectors such as agriculture. The main obstacle has been the restrictiveness imposed by the CAP. In Lomé III the EC made special arrangements for beef, rice, sugar, rum and bananas, plus agreement to broaden and speed up requests for special access. Changes were also made in relation to other schemes and these are discussed below.

STABEX. While the Community's Export Revenue Stabilisation Scheme (STABEX) was predated by the IMF's own compensatory finance scheme, the conditions of STABEX have been less strict and it has given preferential treatment to very disadvantaged countries. The numbers of primary products covered under the scheme have been increased in each Convention and 48 products are listed in the appropriate article of the third ACP-EC Convention. In addition, the restrictive threshold qualifications have been reduced. To obtain assistance the commodity must exceed a dependence threshold of export earnings in the previous year and export earnings have to fall by a minimum amount below a reference level in the four years preceding the claim. The dependence threshold and reference level have been cut from 7.5 per cent in Lomé I to 6.5 per cent in Lomé II and 6 per cent in Lomé III. For the least developed, island and land-locked states, the dependence and reference levels have been reduced from 2.5 per cent in Lomé I to 2 per cent in Lomé II and 1.5 per cent in Lomé III.

A defect of STABEX is its limited funding and with some falling commodity prices for products such as groundnuts and coffee, transfers have had to be scaled down significantly. The importance of these two products in total STABEX expenditure is shown in Table 9.3 for the period 1975–85.

These primary products have influenced the distribution of STABEX expenditure between ACP states, with Senegal topping the list of beneficiaries. This is shown in Table 9.4.

In some respects, the distribution is arbitrary since some poor countries which fail to meet the qualifications have suffered, *vis-à-vis* a few relatively more prosperous countries which have had their export earnings included. Many other criticisms have been levelled at STABEX, such as its bias against countries which have efficient domestic commodity policies and balance of payments management (McQueen 1977; Hewitt 1984; Hine 1985).

SYSMIN. The Système Minérais (SYSMIN) was an innovation in Lomé II and is a similar scheme for mineral products to that for primary products in STABEX. Minerals, with the exception of iron ore, had been excluded from STABEX. Iron ore has been switched

Table 9.3   STABEX 1975–85 — aggregate balance-sheet by product

	Total (in ECU)
All groundnut products	333 780 778
Coffee	282 196 654
All cocoa products	161 299 447
All cotton products	81 330 854
Iron ore	61 789 536
All wood products	45 349 687
Oil cake	45 303 777
All copra and coconut products	42 962 224
Sisal	33 118 052
Bananas	20 034 026
All palm products	18 165 476
Beans	17 838 522
Tea	17 243 689
Cajou kernals	11 458 241
Raw hides and skins	10 006 845
Vanilla	8 173 099
Sesame seeds	5 783 823
Cloves	5 212 874
Kante kernals	1 937 603
Essential oil	1 510 469
Mohair	1 290 959
Gum arabic	848 489
Prawns	710 289
Nutmeg	637 851
Pyrethrum	608 802
Grand total	1 208 592 066

Source: Eurostat, ACP Statistics 1987.

Table 9.4   The top ten beneficiaries from STABEX 1975–85

	Receipts (in ECU)
Senegal	183 257 156
Sudan	125 042 319
Ivory Coast	113 324 801
Ghana	90 647 339
Ethiopia	53 807 619
Papua New Guinea	50 690 742
Tanzania	50 473 947
Kenya	44 865 565
Togo	41 775 242
Mauritania	37 000 450

Source: Eurostat, ACP Statistics 1987.

into SYSMIN along with various other mineral products, though the cost of financing these is less than if they had been included within STABEX (Long 1980, pp. 104–6). The rationale of SYSMIN is to tackle the depletion of mineral resources, although the high demand in the 1960s and the 1970s was in fact dampened by slower economic growth during the 1980s. Africa is very well endowed with minerals and metals, far more than the Caribbean or the Pacific. The scheme helps mineral producers where earnings fall below production costs and where production is threatened. A trigger threshold was set at 10 per cent with a dependence threshold of 15 per cent (and 10 per cent in the case of the least developed, island and land-locked states). The range of products included iron ore, copper, phosphates, manganese, bauxite, alumina and tin.

Criticisms have been levelled at the restrictive coverage of products and countries covered by the scheme. One modification made under Lomé III was the opening of a second 'window' for ACP countries which derived 20 per cent of their export earnings (12 per cent for the least developed, island and land-locked countries), from a combination of mining products – other than precious minerals, oil and gas, but not necessarily those mentioned specifically in the convention. This was expected to broaden the number of beneficiaries, since in the first four years of SYSMIN only four countries benefited: Zambia, Zaire, Guyana and Rwanda. The modified scheme was considered likely to benefit ACP states such as Botswana, Niger and Zimbabwe. It was also agreed that SYSMIN funds could be used to tackle problems emanating from adverse developments like new technology. In addition, SYSMIN ceased to be concerned solely with maintaining productive capacity, and where it was in the interests of the ACP then orderly reductions in capacity could be financed.

The consequences of association with the ACP. ACP countries in association with the EC have naturally derived some economic benefits, although the trading benefits have been less than anticipated. Under both the Yaoundé and the Lomé agreements the associates' share of total EC imports has fallen and surprisingly they have had a slower rate of export growth to the Community than those from some other developing countries. ACP performance has been disappointing in several respects. Its share in all extra-EC imports fell from 8.1 per cent in 1974 to 5.5 per cent in 1982 (Hewitt, 1984; *The Courier* July–August 1986). The ACP share of world trade also fell from 2.5 per cent in 1970 to 1.6 per cent in 1982, excluding Nigeria. Furthermore, the degree of intra-ACP trade has remained low – only about 4 per cent – with a high proportion of this being conducted in regionally-integrated blocs such as the Economic Community of West African States (ECOWAS).

The apparent liberalism of the Lomé agreements, with their lack of formal quantitative restrictions, conceals certain weaknesses. For example, most ACP exports — tropical foodstuffs and raw materials — enter the EC duty free in any case. For those products where the ACP does enjoy an advantageous margin of preference over other LDCs, this has been reduced by multilateral tariff reductions under GATT, plus other special arrangements such as the GSP. The CAP has been mentioned as one obstacle to agricultural exports, while industrially many ACP countries have been unable to benefit significantly because of their low level of industrial development. Furthermore, restrictive rules of origin were imposed under Lomé I, whereby 50 per cent of value added had to take place within ACP states. This was a high level of added value to set for countries with limited manufacturing industry and which needed to co-operate with other non-Lomé states. The EC has responded by making the rules more flexible where they were found to be inhibiting industrial development.

In industries favoured by LDCs, such as textiles, the ACP share of exports by LDCs to the Community has been very low. Furthermore, a few countries, such as Mauritius, have accounted for a high proportion of these exports, having attracted considerable inward investment into the textile industry. The benefits being derived by Mauritius eventually led to national safeguards being imposed in the form of VERs by the UK and France. Another country which has been quite successful in developing and diversifying its trade has been the Ivory Coast. Hence, the consequences of Lomé depend upon which countries are examined and to focus on overall ACP performance, dominated by some countries with poor performance, such as Ghana, Zaire and Zambia, may result in a misleading conclusion (Stevens 1984, Ch. 2).

While ACP trade gains may have been relatively limited, this has not placated other countries which have expressed continuing concern that in the long-run their own exports will tend to be displaced from the Community market. Furthermore, some trade diversion has been observed in particular products (Balassa 1975). However, in many products the ACP preference is ineffective either because the ACP is quite competitive without the preferences, or, at the opposite extreme, even with the benefit of the preferences it still remains insufficiently competitive. Where the ACP preference has been decisive is for products such as palm oil, in which the ACP countries thereby have raised their competitiveness.

The ACP importance as a supplier to the Community is particularly high for specific products. For example, in 1985 they supplied 83 per cent of its sugar imports (though only to top up heavily protected EC beet output), 79 per cent of its cocoa imports, 64 per cent of its aluminium imports, 41 per cent of its coffee imports and 24 per cent of its copper imports.

Outside non-ACP countries have considered it vital to try to reach some agreement with the Community to minimize perceived disadvantages and to safeguard their interests. To outsiders the attraction of the large Community market is very clear and there has been a scramble to reach some kind of trading agreement with it.

C   The generalized system of preferences (GSP)

Those LCDs not in association with the EC have been eligible under the GSP. Both the EC and the UK introduced a GSP scheme in 1971, though the former scheme was less extensive in coverage. The enlarged Community operates one GSP which gives tariff concessions on industrial and agricultural imports − though the agricultural imports are highly restricted by the CAP. GSP has offered much less than either Yaoundé or Lomé since GSP is more restrictive and it excludes many of the products which are important to the associates. It has quotas and covers fewer products, with restrictions on products such as textiles. The GSP lacks the binding and permanent nature of Lomé. Although the GSP covers a given time period, the Community can make withdrawals from it at any time without breaching its legal obligations. Where there has been a surge in imports from the successful NICs the Community has introduced safeguards. The EC also applies rules of origin which do not allow cumulation apart from the imports of regional groupings.

The effects of the GSP have generally been very limited (Balassa 1975; Hine 1985). Most LDCs naturally have only a limited base for the production of industrial exports and it is the NICs which have been most successful; the latter, whilst being relatively efficient, are often not the neediest countries. Seven countries − Yugoslavia, Malaysia, Hong Kong, India, South Korea, Brazil and Romania − have been responsible for over half of the Community's GSP imports (Hine 1985, p. 210).

China is now covered by the GSP. It has been seeking closer links with the Community to offset the dominance of the superpowers. In 1978 a non-preferential trade agreement was signed with China, which was followed in 1985 by a trade and co-operation agreement (Redmond 1987).

Part III   The British Commonwealth

When the UK joined the EC in 1973 it was natural that some arrangements would be made to fit the British Commonwealth into a modified association with the Community. What was at issue was whether this was to embrace both the less developed and the developed countries in the Commonwealth which had enjoyed Imperial preference. Provisions had been made by the EC largely to suit French overseas interests and the overall outcome has tended to reflect a French view of the outside world; but also West Germany's special interests in trade with the GDR were catered for. The UK successfully negotiated agreements to replace its special links with most LDCs and in addition special treatment was provided for New Zealand, despite dissatisfaction by French farmers about imports of New Zealand dairy products. The old dominions, Canada and Australia, though important suppliers of products such as minerals to the EC, have refocused their links in their own region, establishing closer relationships with countries like the USA and Japan.

Even before the UK entered the Community some less developed Commonwealth countries had already reached their own agreements with the EC. They had been encouraged to do so in the expectation that the UK would enter the Community. It was paradoxical that in the 1960s some of these LDCs were successful in joining the EC and began to discriminate in favour of the EC and against the UK. Nigeria was the first Commonwealth country to appreciate the benefits of an agreement with the expanding Community market which was importing more than twice as much of its important cocoa exports than the UK. There was recognition of the need to become associated to prevent a displacement of sales by competitors which already enjoyed association under the Yaoundé Convention.

By 1969 the three East African countries, Tanzania, Uganda and Kenya, had reached agreement with the EC, but their terms were less favourable than those accorded to the Yaoundé associates. They were only able to reach an agreement on trade (not on aid) and in trade they not only had to accept quotas on some of their exports which were in strong competition with the Yaoundé producers but also had to grant even more beneficial reverse preferences to the EC.

The incorporation of 21 Commonwealth countries into the first Lomé Convention helped to bridge Anglo-French divisions which had resulted in a carving up of the African continent. The Commonwealth associates were in many cases more developed than their counterparts and less prepared to accept a subservient position. The UK has helped to turn the Community into a more outward-looking bloc. Prior to UK entry into the Community, UK imports from LDCs were about a quarter of its total imports, whereas about a fifth of total EC imports came from LDCs. The liberal trading policy of the UK, and the support from the USA, moved the Community towards their own approach of requiring no reverse preferences from associated countries. Although today the UK is still a major importer from LDCs, its growth of imports from ACP countries has been relatively slow. France has overtaken the UK as the major market for the ACP, while West Germany imports more manufactured goods from the ACP than does the UK (*The Courier* July/August 1986).

Whereas there was no sugar agreement as part of the Yaoundé Convention – the Congo being the only significant producer until Mauritius joined in 1972 – the Commonwealth sugar agreement with the UK was used as the basis of a new ACP agreement. The Community agreed to buy 1.2 million tonnes of sugar from the ACP; this was about 60 per cent of total exports. While the price had to be negotiated between ACP exporters and EC consuming countries, it could not be lower than the price agreed by the Community for its own producers. The guarantees have been helpful, though unfortunately offset by the EC's over-production of beet sugar and the dumping of this on the world market which has tended to depress world prices.

One area of the Commonwealth which suffered is the part in Asia which was deemed ineligible for inclusion in Lomé. It was argued that Bangladesh, India, Malaya, Pakistan, Sri Lanka, Singapore and Hong Kong differed in economic structure and their inclusion in Lomé would dilute the benefits enjoyed by other ACP associates. They are covered instead by the EC's GSP scheme, though this was tighter than the UK's own GSP. Over time, the UK has fallen in line with a less liberal policy towards those countries not covered by the EC's preferential arrangements. Those groups (ACP) for which the UK was able to negotiate special terms have been able to increase their share of trade with the Community; but other LDCs have been squeezed by such preferential agreements and by the primacy accorded to trade with other blocs such as EFTA and the Mediterranean.

10   Enlargement and integration: prospect and retrospect

Part I   The new Community

The original Six (West Germany, France, Italy, Belgium, the Netherlands and Luxembourg) reflected many differences: for example, Italy with its particular problems in the Mezzogiorno for which special provisions were necessary. Nevertheless, the Six constituted a much more homogeneous and optimal grouping than the current twelve members of the Community today. The first enlargement of the Community in 1973 enhanced its northern bias, bringing in the UK, Ireland and Denmark. Subsequent enlargement in the 1980s has shifted the balance of influence more to southern Europe after the entry of Greece in 1981 and the accession of Spain and Portugal from the first of January 1986.

Why has the Community doubled its membership? It is open to any European country to apply for membership of the EC. Countries outside the Community regard it with awe, seeing it as a much stronger, united and more attractive organization than it often appears to be once they have gained membership. The EC has generally looked on applications favourably since its image is strengthened by its new found popularity, and it has been flattered by applications to join. It has become a more powerful actor with an enhanced capacity to exercise its economic and political influence in international affairs. The EC has been greatly strengthened in size and potential power; for example, its population is some 321.0 million and its share of world trade (excluding intra-EC trade) is 20.9 per cent of exports and 21.9 per cent for imports.

Unfortunately, enlargement of the EC has also multiplied its problems, making it a less optimal grouping. The addition of more members has aggravated procedural difficulties. A system of majority voting on particular issues will help, encouraged by the SEA, though there will be ill-will if countries are outvoted on issues which they perceive to be important. The incorporation of extra members has resulted in new official languages, with the multiplication of interpretation and translation services. The EC has now nine official languages: Danish, Dutch, English, French, German, Greek, Italian, Portuguese and Spanish. Economic disparities have similarly been increased with a lower income per head and wider national and regional variations within an even more agricultural Community. There are also dangers that the less competitive countries which have joined the EC will push it towards more protectionism against non-members.

Part II   Enlargement and integration

A   Southern enlargement

Greece. The entry of Greece as the tenth member of the EC in 1981 completed its links with the Community. These had been established 20 years earlier with the signing of the Athens Agreement in 1961 which had commenced the association of Greece with the Community. Greece has encountered both political and economic problems. Politically it moved from a military coup in 1967 back to a democratic civil regime in 1974. Economically, Greece has a larger percentage of its labour force in agriculture than either Portugal or Spain; furthermore, the contribution of agriculture to Greek GNP is much lower than its contribution to total employment. Nevertheless, Greece enjoyed both a food surplus in its trade with the Community and also with the rest of the world (Tsoukalis 1981). Greece submitted a memorandum to the EC in 1982 outlining the problems of the Greek economy and the inadequacy of Community policies; this included the CAP market organization which covered only 75 per cent of Greek agricultural production compared with 95 per cent of agricultural production in other member countries (Nicholson and East 1987, p. 198). Greece has an overdeveloped service sector whilst its industry manifests serious deficiencies, with some economists having referred to its deindustrialization before even reaching the stage of industrial maturity.

The dissatisfaction of Greece with some aspects of the Community has been alleviated by a positive response to deal with its problems. Currently there seems little likelihood of any withdrawal by Greece from the EC since its net impact on the Greek economy has generally been positive and it is a net beneficiary from the CAP (Yannopoulos 1986). Greece has used its bargaining position to obtain favourable treatment in the Integrated Mediterranean Programmes (IMPs) before agreeing to Iberian enlargement of the EC. Greece has also enjoyed leverage in the Community over its rival, Turkey, and it has taken a hard line because of the occupation by Turkish forces of the northern part of Cyprus.

Portugal. Unlike Greece, which enjoyed close links with the EC over many years, Portugal enjoyed close links with EFTA. It first joined EFTA to retain its close links with the UK. At the time Portugal lacked a democratic political system and was concerned to continue with its colonial links overseas. It fared well in EFTA since it had a long timetable for cutting its tariffs on imports, whereas those tariffs against its exports were eliminated more quickly.

Portugal's decision to become a full member of the EC coincided with its more European outlook and the shedding of its colonial empire. Its trade agreement with the EC in 1973 offered less generous terms than those which had been granted to Greece. With the return to full democracy in Portugal after the departure of Caetano in 1974 public opinion gave wide support to full membership of the EC, even more so than that in Greece. Unlike Greece, Portugal is weaker in agriculture but stronger industrially. However, Portugal has by far the lowest income per head in the Community and faces potential difficulties. In agriculture, Portugal is extremely inefficient, with low agricultural productivity, and for many years it has been a net importer of food. After 1974 its food imports rose again to help feed the people displaced from the colonies (*retornados*). Investment in agriculture has been low since priority was given to industrialization. But Portugal will face intense industrial competition within the EC and in 1986 it lost its narrow trade surplus with the EC. Even in traditional sectors such as textiles which in 1985 accounted for 35 per cent of all Portuguese overseas earnings there is fierce competition: for example, the granting of a large EC textile quota to Turkey has been unpopular.

Portugal also seems likely to suffer in some respects from the opening up of trade in Iberia with Spain. Historically, their joint trade has been low, and in 1984 only 4.4 per cent of Portugal's exports and 7.2 per cent of its imports were conducted with Spain. For Spain, 2.4 per cent of its exports and 0.7 per cent of its imports were with its Portuguese neighbour. Although Portugal has the advantage of lower wages, Spain benefits from its larger home market and stronger companies, reinforced by an influx of much multinational investment in recent years.

Spain. Spanish membership of the Community was a justified reward for its return to democracy, but Spain probably poses the greatest economic challenge for the EC − certainly since the digestion of the UK in 1973. Spain had been very much a closed economy under Franco, and until 1970 it had neither established trading links with EFTA nor with the EC. In 1970 it began a trade agreement with the EC which reduced tariffs, but with some exceptions in sensitive products and with a slower pace for dismantling tariffs on the Spanish side.

Full membership of the Community provides new export opportunities for Spain, but also much stiffer import competition which was previously contained by higher tariffs. This tariff protection was particularly high in sectors such as the car industry and in 1986 the tariff was cut from 36.5 to 22.5 per cent as a first stage towards its eventual removal. The introduction of EC policies such as VAT and abolition of the former tax rebate, plus weak marketing expertise, handicap Spain's export potential and is likely to result in a long-term trade deficit. Community exporters such as West

Germany have taken full advantage of the opening up of the Spanish market, with West Germany replacing the USA as its major supplier. In its first two years of Community membership the Spanish economy grew rapidly with high investment, though the surge of imports resulted in a huge trade deficit. Spain has about a 30 per cent gap in productivity compared with the Community average and also low quality standards. The issue of renegotiation with the EC has already been raised, since its budgetary gains are being outweighed by its massive trade imbalance.

The size of Spanish output poses problems for the Community in agriculture and fishing, and in industry. Although agricultural production in southern Europe is to some extent complementary with that in northern Europe, there are likely to be some adverse effects, especially in southern France and Italy. An even greater problem is the prospect of generating additional farm surpluses; for example, Spanish olive oil production is almost as large as that in the rest of the Community. The dilemma for the Community has been the extent to which it should extend price support to southern European products (Leigh and van Praag 1978). Spanish producers possess a worrying capacity to add to over-production and its fishing fleet tends to complicate agreements to control over-fishing. Industrially, Spain is a major world producer in some staple industries such as steel and shipbuilding in which the EC has already had to introduce policies for restructuring because of over-capacity. Spain will also be a major competitor in other traditional industries, such as footwear and textiles.

Turkey. Will Turkey be the next country to join the Community fully? It has been an associate member of the EC since 1964. It is important strategically in its location as a member of NATO, and in its population size with some 50 million people. However, its economic weaknesses as the 'sick man of Europe' would create indigestible problems for the EC. Turkey's GDP per head is only slightly more than half of that in Portugal (which is by far the poorest member of the EC). Much of Turkey's labour force has been employed in agriculture − more than the total in the whole EC(10) (Rustow and Penrose 1981). Industrially, it was unable to maintain the agreed reductions in its tariffs, and Turkish industries, apart from textiles, are likely to suffer badly from stronger competition. Despite political advantages to the EC and Turkey, Community policy seems likely to be one of delaying Turkish membership to ensure that this does not take place until the beginning of the next century.

B   Differentiated and flexible integration
Enlargement is likely to accelerate the more pragmatic and flexible

approach to integration. However, a range of basic common policies have formed the building blocks of the Community. Countries have to conform to the Treaties and to the ongoing legislation from Community institutions. The basic foundations of the EC, such as the principle of non-discrimination against its members, have to be respected and countries cannot reimpose trading barriers against other members of the Community. Unless these principles are applied, the Community cannot operate effectively and will be undermined. Nevertheless, a pursuit of excessive common standardization and an attempt to impose uniformity for its own sake is undesirable and certainly less practicable for a Community of twelve different countries. The Community has acknowledged this, using various instruments such as gradual and phased Directives, plus some derogations, and some national discretion in how measures are to be applied (Wallace 1985).

Some differentiation in approach has also existed in other organizations, such as French and Spanish arrangements in NATO. The crucial issue, however, is how much flexibility is possible and can it be provided without creating so many exceptions and special cases that ultimately it distorts and discredits the whole organization. In the new Community the less standard and more diverse pattern of integration which has had to emerge is likely to be reinforced in the future. The first enlargement of the EC in 1973 created a situation of differential treatment by the transition phases of adjustment. It is no coincidence that this first enlargement resulted in greater discussion about a two-speed Europe which was suggested by W. Brandt in West Germany in 1974; this was followed by the Tindemans Report in 1976 in which there were further proposals for differentiated development. In a two-speed Europe at least there is an obligation on those countries which are forging ahead faster to help the weaker countries; for example, by greater regional assistance.

There is little doubt that since enlargement the EC has shown a tendency to split into at least two tiers. There is not only a reluctance to support weaker countries sufficiently, but also doubts about whether such fiscal transfers would actually produce long-run convergence. The pattern that is inevitably emerging is one in which some countries, usually the original Six, are better able to push forward with policies in new areas. The two countries, France and Germany, which have taken most initiatives have provided the momentum in fields such as the EMS. Countries not participating in these areas are free to join and encouraged to take up the option when conditions become more propitious for them. The two-tier approach may even prove to be the most practical way of progressing in other fields, such as that of removing tax barriers; otherwise the deadline of 1992 will be difficult to achieve. Tax rates and yields on VAT and excise duties have been much wider in the UK, Denmark and Ireland than in the original Six.

The Community is likely to be confined to core policies though there is no consensus over what they should be; for example, R. Dahrendorf's list in a Europe à la carte included foreign policy, trade, monetary policy and overseas development. France approved a variable geometry Community in the 1970s, particularly in industrial and technological policy. The *'acquis communautaire'* applies to core policies, but in other areas countries may choose whether to participate or not. Even some non-members of the EC have participated in the Eureka project and projects of nuclear fusion, like the Joint European Torus (JET).

The new Community of twelve cannot be optimal for all activities. It has striven hard to obtain basic agreement in key areas and indeed it is surprising in some respects that the Community has been able to make as much progress as it has, given the differences and at times the uncooperativeness of new members. A much looser pattern of integration seems inevitable in the future and the UK may look back wishfully on why it could not attain flexibility to a greater extent in the first place in sectors such as agriculture. A more variegated pattern of integration enables the more dynamic countries to press on ahead, acting as catalysts to new policy areas and providing a way of breaking the soul-destroying deadlock and paralysis of the EC (Langeheine and Weinstock 1985). Perhaps the SEA, with more use of majority voting, will help to lay to rest a damaging split into two groups in the Community.

C   The EC: prospect and retrospect

Integration in the EC has been a major contributor in restoring post-war prosperity after two disastrous world wars. Nations were prepared to surrender some degree of power to supranational institutions, though hopes for a federal Europe have been dashed by the continued dominance of the Council of Ministers in the Community's decision-making process. Progress towards rendering the EC's decision making more democratic has been painfully slow − 27 years elapsed before provisions for direct elections to the EP finally materialized in 1979. Since then the EP has gradually sought an accretion of its powers, and these, such as the co-operation procedure, have been manifested in the SEA.

The economic benefits from the customs union and the growing intra-trade are likely to be enhanced further with the completion of the internal market by 1992. Unfortunately, the CAP, which is a cornerstone of the Community and its most fully-developed policy, has faced continuing problems. Economic events have changed so much since its inception as worries over food shortages have been replaced by massive surpluses. These have arisen as a result of inexorable technical progress and over-generous price-support policies. They have had increasingly adverse effects on the pattern of agricultural trade with the rest of the world. Agricultural reforms have tended to be piecemeal and belated, always falling short of fundamental changes in policy. Prospects for successful reform appear limited, with West Germany holding the Presidency of the Council in 1988 and being expected to solve some of the agricultural problems for which it is partly responsible. The CAP has swallowed up the finance which could have been used far more effectively in other ways, such as much needed support to expand high-technology industry to keep pace with the USA and Japan. The Budget is dominated by agriculture, with spending tending to outgrow revenue and even by 1992 agriculture is still expected to account for half of budgetary expenditure. Despite attempts to reorientate the Budget towards industrial and regional policies, spending on these is still small compared with national expenditure, and regional policy still bears a marked agricultural imprint.

Progress in the Community has been gradual and largely incremental, running into periodic crises. Proposals for a great leap forward towards a major transformation, such as that towards EMU in the 1970s, failed, partly as a result of the oil crisis and a move to floating exchange rates. Hence since 1979 this has given way to the EMS which has had to operate more flexibly. In addition, enlargement of the Community has held back progress as new members have become preoccupied with their own particular problems. Nevertheless, while any annual appraisal of progress might indicate that this has occurred at a snail's pace, and at times the Community has had to back-pedal, when one cumulates the developments retrospectively over a period of 30 years it indicates a massive step forward. On its thirtieth anniversary on 25 March 1987, the EEC could look back on the outcome of its complex bargaining. It is a Community enlarged from six to twelve members which has manifested not only its durability but also its attractiveness to other countries. In addition, countries outside have recognized the EC as the world's economic trading giant and have clamoured to reach some kind of trading arrangement with it.

Any temporary loss of momentum towards integration is inevitable at times, and especially after the early idealism and the dynamism of super-economic growth of the 1960s. The most recent attempt to restore a new sense of direction to the Community has been provided by the SEA which came into force in 1987. This is much less ambitious than many supporters of European union had hoped for, and in some respects is the lowest common denominator which could be agreed by the twelve. Even so, it represents a recommitment to real completion of the internal market; to co-operation in economic and monetary policy; economic and social cohesion; research and technological development; the environment; and greater political co-operation, leading towards a common foreign policy. It became necessary to refocus the Community's activities, since some new policies had begun to operate outside the Community's framework, with also a trend towards inter-governmental integration. A greater use of majority voting became a prime requirement if the enlarged Community was to work more effectively and not become almost paralysed in its decision-making. Majority voting has been introduced in areas which are important in revitalizing the EC, such as the internal market. The fact that a vote can be taken is likely to encourage compromise, though there are still many areas where unanimity is necessary. While the co-operation procedure with Parliament injects greater democracy into the Community, this may tend to prolong the decision-making procedure.

The EC is aware that it needs to confine itself to those areas where it can demonstrate a clear superiority of competence and performance over nation states. In moving forward in new areas it cannot assume or take for granted that all the problems have been solved in existing areas of integration. In addition the enlarged Community is likely to experience greater internal problems since it now comprises a much less optimal grouping in its membership. Only a looser pattern of integration appears compatible and suitable for the new Community in the future.

As a postscript, there is little doubt that the internal market will become the prime focus of economic interest and activity over the next few years. Since this chapter was completed, glittering economic prospects have been painted from the realization of a single domestic market in the European Community (Pelkmans and Winters 1988; Cecchini 1988). For example, potential microeconomic gains in welfare of some ECU 216 billion have been estimated for the EC(12) equal to some 5.3 per cent of GDP. A virtuous circle of benefits is expected, especially in the long-term from industrial reorganization, the reaping of economies of scale and through greater innovation. At a macroeconomic level the benefits accruing from the successful completion of a single market are likely to help the European Community to attain a better trade-off between conflicting policy objectives. The rate of inflation can be lowered (an average of 6.1 per cent); economic growth can be raised (on average by 4.5 per cent), leading to the creation of new employment opportunities (some 1.8 million jobs). The constraints provided by both budgetary and balance of payments deficits will be loosened. Although in the short-run some job change and displacement will occur, in the medium- and long-term the employment gain could be enormous (some 5 million new jobs, if accompanied by reflationary policies) (Cecchini 1988, Table on p. 101).

Part III   Integration and the UK

The UK in joining the EC in 1973 had to adjust to an organization which it had not initiated itself and which was not the one most suited to displaying its strengths. By joining too late, its industrial competitiveness had diminished, and Community concern with agriculture seems singularly inappropriate for the UK, with such a small agricultural sector. Nevertheless, the UK continues to seek industrial gains and in particular is trying to exploit its comparative advantage in the tertiary sector of the economy, such as financial services. This partly explains why the UK has become a major proponent of opening up the internal market.

If the UK is to take full advantage of the internal market, steps will have to be taken to improve its competitiveness further, after years of under-investment in capital and the skills of employees. In terms of better communications, the Channel Tunnel may make a marginal improvement to the competitiveness of UK exports on the continent. It is yet another indication of how the UK is being brought ever closer to continental Europe. Economically, the EC has only offered potential opportunities for business from a larger market, with no guarantee of economic success. Without major efforts to keep up with the implications of the internal market, then British business will continue to lag behind its major European competitors.

There has not been much evidence of major economic benefits to the UK and if it has become more *communautaire* this is partly relative to the situation of some other new members; for example, Greece and Denmark, which refused initially to sign the SEA, though later relented after the Danish referendum. Use of a referendum in Denmark, and also in the UK in 1975, has proved a significant supportive element in confirming membership of the Community. Since the Fontainebleau Summit in 1984 the UK has gone through a better phase in the EC, taking advantage of its Presidency of the Council of Ministers in 1986 to provide a new direction. It is attuned to specific developments such as the internal market, though basic differences have continued over interventionist policies; for example, the CAP and EMS. Furthermore, any future Labour government might encounter even greater problems with Community integration in areas such as the internal market.

The UK's relative GDP per head continued to deteriorate in the EC(9), though economically there has been a relative improvement in the UK's performance during the 1980s in the EC(12). This is partly a reflection of a long overdue improvement in UK economic performance, but is mainly a consequence of the lower GDP per head of the three new Mediterranean entrants – Greece, Spain and Portugal. Given that the UK in the past tended to consider itself a special case, meriting distinctive budgetary treatment, it has in retrospect provided an unfortunate precedent. This is because the new Mediterranean entrants have even greater special needs, and meeting these is likely to result in further problems in constraining agricultural and budgetary expenditure, while redirecting regional finance from declining industrial areas to underdeveloped Mediterranean areas.

Southern enlargement tips the balance of Community influence towards the problems of southern Europe and is likely to result in additional difficulties for the UK. Although UK farmers may not be directly affected by agricultural competition as are farmers in the south of France and Italy, the financial implications of integrating southern Europe are enormous. The undoubted gains lie in expanding UK industrial exports to southern Europe, and the British Overseas Trade Board has pinpointed several areas of potential growth. Nevertheless, industrial competitors such as West Germany appear better placed to take advantage of these new export opportunities, if past UK performance is any guide. Much hinges on a positive business response and there is some evidence of considerable British investment in traditional markets such as Portugal. Furthermore, existing companies have started to develop new strategies; for example, Unilever has decided to close its labour-intensive soap-making operations in Spain and produce in Portugal where labour costs are lower, and to concentrate its more capital-intensive scouring powder production in Spain.

The British economy seems destined to continue with high unemployment and major regional imbalance. Any British attachment to the exchange rate mechanism of the EMS — a vital part of future integration — is likely to necessitate high unemployment to dampen the inflation-prone tendencies of the British economy towards the lower level in West Germany. The UK economy also faces stiff intra-EC competition which will grow more intense in the single internal market, and which is likely to exacerbate regional imbalance. There is strong extra-competitiveness in down-market products from the NICs and any incapacity to compete effectively by member states such as the UK could result in an even more protectionist policy by the Community towards outside countries. Although, so far, the EC has not proved as inward-looking as many feared, it would be unfortunate if progress towards an internal market was maintained only at the expense of externalizing its problems, leading to some disintegration in the Community's trading relationship with the rest of the world.

Bibliography

Ackermann, C. and Harrop, J. (1985) 'The Management of Technological Innovation in the Machine Tool Industry: A Cross-National Regional Survey of Britain and Switzerland', *R and D Management*, Vol. 15, No. 3, July.

Albert, M and Ball, R. J. (1983) *Towards European Economic Recovery in the 1980s*, Report for the European Parliament, Brussels.

Aldcroft, D. H. (1978) *The European Economy 1914–1970*, London, Croom Helm.

Allen, H. (1979) *Norway and Europe in the 1970s*, London, Global Book Resources Ltd.

Arbuthnott, H. and Edwards, G. (1979) *A Common Man's Guide to the Common Market*, London, Macmillan.

Ardagh, J. (1982) *France in the 1980s*, Harmondsworth, Penguin.

Armstrong, H. and Taylor, J. (1986) 'An Evaluation of Current Regional Policy', *The Economic Review*, Vol. 4, No. 2, November.

Armstrong, H. and Taylor, J. (1987) *The Way Forward*, London, Employment Institute.

Balassa, B. (1967) 'Trade Creation and Trade Diversion in the European Common Market', *Economic Journal*, Vol. 77.

Balassa, B. (1975) *European Economic Integration*, Amsterdam, North-Holland.

Barber, J. and Reed, B. (eds) (1973) *European Community: Vision and Reality*, London, Croom Helm.

Barclays Bank (1985) 'Comecon', *Barclays Bank Review*, August.

Bayliss, B. T. (1985) 'Competition and Industrial Policy' in A. M. El-Agraa (ed.), *The Economics of the European Community*, Oxford, Philip Allan.

Blackwell, M. (1985) 'Lomé III: the Search for Greater Effectiveness', *Finance and Development*, Vol. 22, No. 3, September.

Booz Allen and Hamilton Inc. (1986) *Europe's Fragmented Markets – a Survey of European Chief Executives*, The Wall Street Journal/Europe.

Bourguignon-Wittke, R., Grabitz, E., Schmuck, O., Steppat, S. and Wessels, W. (1985) 'Five Years of the Directly Elected European Parliament: Performance and Prospects', *Journal of Common Market Studies*, Vol. XXIV, No. 1, September.

Bracewell-Milnes, B. (1976) *Economic Integration in East and West*, London, Croom Helm.

Brewin, C. and McAllister, R. (1986) 'Annual Review of the Activities of the European Communities in 1986', *Journal of Common Market Studies*, Vol. XXV, No. 4, June.

Brown, A. J. (1985) 'The General Budget', in A. M. El-Agraa (ed.) *The Economics of the European Community*, Oxford, Philip Allan.

Buckwell, A., Harvey, D., Thomson, K. and Parton, K. (1982) *The Costs of the Common Agricultural Policy*, London, Croom Helm.

Budd, S. A. (1987) *The EEC: A Guide to the Maze*, London, Kogan Page.

Butler, M. (1986) *Europe: More than a Continent*, London, Heinemann.

Butt Philip, A. (1983) 'Industrial and Competition Policies: A New Look' in A. M. El-Agraa, *Britain within the European Community: The Way Forward*, London, Macmillan.

Cairncross, A. *et al.* (eds) (1974) *Economic Policy for the European Community: The Way Forward*, London, Macmillan.

Capstick, M. (1970) *The Economics of Agriculture*, London, Allen and Unwin.

Castles, S. and Kosack, G. (1973) *Immigrant Workers and Class Structure in Western Europe*, London, Oxford University Press.

Cecchini, P. (1988) *The European Challenge 1992*, Aldershot, Wildwood House, Gower.

Chalkley, M. (1986) 'Selling Mountains and Lakes', *The Economic Review*, Vol. 4, No. 2, November.

Coffey, P. (1975) 'The Lomé Agreement and the EEC: Implications and Problems', *The Three Banks Review*, No. 108, December.

Coffey, P. (1976) *The External Relations of the EEC*, London, Macmillan.

Coffey, P. (1977) *Europe and Money*, London, Macmillan.

Coffey, P. (1979) *Economic Policies of the Common Market*, London, Macmillan.

Coffey, P. (ed.) (1983) *Main Economic Policy Areas of the EEC*, The Hague, Martinus Nijhoff.

Coffey, P. and Presley, J. (1971) *European Monetary Integration*, London, Macmillan.

Cohen, C. D. (ed.) (1983) *The Common Market – Ten Years After*, Oxford, Philip Allan.

Collins, C. D. E. (1985) 'Social Policy' in A. M. El-Agraa, *The Economics of the European Community*, Oxford, Philip Allan.

Commission of the European Communities (1984) *Working for Europe*, Luxembourg.

Commission of the European Communities (1987) *Twelfth Annual Report of the Regional Development Fund for 1986*; also earlier Reports.

Commission of the European Communities (1986) *The Agricultural Situation in the Community*, Brussels.

Commission of the European Communities (1987) *Bulletin* Nos. 1, 2 and 3, Vol. 20, Brussels.

Commission of the European Communities (1987) *Twentieth General Report on the Activities of the European Communities (1986)*, Brussels/ Luxembourg.

Commission of the European Communities (1987) *Report by the Commission to the Council and Parliament on the Financing of the Budget*, COM(87) 101 Final 1/2, Brussels.

Commission of the European Communities (1987) *Commission Communication on Budgetary Discipline*, COM(87) 430 Final, Brussels.

Commission of the European Communities (1987) *Reform of the Structural Funds*, COM(87) 376 Final, Brussels.

Commission of the European Communities (1987) *Making a Success of the Single Act*, February, Brussels.

Commission of the European Communities (1987) *A New Frontier for Europe*, COM(87) 100 Final, Brussels.

Commission of the European Communities (1987) *Own Resources Decision*, COM(87) 420 Final, Brussels.

Commission of the European Communities (1987) *Review of Action Taken to Control the Agricultural Markets and Outlook for the Agricultural Policy*, COM(87) 410 Final, Brussels.

Commission of the European Communities (1987) *Research and Technological Development in the Less Favoured Regions of the Community*, (STRIDE), Final Report, Brussels.

Coombes, D. (1970) *Politics and Bureaucracy in the European Community*, London, Allen and Unwin.

Cooper, C. A. and Massel, B. F. (1965) 'A New Look at Customs Union Theory', *Economic Journal*, Vol. 75.

Cosgrave, C. A. (1969) 'The EEC and Developing Countries' in G. R. Denton (ed.) *Economic Integration in Europe*, London, Weidenfeld and Nicholson.

Cosgrave-Twitchett, C. (1981) *A Framework for Development?: The EEC and the ACP*, London, Allen and Unwin.

Council (1986) *Single European Act*, Brussels.

The Courier (1986) No. 98, July–August.

Daltrop, A. (1982) *Politics and the European Community*, London, Longman.

Dearden, S. (1986) 'EEC Membership and the United Kingdom's Trade in Manufactured Goods', *National Westminster Bank Quarterly Review*, February.

Dennis, G. (1985) 'The European Monetary System' in A. M. El-Agraa (ed.) *The Economics of the European Community*, Oxford, Philip Allan.

Denton, G., Forsyth, M. and Maclennan, M. (1968) *Economic Planning and Policies in Britain, France and Germany*, London, Allen and Unwin.

Denton, G. (ed.) (1969) *Economic Integration in Europe*, London, Weidenfeld and Nicholson.

Denton, G. (ed.) (1974) *Economic and Monetary Union in Europe*, London, Croom Helm.

Denton, G. (1984) 'Restructuring the European Community Budget', *Journal of Common Market Studies*, Vol. XXIII, No. 2, December.

Department of Industry (1981) *An Investigation into the Woollen and Worsted Sector of the Textile and Garment Making Industries in the United Kingdom, France, Germany and Italy*, London.

Dinkelspiel, U. (1987) 'Eureka: Co-operation in High Technology', *EFTA Bulletin*, Vol. XXVIII, No. 1, January–March.

Dosser, D., Gowland, D. and Hartley, K. (eds) (1982) *The Collaboration of Nations*, Oxford, Martin Robertson.

Drenowski, J. (ed.) (1982) *Crisis in the Eastern European Economy*, London, Croom Helm.

Duchêne, F., Szczepanik, E. and Legg, W. (1985) *New Limits on Agriculture*, London, Croom Helm.

Einzig, P. (1971) *The Case Against Joining the Common Market*, London, Macmillan.

El-Agraa, A. M. (ed.) (1983) *Britain Within the European Community: The Way Forward*, London, Macmillan.

El-Agraa, A. M. (ed.) (1985) *The Economics of the European Community*, Oxford, Philip Allan.

The European (1987) Vol. 1, No. 3, May–June, and No. 5, September–October, Oxford, Pergamon Press.

European Documentation (1986) *The European Community's Budget*, Luxembourg.

European Investment Bank (1986) *Annual Report*, Luxembourg.

European Parliament (1978) *Powers of the European Parliament*, London.

Eurostat (1984) *Basic Statistics of the Community*, Commission, Brussels.

Eurostat (1986) *ACP, Basic Statistics*, Commission, Brussels.

Evans, D. (ed.) (1973) *Britain in the EC*, London, Gollancz.

Fennell, R. (1985) 'A Re-consideration of the Objectives of the Common Agricultural Policy', *Journal of Common Market Studies*, Vol. XXIII, No. 3, March.

Fennell, R. (1979 and 1988) *The Common Agricultural Policy of the Community*, London, Granada.

George, K. D. and Joll, C. (1975) *Competition Policy in the United Kingdom and the European Economic Community*, Cambridge University Press.

George, K. D. and Ward, T. S. (1975) *The Structure of Industry in the EEC*, Cambridge Occasional Paper.

George, K. D. and Joll, C. (1978) 'EEC Competition Policy', *The Three Banks Review*, March.

George, S. (1985) *Politics and Policy in the European Community*, Oxford, Clarendon.

George, S. (1987) *The British Government and the European Community since 1984*, University Association for Contemporary European Studies No. 4.

Greenaway, D. (1987) 'Intra-Industry Trade, Intra-Firm Trade and European Integration', *Journal of Common Market Studies*, Vol. XXVI, No. 2, December.

Groeben, H. von der (1985) *The European Community: the Formative Years*, Commission, Brussels/Luxembourg.

Han, S. S. and Liesner, H. H. (1970) *Britain and the Common Market*, Cambridge Occasional Paper No. 27.

Harrop, J. (1973) 'The Rise and Fall of EFTA', *The Bankers' Magazine*, March.

Harrop, J. (1978) 'The European Investment Bank', *National Westminster Bank Quarterly Review*, May.

Harrop, J. (1978) 'An Evaluation of the European Investment Bank', *23A Société Universitaire Européene de Recherches Financières*, Tilburg, Netherlands.

Harrop, J. (1978) 'Convergence in Europe', in R. D. Wilson (ed.) *Workbook on Testing Ten Economies*, Sutton, Economics Association.

Harrop, J. (1985) 'Crisis in the Machine Tool Industry: A Policy Dilemma for the European Community', *Journal of Common Market Studies*, Vol. XXIV, No. 1, September.

Hartley, K. (1982) 'Defence and Advanced Technology', in D. Dosser, D. Gowland and K. Hartley (eds) *The Collaboration of Nations*, Oxford, Martin Robertson.

Healey, N. M. (1988) 'The Case for Britain Joining the EMS', *Economic Affairs*, February/March.

Heertje, A. (ed.) (1983) *Investing in Europe's Future*, Oxford, Blackwell.

Heller, R. and Willat, N. (1975) *The European Revenge: How the American Challenge was Rebuffed*, London, Barrie and Jenkins.

Henderson, P. D. (1977) 'Two British Errors: Their Probable Size and Some Possible Lessons', *Oxford Economic Papers*, No. 2, July.

Henig, S. (1980) *Power and Decision in Europe*, London, Europotentials Press.

Hewitt, A. (1984) 'The Lomé Conventions: Entering a Second Decade', *Journal of Common Market Studies*, Vol. XXIII, No. 2, December.

Hewstone, M. (1986) *Understanding Attitudes to the European Community*, Cambridge University Press.

Hill, B. E. (1984) *The Common Agricultural Policy: Past, Present and Future*, London, Methuen.

Hine, R. C. (1985) *The Political Economy of European Trade*, Brighton, Wheatsheaf.

HMSO (1971) White Paper, *The United Kingdom and the European Communities*, Cmnd 4715, London.

HMSO (1978) Green Paper, The European Monetary System, Cmnd 7405, November, London.

HMSO (1987) Central Statistical Office, Pink Book, *United Kingdom Balance of Payments*, London.

Hodges, M. (ed.) (1972) *European Integration*, Harmondsworth, Penguin.

Hoffman, G. (ed.) (1983) *A Geography of Europe*, 5th Ed., New York, USA, John Wiley.

Holland, S. (ed.) (1972) *The State as Entrepreneur*, London, Weidenfeld and Nicholson.

Holland, S. (1976) *Capital versus the Regions*, London, Macmillan.

Holland, S. (1976) *The Regional Problem*, London, Macmillan.

Holland, S. (1980) *Uncommon Market: Capital, Class and Power in the European Community*, London, Macmillan.

Holmes, P. (1983) 'The EEC and British Trade' in C. D. Cohen (ed.) *The Common Market: Ten Years After*, Oxford, Philip Allan.

Holt, S. (1967) *The Common Market*, London, Hamish Hamilton.

House of Lords (1983) Select Committee on the European Communities, *European Monetary System*, Fifth Report.

House of Lords (1984) Select Committee on the European Communities, *The Common Fisheries Policy*, December.

House of Lords (1985) Select Committee on the European Communities, *The 1985 Farm Price Proposals: Agricultural Price Review*, Vols I and II, March.

House of Lords (1986) Select Committee on the European Communities, *Socio-Structural Policy in Agriculture*, July.

Hu, Yao-Su (1981) *Europe Under Stress*, London, Butterworths.

Ionescu, G. (ed.) (1979) *The European Alternatives*, The Netherlands, Sijthoff and Noordhoff.

Jacquemin, A. P. (1974) 'Size, Structure and Performance of the Largest European Firms' *The Three Banks Review*, June.

Jacquemin, A. P. and de Jong, H. W. (1977) *European Industrial Organisation*, London, Macmillan.

Jay, D. (1968) *After the Common Market*, Harmondsworth, Penguin.

Jenkins, R. (1978) 'European Monetary Union', *Lloyds Bank Review*, January.

Jenkins, R. (ed.) (1983) *Britain and the EEC*, London, Macmillan.

Johnson, C. (1982) 'The Fall in Farm Prices', *Lloyds Bank Economic Bulletin*, No. 41, May.

Johnson, C. (1987) 'How Well Are We Doing?' *Lloyds Bank Economic Bulletin*, No. 100, April.

Johnson, H. G. (1973) 'An Economic Theory of Protectionism, Tariff Bargaining and the Formation of Customs Unions', in M. B. Krauss (ed.) *The Economics of Integration*, London, Allen and Unwin.

Jones, A. J. (1979) 'The Theory of Economic Integration' in J. K. Bowers (ed.) *Inflation, Development and Integration: Essays in Honour of A. J. Brown*, Leeds University Press.

Jones, A.J. (1985) 'The Theory of Economic Integration' in A.M. El-Agraa (ed.) *The Economics of the European Community*, Oxford, Philip Allan.

Josling, T. and Harris, J. (1976) 'Europe's Green Money', *The Three Banks Review*, March.

Josling, T. (1984) 'US and EC Farm Policies: An Eclectic Comparison', in K.J. Thomson and R.M. Warren (eds) *Price and Market Policies in European Agriculture*, Dept. of Agricultural Economics, University of Newcastle upon Tyne.

Josling, T. (1986) 'Agricultural Policies and World Trade' in L. Tsoukalis (ed.) *Europe, America and the World Economy*, Oxford, Basil Blackwell for the College of Europe.

Kaldor, N. (1971) 'The Truth about the Dynamic Effects', *New Statesman*, 12 March.

The Kangaroo News (1987) No. 20, May, London.

Keating, M. and Jones, B. (1985) *Regions in the Community*, Oxford, Clarendon.

Kenen, P.B. (1969) 'The Theory of Optimum Currency Areas: An Eclectic View' in R.A. Mundell and A.K. Swoboda (eds) *Monetary Problems of the International Economy*, Chicago University Press, USA.

Klassen, L.H. and Molle, W.T. (1983) *Industrial Mobility and Migration in the European Community*, Aldershot, Gower.

Krauss, M.B. (ed.) (1973) *The Economics of Integration*, London, Allen and Unwin.

Kreinin, M.E. (1974) *Trade Relations of the EEC*, London, Praeger.

Kruse, D.C. (1980) *Monetary Integration in Western Europe: EMU, EMS and Beyond*, London, Butterworths.

Langeheine, B. and Weinstock, U. (1985) 'Graduated Integration: A Modest Path Towards Progress', *Journal of Common Market Studies*, Vol. XXIII, No. 3, March.

Layton, C. (1969) *European Advanced Technology*, London, Allen and Unwin.

Lee, R. and Ogden, P.E. (1976) *Economy and Society in the EEC*, Farnborough, Saxon House.

Leigh, M. and van Praag, N. (1978) *The Mediterranean Challenge: 1*, Sussex European Research Paper No. 2.

Lewenhak, S. (1982) *The Role of the European Investment Bank*, London, Croom Helm.

Lewis, D.E.S. (1978) *Britain and the European Community*, London, Heinemann.

Lodge, J. and Herman, V. (1978) *The European Parliament and the European Community*, London, Macmillan.

Lodge, J. (1983) *Institutions and Policies of the European Community*, London, Frances Pinter.

Lodge, J. (ed.) (1986) *European Union: The European Community in Search of a Future*, London, Macmillan.

Long, F. (ed.) (1980) *The Political Economy of EEC Relations with African, Caribbean and Pacific States*, Oxford, Pergamon.

Ludlow, P. (1982) *The Making of the European Monetary System*, London, Butterworths.

Lundgren, N. (1969) 'Customs Unions of Industrialised West European Countries' in G.R. Denton (ed.) *Economic Integration in Europe*, London, Weidenfeld and Nicholson.

Mackel, C. (1978) 'Green Money and the Common Agricultural Policy', *National Westminster Bank Quarterly Review*, February.

McKinnon, R. I. (1963) 'Optimum Currency Areas', *American Economic Review*, No. 53.

Maclennan, R. (1978) 'Food Prices and the Common Agricultural Policy', *The Three Banks Review*, September.

McQueen, M. (1977) *Britain, The EEC and the Developing World*, London, Heinemann.

Macsween, I. (1987) 'The Common Fisheries Policy', *The Royal Bank of Scotland Review*, No. 154, June.

Magnifico, G. (1973) *European Monetary Unification*, London, Macmillan.

Mahotière, de la, S. (1970) *Towards One Europe*, Harmondsworth, Penguin.

Marques Mendes, A. J. (1987) *Economic Integration and Growth in Europe*, London, Croom Helm.

Marsh, J. S. and Swanney, P. J. (1980) *Agriculture and the European Community*, London, Allen and Unwin.

Mathijsen, P. S. R. F. (1985) *A Guide to European Community Law*, London, Sweet and Maxwell.

Mayne, R. (ed.) (1972) *Europe Tomorrow*, London, Fontana/Collins.

Midland Bank (1977) 'European Monetary Union', *Midland Bank Review*, Winter.

Midland Bank (1986) 'On Joining the EMS', *Midland Bank Review*, Winter.

Midland Bank (1987) 'Setting Priorities for Science and Technology', *Midland Bank Review*, Winter.

Morgan, A. (1980) 'The Balance of Payments and British Membership of the EEC' in W. Wallace (ed.) *Britain in Europe*, London, Heinemann.

Morgan, A. (1984) 'Protectionism and European Trade in Manufactures', *National Institute Economic Review*, No. 109, August.

Moussis, N. (1982) *Les Politiques de la Communauté Economique Européene*, Paris, Dalloz.

Mundell, R. A. (1961) 'A Theory of Optimum Currency Areas', *American Economic Review*, No. 51.

Myrdal, G. (1957) *Economic Theory and Underdeveloped Regions*, London, Duckworth.

National Institute of Economic and Social Research (1983) 'The European Monetary System', *National Institute Economic Review*, February.

Nicholson, F. and East, R. (1987) *From the Six to the Twelve: The Enlargement of the European Communities*, Harlow, Longman.

Nicoll, W. (1984) 'The Luxembourg Compromise', *Journal of Common Market Market Studies*, Vol. XXIII, No. 1, September.

Noel, E. (1985) *The Institutions of the European Community*, Luxembourg.

Noort, van den, P. C. (1983) 'Agricultural Policy' in P. Coffey (ed.) *Main Economic Policy Areas of the EEC*, The Hague, Martinus Nijhoff.

Open University (1973) *The European Economic Community: History and Institutions, National and International Impact*, Open University Press.

Owen, N. (1983) *Economies of Scale, Competitiveness and Trade Patterns Within the European Community*, Oxford University Press.

Padoa-Schioppa, T. (1984) *Money, Economic Policy and Europe*, The European Perspective Series, Commission, Brussels.

Palmer, M. and Lambert, J. (1968) *European Unity: A Survey of the European Organisations*, London, Allen and Unwin.

Parr, M. and Day, J. (1977) 'Value Added Tax in the United Kingdom' *National Westminster Bank Quarterly Review*, May.

Pearce, J. (1981) *The Common Agricultural Policy*, Chatham House Paper, No. 13, London, Routledge and Kegan Paul.

Pearce, J. and Sutton, J. (1986) *Protection and Industrial Policy in Europe*, London, Routledge and Kegan Paul.

Pelkmans, J. and Winters, A. (1988) *Europe's Domestic Market*, London, Chatham House, Paper No. 43, The Royal Institute of International Affairs, Routledge.

Petith, H. C. (1977) 'European Integration and the Terms of Trade', *Economic Journal*, Vol. 87.

Pinder, D. A. (1986) 'Small Firms, Regional Development and the European Investment Bank', *Journal of Common Market Studies*, Vol. XXIV, No. 3, March.

Pinder, J. (1987) 'Is the Single European Act a Step Towards a Federal Europe?' *The Journal of Policy Studies*, Vol. 7, Part 4, April.

Pollard, S. (1974) *European Economic Integration 1815–1970*, London, Thames and Hudson.

Pomfret, R. (1986) *Mediterranean Policy of the European Community*, London, Macmillan.

Postan, M. M. (1967) *An Economic History of Western Europe 1945–1964*, London, Methuen.

Presley, J. R. and Coffey, P. (1974) *European Monetary Integration*, London, Macmillan.

Presley, J. R. and Dennis, C. E. J. (1976) *Currency Areas: Theory and Practice*, London, Macmillan.

Prest, A. R. (1983) 'Fiscal Policy' in P. Coffey (ed.) *Main Policy Areas of the EEC*, The Hague, Martinus Nijhoff.

Pridham, G. (1986) 'European Elections, Political Parties and Trends of Internalization in Community Affairs', *Journal of Common Market Studies*, Vol. XXIV, No. 4, June.

Priebe, H. (1980) 'German Agricultural Policy and the European Community', in W. L. Kohl and G. Basevi (eds) *West Germany: A European and Global Power*, Lexington, Mass., USA, Heath.

Pryce, R. (ed.) (1987) *The Dynamics of European Union*, London, Croom Helm.

Ransom, C. (1973) *The European Community and Eastern Europe*, London, Butterworths.

Redmond, J. (1987) 'Trade Between China and the European Community: A New Relationship?', *National Westminster Bank Quarterly Review*, May.

Ritson, C. (1977) *Agricultural Economics*, St. Albans, Granada.

Roarty, M. J. (1987) 'The Impact of the Common Agricultural Policy on Agricultural Trade and Development', *National Westminster Bank Quarterly Review*, February.

Robson, P. (1980) *The Economics of International Integration*, London, Allen and Unwin.

Rustow, D. and Penrose, T. (1981) *Turkey and the Community, The Mediterranean Challenge: V*, Sussex European Research Centre, Paper 10, Brighton.

Science et Vie Economie (1987) No. 25.

Scott, A. (1986) 'Britain and the EMS: an Appraisal of the Report of the Treasury and Civil Service Committee', *Journal of Common Market Studies*, Vol. XXIV, No. 3, March.

Seers, D. and Vaitsos, S. (1980) *Integration and Unequal Development*, London, Macmillan.

Servan Schreiber, J. J. (1968) *The American Challenge*, London, Hamish Hamilton.

Shanks, M. (1977) *European Social Policy Today and Tomorrow*, Oxford, Pergamon Press.

Sharp, M. (ed.) (1985) *Europe and the New Technologies*, London, Frances Pinter.

Shonfield, A. (1973) *Europe: Journey to an Unknown Destination*, Harmondsworth, Penguin.

Stevens, C. (ed.) (1984) *EEC and the Third World: A Survey*, No. 4, ODI/IDS, London, Hodder and Stoughton.

Strange, S. (1980) 'Germany and the World Monetary System' in W. L. Kohl and G. Basevi (eds) *West Germany: A European and Global Power*, Massachussets, USA, Heath Lexington.

Svennilson, I. (1954) *Growth and Stagnation in the European Economy*, Geneva, United Nations Economic Commission for Europe.

Swann, D. (1983) *Competition and Industrial Policy*, London, Methuen.

Swann, D. (1985) *The Economics of the Common Market*, 5th Ed., Harmondsworth, Penguin.

Tarditi, S. (1984) 'Price Policies and European Economic Integration' in K. J. Thomson and R. M. Warren (eds) *Price and Market Policies in European Agriculture*, Dept. of Agricultural Economics, University of Newcastle upon Tyne.

Taylor, P. (1983) *The Limits of European Integration*, London, Croom Helm.

Treaties Establishing the European Communities (1987) Abridged Ed., Brussels/Luxembourg.

Tsoukalis, L. (1977) *The Politics and Economics of European Monetary Integration*, London, Allen and Unwin.

Tsoukalis, L. (ed.) (1981) *The European Community and its Mediterranean Enlargement*, London, Allen and Unwin.

Tsoukalis, L. (ed.) (1986) *Europe, America and the World Economy*, Oxford, Basil Blackwell for the College of Europe.

Tugendhat, C. (1986) *Making Sense of Europe*, London, Viking; paperback Harmondsworth, Penguin, 1987.

Turner, G. (1986) 'Inside Europe's Giant Companies: Cultural Revolution at Philips', *Long Range Planning*, Vol. 19/4, No. 98, August.

Utne, A. (1986) 'EFTA's Importance as a Trading Partner for the EC', *EFTA Bulletin*, Vol. XXVII, October–December.

Vanhove, N. and Klassen, L. H. (1980) *Regional Policy: A European Approach*, Farnborough, Saxon House.

Wallace, H., Wallace, W. and Webb, C. (eds) (1977) *Policy-Making in the European Communities*, London, John Wiley.

Wallace, W. (ed.) (1980) *Britain in Europe*, London, Heinemann.

Wallace, H. (1985) *The Challenge of Diversity*, London, Routledge and Keegan Paul.

Whitby, M. (ed.) (1979) *The Net Cost and Benefit of EEC Membership*, London, Wye College.

Williams, M. (1977) *Teaching European Studies*, London, Heinemann.

Winters, A. (1987) 'Britain in Europe: A Survey of Quantitative Trade Studies', *Journal of Common Market Studies*, Vol. XXV, No. 4, June.

Yannopoulos, G. N. (1985) 'EC External Commercial Policies and

East-West Trade in Europe', *Journal of Common Market Studies*, Vol. XXIV, No. 1, September.

Yannopoulos, G. N. (ed.) (1986) *Greece and the EEC*, Basingstoke, Macmillan.

Ypersele, J. van and Koeune, J. C. (1985) *The European Monetary System*, Cambridge, Woodhead-Faulker.

Zis, G. (1984) 'The European Monetary System 1979–1984: An Assessment', *Journal of Common Market Studies*, Vol. XXIII, No. 1, September.

Index

64853